SEAMUS HEANEY

Seamus Heaney

SEAMUS HEANEY

The Shaping Spirit

Edited by

Catharine Malloy
and Phyllis Carey

DELAWARE

Newark: University of Delaware Press
London: Associated University Presses

Associated University Presses
440 Forsgate Drive
Cranbury, NJ 08512

Associated University Presses
16 Barter Street
London WC1A 2AH, England

Associated University Presses
P.O. Box 338, Port Credit
Mississauga, Ontario
Canada L5G 4L8

The paper used in this publication meets the requirements of the American National Standard for Permanence of Paper for Printed Library Materials Z39.48-1984

Library of Congress Cataloging in Publication Data

Seamus Heaney—the shaping spirit / edited by Catharine Malloy and Phyllis Carey.
    p. cm.
    Includes bibliographical references and index.
    ISBN 0-87413-581-8 (alk. paper)
    1. Heaney, Seamus—Criticism and interpretation. 2. Northern Ireland—In literature. I. Malloy, Catharine, 1941– .
II. Carey, Phyllis.
PR6058.E2Z885 1996
821'.914—dc20   95-33643
                                       CIP

SECOND PRINTING 1997
PRINTED IN THE UNITED STATES OF AMERICA

For
our mothers
and fathers

Contents

Abbreviations

CT   *The Cure at Troy.* London: Faber and Faber, 1990.

DD   *Door into the Dark.* London: Faber and Faber, 1969.

DN   *Death of a Naturalist.* New York: Oxford University Press, 1966.

FW   *Field Work.* New York: Farrar, Straus & Giroux, 1979.

GT   *The Government of the Tongue.* New York: Farrar, Straus & Giroux, 1988.

HL   *The Haw Lantern.* New York: Farrar, Straus & Giroux, 1987.

N   *North.* London: Faber and Faber, 1975.

Poems   *Poems, 1965–1975.* New York: Farrar, Straus & Giroux, 1980.

Pr   *Preoccupations: Selected Prose, 1966–1978.* New York: Farrar, Straus & Giroux, 1980.

PW   *The Place of Writing.* Atlanta: The Scholars' Press, 1989.

RP   "The Redress of Poetry." *Times Literary Supplement,* 22–28 December 1989, 1412/13/18.

SA   *Sweeney Astray.* New York: Farrar, Straus & Giroux, 1984.

SI   *Station Island.* London: Faber and Faber, 1984.

SP   *Selected Poems, 1966–1987.* New York: Farrar, Straus & Giroux, 1990.

ST   *Seeing Things.* London: Faber and Faber, 1991.

WO   *Wintering Out.* London: Faber and Faber, 1972.

Acknowledgments

When we began to collect these essays on selected works by Seamus Heaney, we could not have anticipated the support and encouragement of so many of our colleagues and friends. Throughout the project, Michael Patrick Gillespie of Marquette University and Michael Durkan of Swarthmore College have given helpful suggestions and support. Special thanks to Patricia Donlon of the National Library of Ireland for her interest in this project throughout its course and to Seamus Deane, whose conversation with us at a memorable dinner in South Bend figured significantly in our own re-shaping of the volume.

We also wish to acknowledge Boltin Picture Library for supplying the photograph of the Bone Trial piece, Dungarvan, County Waterford, and the *Irish Times* and The National Library of Ireland for providing the photograph of Seamus Heaney.

We are grateful to our colleagues in the Mount Mary College English Department and to the staff at the Haggerty Library for their help and support. We also wish to thank Sister Theresa Lamy and Kathleen Scullin for their kindness and generosity, Mary Kay Mader for many hours of typing and retyping portions of the manuscript, and Clare Elizabeth Malloy for her imaginative cover design.

For their encouragement and patience, we thank our families.

We are most grateful, of course, to Seamus Heaney, whose work inspired this collection in the first place.

Permissions

For permission to reprint copyright material, the publishers gratefully acknowledge the following:

Seamus Heaney for permission to use excerpts from his translation of Dante's *Inferno.*

Faber and Faber Ltd. and Farrar, Straus & Giroux, Inc. for excerpts from *Death of a Naturalist, Wintering Out, North, Field Work, Preoccupations, Station Island, The Haw Lantern, Selected Poems, 1966–1987, The Cure at Troy,* and *Seeing Things,* all by Seamus Heaney, who is the copyright holder.

Boltin Picture Library for permission to use the photograph of the Bone Trial piece, Dungarvan, County Waterford.

The Critic, for excerpts from "Making Connections, An Interview with Seamus Deane" (Spring 1994) by Catharine Malloy and Phyllis Carey.

Frank Miller of *The Irish Times* and The National Library of Ireland for providing the photo of Seamus Heaney.

Johns Hopkins University Press, for excerpts from *Violence and the Sacred* (1977) by R. Girard.

Scholars Press, Atlanta, for excerpts from *The Place of Writing* (1989) by Seamus Heaney.

Colin Smythe Limited, Publishers, Gerrards Cross, Buckinghamshire, for excerpts from *The Irish Hand* (The Dolmen Press, 1984) by Timothy O'Neill.

Times Literary Supplement (London), 16–22 March 1990, for permission to reprint "Powers of Earth and Visions of Air" by Seamus Deane.

Wake Forest University Press, for excerpts from "Wyncote Pennsylvania: A Gloss" from *Poems, 1956–1973* (1979).

The editors apologize for any errors or omissions in the above list and would be grateful to be notified of any corrections that should be incorporated in the next edition of this volume.

Introduction

how deeply structured in all our thinking is this idea of imagination as a
shaping spirit which it is wrong to disobey
— *The Government of the Tongue*

"It's the shape that matters."[1] The often-quoted words of Samuel Beckett,
whom Seamus Heaney has described as "the most admirable writer we've
known in our time,"[2] could apply as well to Heaney himself, perhaps the
most renowned Irish poet we've known in our time. In "The Government
of the Tongue," Heaney explores and confirms Osip Mandelstam's insight
into Dante's aesthetic: The poet is not governed by the rules of meter, by
social pressure, or by "an orthodoxy or system," but, rather, poetry is "formed
from within, like a crystal, not cut on the outside like a stone." The "shaping spirit," Heaney goes on to note, is itself governed by the artistic experience: "The fact is that poetry is its own reality and no matter how much a
poet may concede to the corrective pressures of social, moral, political and
historical reality, the ultimate fidelity must be to the demands and promise
of the artistic event" (*GT* 301).

Frequently in his essays and interviews, Heaney has alluded to the pre-
eminence of shapes and shaping in his own aesthetic. Heaney's "shaping
spirit," moreover, has undergone various metamorphoses since he began
publishing poetry in the sixties. In the early poetry of *Death of a Naturalist*
(1966) and *Door into the Dark* (1969), for example, the language has a gritty,
grainy texture: Heaney's artistic process, initially, is one that uncovers, digs,
tills, seeks to crystallize experience through language.

In *Wintering Out* (1972), Heaney himself has pointed to the "first moment of change and therefore refreshment and shift of direction . . . in small
wafts of stanzas."[3] In *Wintering Out*, Heaney preserves as he remembers; in
North (1975), the volume that followed, he connects and distances himself to
both origin and place by making the local psychologically universal. In the

13

Richard Ellmann Lectures in Modern Literature delivered at Emory University, Heaney spoke of Yeats's tower at Thor Ballylee and emphasized the importance of the imagination in forming *place*: "The poetic imagination in its strongest manifestation imposes its vision upon a place rather than accepts a vision from it; . . . this visionary imposition is never exempt from the imagination's antithetical ability to subvert its own creation" (*PW* 21). Heaney's shaping spirit at work in the early seventies focused on actively creating imaginative spaces that resonate with actual places. Such spaces, as he later described them in analyzing Yeats's "The Fisherman" and Brian Friel's *Faith Healer*, "open the door between hope and reality, into an effulgence that most of us prefer to close our eyes to, the light of imagination which invites us to sacrifice our actual situation to a vision of our possibilities, which is doomed to fail" (*PW* 65). For Heaney, however, such failure can itself be enabling as imagination's *via negativa*.

After the landscapes of *North*, with their mythical and historical resonances, Heaney moved into a "more metrical, more stated" stance,[4] more dependent on the personal for inspiration. In *Field Work* (1979), political atrocities find expression in the personal and the elegiac and offer a penetrating look at the sorrow and sense of hopelessness prevalent in Northern Ireland. By the time he wrote *Station Island* (1984), Heaney in its title poem is boldly confessional, refusing the sweetness of lyric poetry for incisive dialogues with shades. Here, as Henry Hart has characterized it, "Heaney's artistic conscience . . . is painfully at odds with those two other internal gorgons, his political conscience and his religious conscience."[5] In Dantesque fashion, Heaney moves toward a shaping that reveals both torment and evanescence.

With his more recent poetry in *The Haw Lantern* (1987) and *Seeing Things* (1991), Heaney frequently shapes *things* to affirm their potentialities, some of which approach visions bordering on the sacred. In *The Haw Lantern*, local images and places promote a source of ferment upon which the creative imagination may flourish. Here the search for origins as influences looks toward the small and minute—"The Haw Lantern," "The Spoonbait," "Alphabets"—emphasizing that the smallest entity or shape may be capable of far-reaching importance in achieving self-definition. Heaney has moved from his personal encounters with the haunting, echoing presence of the shades in "Station Island" to a position where images remembered, rather than "spirits," encourage the speaker's migration to another realm, a place, nevertheless, that has spiritual overtones.

Heaney has recently addressed the conflicting influences of the secular and the sacred on the imagination of the poet: "If we are alive intellectually . . . we find ourselves in a bind, having educated ourselves towards exile from meaning and at the same time being still possessed by a half-trust in that which has been relinquished. Here, I think, is where poetry and the arts and maybe religion, too, have their role to play: to make sense of what we don't know, to make up works that satisfy a sense of form and represent the possibility of perceiving a whole truth."[6] Heaney's poetry attempts to stay the confusion in its continuous evolving toward a place of wholeness, integrity.

In an interview with Catharine Malloy, Heaney revealed his own awareness of the emerging shapes in his poetry: "What may have emerged in the last ten or twelve years is a sense of purpose that wasn't necessarily there before and some sense of controlling, underlying shapes. . . ."[7] He went on to describe his growing desire to "see from the circumference towards the center and to displace the autobiographical eye or to displace that with some fictional figure or other perspective." The "displacement" that Heaney's poetry moves toward encompasses both presence and absence: "I'm much devoted to the idea of a space that is both full and empty, like a disappearing island or the Lough Derg space or Station Island, which is both an empty repetition and a resource—the idea of fullness and emptiness."[8]

The shaping of spaces that are both full and empty contributes to making poetry what Heaney calls elsewhere "a threshold": "one constantly approached and constantly departed from, at which reader and writer undergo in their different ways the experience of being summoned and released" (*GT* 108). Exploring how Heaney's poetry both summons and releases, how "the shaping spirit" operates in Heaney's poetry as it responds to the possibilities of language and events, is the central concern of this collection of essays.

Previous collections of essays on Heaney's poetry have taken widely divergent forms. The first volume, *The Art of Seamus Heaney*, edited by Tony Curtis and published over a dozen years ago (1982), is distinctive in that seven of the eight contributors—including Ciaran Carson, Dick Davis, and Barbara Hardy—were creative writers themselves. The essays in the Curtis collection discuss individual works chronologically through *Station Island*. Harold Bloom's *Seamus Heaney* (1986) brings together selected essays published between 1977 and 1985, which are intended to represent "the best criticism"[9] on Heaney up to 1985. Bloom's volume, arranged chronologically according to when the contributors' essays were originally published, provides easy access to well-known critics on a wide range of topics related to Heaney. Jacqueline Genet's *Studies on Seamus Heaney* (1987) offers a bilingual collection with three essays in French by French critics and five essays in English. The essays range from a close reading of one poem to stylistic techniques to thematic overviews. More recently, *Seamus Heaney: A Collection of Critical Essays*, edited by Elmer Andrews (1992), provides in nine of its eleven essays various overviews of Heaney's poetic career. Special journal issues devoted to Heaney have occurred over the years, for example, *Salmagundi* (Fall 1988) and most recently, *Colby Quarterly* (March 1994). The latter contains essays by six writers, three of whom are represented in this collection: Catharine Malloy, Jonathan Allison, and Rand Brandes.

The present collection differs from previous volumes in that its essays, while offering a wide diversity of approaches, all concern themselves with the central critical issue of Heaney's artistic "shaping." Arranged loosely in a chronological pattern corresponding to Heaney's poetic career, the essays offer insights into concerns ranging from Heaney's reshaping of the mythological, to his use of individual images, to the influence of such "mentors" as Dante and Joyce, to Heaney's attempts to shape the numinous, to his unique rendering of the words of others through translation. The twofold purpose of the collection is to illuminate the protean nature of Heaney's poetic achievement—to examine the variety of inchoate energies influencing Heaney's shaping processes—and to relate those processes to larger political, social, and aesthetic contexts.

Robert Welch has characterized the thrust of Heaney's poetry as "total absorption and trance, a world transformed and translated from singleness and separateness, to integrity. This knowledge is poetic knowledge, an order of understanding capable of a sense of wholeness."[10] Welch emphasizes the shaping influence of Heaney's Irish background, where translation is a vital activity and where for two hundred years, Irish culture has "been in the business of translating itself to itself and to the outside world."[11] Seamus Deane, in the leadoff essay of this volume, suggests a fascinating twist on this idea as he provides an overview of Heaney's ability to translate the world into poetry. Contrasting Heaney's aesthetic with those of Yeats and Kinsella, Deane notes that Heaney's poetry recognizes the absence of a center, that it is "an attempt to voice that pure emptiness, to put the tongue in that 'O,' the vowel that is the precondition of speech." Deane demonstrates how Heaney translates the "pure emptiness" into the actual in his poetry: "[I]t is only through the poetry that the world to which it refers comes fully into existence." Rather than rendering the separateness into a wholeness, Deane argues that Heaney shapes the emptiness at the center of language to create the real world.

Deane's reading of Heaney's decentering process offers but one of many widely varying interpretations of his poetry. That Heaney can elicit the highest praise ("the finest poet in the English language")[12] as well as disdain ("he certainly can evoke place and mood, but his thoughts and his spiritual hauntings are blurred and vain")[13] derives in part from how one "reads" Heaney's attempts to "displace" and "to see from the circumference towards the center." In his provocative and witty essay, "Moments of

Misremembrance: A Poem and Its Audiences," John Boly explores the continuous and erratic *misshaping* that he sees arising from the persona-audience dialectic in "Death of a Naturalist." Boly uses a lexeographic reading of the poem to deconstruct the "master narrative" and to open it to elements that cannot be controlled by its author. For Boly, Heaney's persona miscasts the audience into various roles as readers as they are led into the past, but the "misremembrance" in its attempt to conceal can itself become a source of comic regeneration for the reader.

Heaney himself, of course, is keenly aware of the vicissitudes of writing at a time when language has lost its representative status:

> in the postmodern age, the very vocabulary has become untrustworthy, undermined by our awareness of its collusion with all kinds of secluded ideologies, based (depending upon your suspicion) upon gender or *imperium* or, indeed, subversions, and from this acknowledgement of language's duplicitousness arises a doubt about the very possibility of ever pronouncing the authentic persuasive word. . . . Thus, under the pressure of conflicting recognitions, in love with the literature of the past but sceptical of the language of the present, self-divided and self-rebuking, the poet stands like an embodiment of both the loaded scales and the trembling pointer needle. (*RP* 1412–13)

The dilemma of attempting to shape language that carries with it its own web of disjunctive, fragmented meanings becomes for Heaney, however, yet another source for poetic imagery. Rand Brandes in his "'Inscribed in Sheets': Seamus Heaney's Scribal Matrix" sees the recurring figure of the scribe in Heaney's poetry as Heaney's attempt to image the struggles and dilemmas of the writing process itself. Brandes argues that in *Sweeney Astray, Station Island* and *The Haw Lantern*, the scribe becomes a self-reflexive image, a trope the poet can use to contemplate the art of writing in a poststructuralist age that views texts in terms of the semiotic systems that structure society.

Heaney's use of pastoral images to shape the contradictions inherent in the poetic process is the focus of Jonathan Allison's essay, "Seamus Heaney's Anti-Transcendental Corncrake." That much of Heaney's poetry invokes the pastoral tradition has itself been the subject of a monograph on Heaney: *The Poetry of Resistance: Seamus Heaney and the Pastoral Tradition* by Sidney Burris. Burris argues that Heaney's poetry "while it remains sensitive to his country's abiding public demands, a pastoral concern, cultivates simultaneously the lyrical freedom that renders such demands palatable."[14] While Burris explores Heaney's pervasive use of the pastoral to conjoin the public with the lyrical, Allison, in exploring one image—the corncrake—provides an analytic microcosm of Heaney's penchant for the pastoral in his poetry. Allison contextualizes his discussion in corncrake poems and bird poems generally and compares and contrasts Heaney's use of the bird to that of other Irish poets (e.g., John Hewitt, Ciaran Carson, Norman Dugdale, Richard Murphy). Allison demonstrates how Heaney shapes this image to express the dialectic concerns—cultural, aesthetic, political—of the poetic voice. Allison's and Brandes's essays enable the reader to see how Heaney enlists recurring, dynamic images to resonate with larger cultural and metapoetic discourses.

Besides pastoral elements, the poetic world that Heaney forges encompasses his own past experiences, ancient myths and Irish folklore, the British-Irish troubles in Northern Ireland, and the poetic heritage of Dante, Wordsworth, Keats, Hopkins, Yeats, Frost, and Kavanagh. In a reference to Derek Mahon, Heaney has affirmed the purpose of poetry as "keep[ing] the colours new. They rinse things . . . first of all rinse the words, yes. But also perhaps rinse—and hang out again on the line—values . . . which are fundamental to the culture, the myth values of the culture."[15]

How the poet reshapes the mythical and merges it with the autobiographical is the focus of David Lloyd's essay, "Fusions in Heaney's *North*." Lloyd demonstrates how Heaney unites ancient impulse and present reality in *North*. By merging his voice and sensibility with figures from mythology and literary texts, Heaney's poetic shaping reveals how archaic elements underpin and partially direct contemporary consciousness. As a result, the political dilemmas of Northern Ireland can be viewed in wider mythological and historical contexts, providing perspectives beyond the sectarian.

The current resurgence in Northern Irish poetry that Heaney exemplifies, along with such writers as Derek Mahon, Medbh McGuckian, Ciaran Carson, Michael Longley, and others, raises the question of the relationship of literature and the political violence with which it coincides. Seamus Deane in an interview with the editors of this volume pondered this question:

> I think [the literary revival and the violence] are connected, but what one would understand in the connection is still problematic. One of the questions that has to be addressed in Ireland is the relationship between violent change and literary revival. Twice in this century there has been a political crisis in Ireland: once in the early century and once in '68, and both of them have coincided with a revival in various modes of writing and discourse. The almost perfect coincidence between the publication of the Northern poets and the outbreak of the troubles is surely more than coincidental, but at the same time I hesitate to say that either one caused the other. . . . Much of the

literature [of the Irish revival between 1880 and 1930] could almost be classified as "Studies in a Dying Culture," a culture that is fading, a culture that is about to go under, and yet, it's precisely because it is "dying" that it is able to produce this golden moment of articulation before its extinction—whether it's O'Casey's tenements or Synge's West or the Yeatsian dream of an Ireland combining the nobleman and the beggarman or, of course, the famous paralysis of the Dublin of the early Joyce. Even there, there is a connection that is now necessary to reinterpret, or it's that kind of connection that has now become pronouncedly important for us because it's saying something about our own position in the North.[16]

Heaney's own treatment of the troubles in Northern Ireland has met with a great deal of controversy. Early in Heaney's career, for example, the Northern poet Ciaran Carson took issue with Heaney in a 1975 issue of the *Honest Ulsterman*. At the time Carson was concerned that Heaney was becoming "the laureate of violence—a mythmaker, an anthropologist of ritual killing, an apologist for 'the situation,' in the last resort, a mystifier."[17] While not responding directly to Carson, Heaney has written about his own view on the relationship between myth and the political realities of his homeland:

The poet is stretched between politics and transcendence, and is often displaced from a confidence in a single position by his disposition to be affected by all positions, negatively rather than positively capable. This, and the complexity of the present conditions, may go some way to explain the large number of poems in which the Northern Irish writer views the world from a great spatial or temporal distance, the number of poems imagined from beyond the grave, from the perspective of mythological or historically remote characters. . . .[18]

The distancing that the use of mythology provides enables Heaney to "unplug a political undercurrent in the poetry."[19] Charles O'Neill explores that undercurrent, specifically the mechanisms of violence and representation in Heaney's myth of *North*. Using René Girard's theory of the relationship between violence and the sacred, O'Neill demonstrates how Heaney's reshaping of myth allows it to speak its timeless human truths, the complicity of all in violence and its connection with what Heaney has termed "this terrible sacrificial religious thing."[20] Together, Lloyd's and O'Neill's essays provide widely divergent yet complementary readings of *North* that reveal the complexities of Heaney's transformation of myth into living, universal reality. As Elmer Andrews has noted in *The Poetry of Seamus Heaney:* "[Heaney] seeks to compose, not a pseudo-reality, but those facets of reality that bring what we do not know—or do not want to know—about ourselves to light."[21]

Reseeing and reshaping the past is a continuous concern for Heaney, whether it is the ancestral past, his literary heritage, or his own personal past. That meaning can arise out of the purifying process of examining the past is a major shaping impetus in Heaney's poetry from *Station Island* to the present. According to Heaney, "[T]he best poetry will not only register the assault of the actual and the brunt of necessity; it will also embody the spirit's protest against all that" (*RP* 1413). In Heaney's poetry, the affirmative aspect of the "spirit's protest" involves what he calls elsewhere "purifying language" with a kind of shaping that "lets a blind up for a moment," revealing a fragment of truth: "The kinds of truth that art gives us many, many times are small truths. They don't have the resonance of an encyclical from the Pope stating an eternal truth, but they partake of the quality of eternity." "Purifying language" for Heaney includes using words, which in the current age have become only words, "like soul and spirit. You want them to . . . yes, to be available, to purify possibilities again."[22]

Station Island becomes one of Heaney's major attempts to "embody the spirit's protest" and to purify language by boldly confronting the past. Sammye Crawford Greer in her essay, "'Station Island' and the Poet's Progress," analyzes Heaney's "paradigmatic descent into the land of the dead" where he discovers a counterweight to the emptiness at the center: the poetic act of "salvaging"—"to re-envisage / the zenith" (*SP* 208) itself becomes the tangent leading from the abyss.

Confronting the past by examining Irish cultural memory is the focus of Michael Patrick Gillespie in his "Aesthetic and Cultural Memory in Joyce and Heaney." Gillespie, a noted Joyce scholar, examines "Station Island" to show how Heaney uses the Joycean influence "to validate Heaney's own poetic efforts." Gillespie argues that Joyce becomes for Heaney a way of articulating the struggle Heaney himself feels between the inspiration of the culture he comes from and its parochial concerns. As Heaney himself has observed, "Joyce de-provincialized the Irish reader of various writers and in that way he is extremely enabling. . . . [His] significance [is] as somebody who helped to enable the writer from the region to be fortified in relation to the center because he amplified and verified that pleasure in language. There was the pleasure of recognition and the pleasure of feeling that your world was becoming word, and that is tremendously gratifying."[23]

Heaney's recognition of Joyce's ability to translate "the region" into word complements his refusal to abdicate his own "region." In a Field Day pamphlet, Heaney responded to the editors of *Contemporary British Verse* that his "anxious muse, / Roused on her bed among the furze / has to refuse / the adjective . . . 'British.'"[24] The attempt to amplify the local without betraying it accounts to some extent for Heaney's attraction to writers from the Eastern bloc, e.g., Osip Mandelstam, Czeslaw Milosz, and Zbigniew

Herbert, writers whose homelands had been politically betrayed. It also accounts for Heaney's role as a director of and his contributions to the Field Day enterprise, an attempt, according to Seamus Deane "to redefine or open up . . . a cultural space—also to some extent a political space as we envisioned it—to escape from the cul de sac, stereotypes, and political collapse of Northern Ireland."[25] Heaney translated Sophocles' *Philoctetes* for a Field Day production in 1990, and in her essay on *The Cure at Troy*, Phyllis Carey argues that in Heaney's version the focus is on awakening the audience/ reader to the possibilities of seeing through poetry. What is suggested by the play is the need to move beyond retribution to imagined possibilities. Poetry itself becomes the threshold in the play, summoning the reader/ viewer to release from the isolating prison of a politics based on revenge. Carey uses Václav Havel's *Largo Desolato* as a foil for *The Cure at Troy*. Both political dramas, whose writers have each experienced various kinds of colonization, are created as dissident parables.

In *Seeing Things,* Heaney moves to a kind of shaping that attempts to invest the concrete image with nearly mystical qualities. Heaney himself has said that in *Seeing Things* there is the "sense of an airiness as well as the double take . . . a downbeat, flat, looking-at-things mood and at the same time a hallucinatory experience, a dubiousness about what you're seeing when you're seeing things."[26] Catharine Malloy in her "Seamus Heaney's *Seeing Things:* 'Retracing the path back . . .'" examines the importance of language as a guide that facilitates memories of places, things, and family, and subsequently shapes experiences emanating from past sources and presences into a momentary wholeness.

The attempt to resee, to reshape, to "re-envisage the zenith," to "purify" language—all marks of Heaney's latest poetry—reveals also the formative influence of Dante on Heaney. Darcy O'Brien in his "Ways of *Seeing Things*" provides with the author's permission selections from Heaney's previously unpublished translation of Dante's *Inferno.* O'Brien argues that Heaney's translation is so guided by his own "shaping spirit" that the poetry seems to be as much Heaney's as Dante's, that Heaney has rendered the vision of the Florentine into twentieth-century reality. According to O'Brien, Heaney's translation of Dante in turn has enabled him in *Seeing Things* to "rekindle the numinous." Starting with the actual, Heaney shapes it into a "sign that is part of a larger pattern, shape or trajectory of action, that implies order and imparts mysterious joy."

Translating—whether it be the shaping of language to represent a vision, or, as an Irish writer, the attempt to articulate in a language laden with political implications, or the re-shaping in English of Greek, Italian, and Irish writing—becomes in many ways a paradigm for Heaney's aesthetic. Besides selections from Dante and Sophocles, Heaney has recently translated portions of Ovid's *Metamorphoses*, using them as frames for a translated excerpt from the Irish of Brian Merriman's *Cúirt an Mheón-Oíche* (1780). Heaney's explanation reveals his sensitivity to nuance and context: "It seemed in particular that the end of *The Midnight Court* took on a new resonance if it was read within the acoustic of the classical myth."[27] The juxtaposing of the Irish and the Greek, however, provides new resonances for both the Irish tale and Ovid's "Orpheus and Eurydice." Shaping anew the legacy of the past is a way of reshaping the present.

In December 1995, as this volume is going to press, Seamus Heaney has just received the 1995 Nobel Prize for Literature. He has just published his Oxford lectures, and his latest poetic explorations, *The Spirit Level*, will appear in early 1996. The contributors to this volume, following the lead of Heaney's "shaping spirit," have probed his poetry to suggest the protean energies and forces at work in a wide selection of Heaney's writings. In attempting to explore the dynamic modes of representation in Heaney's works, the following essays are offered as "field work" in Heaney criticism, digging into and opening up shapes and shaping processes, which, in turn, exceed the critical tools that have helped unearth them:

> And then when he thought of probes that reached the farthest,
> He would see the shaft of a pitchfork sailing past
> Evenly, imperturbably through space,
> Its prongs starlit and absolutely soundless—
>
> But has learned at last to follow that simple lead
> Past its own aim, out to an other side
> Where perfection—or nearness to it—is imagined
> Not in the aiming but the opening hand.
>
> "The Pitchfork" (*ST* 25)

Notes

1. Samuel Beckett, quoted in Bert States, *The Shape of Paradox: An Essay on Waiting for Godot* (Berkeley: University of California Press, 1978), 9.

2. Seamus Heaney, "Bard of Hope and Harp," interview by John Walsh, *Sunday Times* (7 October 1990): 7–4.

3. Seamus Heaney, "John Breslin interviews Seamus Heaney," interview by John Breslin, *Critic*, Winter 1991, 29.

4. Seamus Heaney, quoted in ibid.

5. Henry Hart, *Seamus Heaney: Poet of Contrary Progressions* (Syracuse, N.Y.: Syracuse University Press, 1992), 7.

6. Heaney, "John Breslin interviews," 34.

7. Seamus Heaney, interview by Catharine Malloy, Harvard University, March 1990.

8. Ibid.

9. Harold Bloom, ed., *Seamus Heaney* (New Haven: Chelsea House, 1986), vii.

10. Robert Welch, *Changing States: Transformations in Modern Irish Writing* (London: Routledge, 1993), 269.

11. Ibid., xi.

12. Heaney, "Bard of Hope and Harp," 7.2.

13. James Simmons, "The Trouble with Seamus," in *Seamus Heaney: A Collection of Critical Essays*, ed. Elmer Andrews (New York: St. Martin's Press, 1992), 60.

14. Sidney Burris, *The Poetry of Resistance: Seamus Heaney and the Pastoral Tradition* (Athens: Ohio University Press, 1990), xiii.

15. Seamus Heaney, "A Soul on the Washing Line," interview, *Economist* 319 (22 June 1991): 100.

16. Seamus Deane, "Making Connections: An Interview with Seamus Deane," interview by Phyllis Carey and Catharine Malloy, *Critic* 48 (Spring 1994): 35–36.

17. Ciaran Carson, "Escaped from the Massacre?" *Honest Ulsterman*, no. 50 (Winter 1975): 183–86.

18. Seamus Heaney, "The Peter Laver Memorial Lecture: 'Place and Displacement': Recent Poetry from Northern Ireland," *Wordsworth Circle* 16 (Spring 1985): 50–51.

19. Eileen Cahill, "A silent voice: Seamus Heaney and Ulster Politics," *Critical Quarterly* 29, no. 3 (Autumn 1987): 57.

20. Seamus Heaney, interview by James Randall, *Ploughshares* 5 (1979): 18.

21. Elmer Andrews, *The Poetry of Seamus Heaney: All the Realms of Whisper* (New York: St. Martin's Press, 1988), 202.

22. Heaney, "A Soul," *Economist*, 100–102.

23. Heaney, interview by Catharine Malloy.

24. Seamus Heaney, *An Open Letter by Seamus Heaney*, Field Day Theatre pamphlet, no. 2 (Derry: Field Day Theatre Company, 1983), 7.

25. Deane, "Making Connections," 31.

26. Heaney, "John Breslin interviews," 28.

27. Seamus Heaney, *The Midnight Verdict* (Loughcrew, Oldcastle, County Meath, Ireland: The Gallery Press, 1993), 11.

Works Cited

Andrews, Elmer. *The Poetry of Seamus Heaney: All the Realms of Whisper.* New York: St. Martin's Press, 1988.

———, ed. *Seamus Heaney: A Collection of Critical Essays.* New York: St. Martin's Press, 1992.

Bloom, Harold, ed. *Seamus Heaney.* New Haven, Conn.: Chelsea House, 1986.

Burris, Sidney. *The Poetry of Resistance: Seamus Heaney and the Pastoral Tradition.* Athens: Ohio University Press, 1990.

Cahill, Eileen. "A silent voice: Seamus Heaney and Ulster Politics." *Critical Quarterly* 29, no. 3 (Autumn 1987): 55–70.

Carson, Ciaran. "Escaped from the Massacre?" *The Honest Ulsterman*, no. 50 (Winter 1975): 183–86.

Curtis, Tony, ed. *The Art of Seamus Heaney.* Mid Glamorgan, Wales: Poetry Wales Press, 1982.

Deane, Seamus. "Making Connections: An Interview with Seamus Deane." Interview by Phyllis Carey and Catharine Malloy. *The Critic* 48 (Spring 1994): 29–37.

Genet, Jacqueline. *Studies on Seamus Heaney*. Caen, France: Centre de Publications de l'Université de Caen, 1987.

Hart, Henry. *Seamus Heaney: Poet of Contrary Progressions*. Syracuse, N.Y.: Syracuse University Press, 1992.

Heaney, Seamus. "Bard of Hope and Harp." Interview by John Walsh. *The Sunday Times*, 7 October 1990, 7.2–7.4.

———. Interview by Catharine Malloy. Harvard University, March 1990. Unpublished.

———. Interview by James Randall. *Ploughshares* 5 (1979): 7–22.

———. "Seeing Things: John Breslin interviews Seamus Heaney." Interview by John Breslin. *The Critic* 46 (Winter 1991): 26–35.

———. *The Midnight Verdict*. Loughcrew, Oldcastle, County Meath, Ireland: The Gallery Press, 1993.

———. *An Open Letter by Seamus Heaney*. Field Day Theatre Pamphlet, no. 2. Derry: Field Day Theatre Company Ltd., 1983.

———. "The Peter Laver Memorial Lecture: 'Place and Displacement': Recent Poetry from Northern Ireland." *The Wordsworth Circle* 16 (Spring 1985): 48–56.

———. *The Redress of Poetry: Oxford Lectures*. London: Faber and Faber, 1995.

———. "A Soul on the Washing Line." Interview. *The Economist*. 319, no. 7712 (22 June 1991): 98–102.

———. *The Spirit Level*. New York: Farrar, Straus & Giroux, 1996.

Simmons, James. "The Trouble with Seamus." In *Seamus Heaney: A Collection of Critical Essays*, edited by Elmer Andrews, 39–66. New York: St. Martin's Press, 1992.

States, Bert O. *The Shape of Paradox: An Essay on Waiting for Godot*. Berkeley: University of California Press, 1978.

Welch, Robert. *Changing States: Transformations in Modern Irish Writing*. London: Routledge, 1993.

SEAMUS HEANEY

Powers of Earth and
Visions of Air

SEAMUS DEANE

Since his first book, *Death of a Naturalist* (1966), Seamus Heaney has been
much concerned with deaths of various kinds. His life as a writer has almost
exactly coincided with the most recent period of crisis in Northern Ireland,
and the degeneration of that rancid statelet over the past twenty years has
provided enough violent killings to deepen a preoccupation that was already there in the early work. In Heaney's poetry, as in the political world
that subsists with it, there is a need to possess or to repossess a territory that
is always there in its specific actuality and yet evades all attempts to seize
and hold it in one stabilizing grasp.

It has often been observed that Heaney's work—especially the first four
volumes, including *Door into the Dark* (1969), *Wintering Out* (1972) and *North*
(1975)—has a remarkably large vocabulary for earth, especially earth in a
state of deliquescence, earth mixed with water. *Mud, slime, mould, silt,* and
slicks are words that note the ambiguity of the ground itself; they appear in
those man-made workings that Heaney endlessly explores, in trenches,
drains, pits, wells and furrows. These in turn belong to particular kinds of
territory—fens, bogs, loanings, keshes—and all of these are finally embed-
ded in political and religious division of the land: baronies, parishes, counties,
and parklands. Even the local place-names are seduced into their alluvial
origins. To name a place is to pronounce the kind of ground it occupies; to
fail to pronounce the name properly is to fail to possess it truly, to be foreign.
This devotion to the ground and its names, the constant ascent from original slime to the nominations of geography and history, provides Heaney's
poetry with a highly complex sonar architecture in which vowels and consonants dispute between themselves for an equilibrium that will allow to each
its separate function and yet acknowledge for both their interdependence. The

Extracted and reprinted with permission of the author from the *Times Literary Supplement*, 16 March 1990, 275–76.

27

vowel, especially the vowel *O,* is originary: but it cannot speak the emptiness it represents without the consonantal surround. Looms and honeycombs, seeds splitting into root systems, interconnected deltas of archaeological remains, develop their ramifications around these gaping open ground vowels, the eyes, sores, valves and wounds that are the characteristic marks of the creature who is the ultimate victim of and possessor of the ground—the buried corpse.

In *Wintering Out* and in *North,* more than in any previous volume, Heaney found a way to make the ground speak in a human voice. The act of ventriloquism by which he made the Viking dead speak for the contemporary victims of violence in Ireland was a brilliant stroke—it enabled to a higher degree than before the tone of reverence and piety that had been and has continued to be the most notable aspect of Heaney's mode of address to his subject. The violence of the actions that had produced these sacrificial victims was only partly muted. By deflecting it to these archaeological remains, he could brood on it without risking that pornographic observation of atrocity which is so frequently found in the reportage of political crises. More importantly, though, it brought him back to the inexhaustible trope of origin (since the violence is, in a sense, originary, prehistoric) and death as manifested in the earth itself. The territory now assumes yet another vocabulary—of souterrain, flint, and hoard—the words of archaeology that support and reproduce the words of farming and cultivation. A digging is now both a cultivation of the ground and an exploration of it. The ground is never firm; like the bog, with its moss and peat and its aqueous nervous system, it absorbs and preserves the dead it receives, making them like itself but allowing them to retain their own identity, an embrace of vowel and consonant. For Heaney, this is a linguistic as well as a historical and political drama, an actual place in time, geography intersecting history, in and through which he can gaze at the nub, node, or center his poetry craves.

For all the consolations Heaney's poetry is supposed to offer, it is, in truth, unconsoling. Its evocation of tradition, rural landscape, folk custom and deep historical time in tones that bespeak healing, annealment, reverence and peace is powerful indeed. Yet the quest for a center, for what he calls an "omphalos," is darkly stimulated by his recognition that the idea of a center is fictive. The tree that he remembers from his childhood as part of the garden hedge has been cut down, and in the eighth and last poem of the sequence called "Clearances" (from *The Haw Lantern,* 1987), he writes of the empty source it has become:

> I thought of walking round and round a space
> Utterly empty, utterly a source . . .

Finally it has, marvelously, become

> a bright nowhere,
> A soul ramifying and forever
> Silent, beyond silence listened for.

"Ramifying" is the key word here. As Heaney's poetry has changed, the thick trellises of earth and water have become more and more etherealized, as he dwells more and more somberly on that ultimate emptiness which death, like that of his mother and of the several victims of political violence, commemorated particularly in poems such as "The Strand at Lough Beg," "Casualty" and "Triptych" (all in *Field Work,* 1979), make more acute. The tree that is cut down in the eighth poem of "Clearances" is anticipated in the immediately preceding sonnet, which ends with a similarly emptied space in which cries, not a tree, are felled. Ultimately, everything that has a physical actuality is translated into a voice. Silence is the voice of emptiness.

> The space we stood around had been emptied
> Into us to keep, it penetrated
> Clearances that suddenly stood open.
> High cries were felled and a pure change happened.

Heaney's poetry is an attempt to voice that pure emptiness, to put the tongue in that *O,* the vowel that is the precondition of speech and that is altered by it. In *North,* he found a way to figure this issue in the opposition between Antaeus, the hugger of the ground, from which came his strength, and Hercules, who defeats Antaeus by lifting him off the ground into the air. The elemental territories are, of course, incorporated in this figure; earth and water vie with air and fire. It is Heaney's emblem for his own version of his development as a writer. He asks a severe question here. Is the emptiness actual or is it a virtual absence that produces a real poetry? Conversely, if it is a real absence, is the poetry that engages with it merely virtual? The terms in which he conducts this investigation are recognizably ones that recur in Irish poetry, particularly in this century. It is in *Station Island* (1984) that Heaney opens the debate into a series of encounters that take place at Lough Derg, a traditional site of pilgrimage in Ireland since early medieval times and a place of literary pilgrimage for a number of writers before him—William Carleton, Patrick Kavanagh, Denis Devlin, and Sean O'Faoláin.

All of these, in their different ways, represented Lough Derg as a place of ancestral faith, profoundly disturbing to the secular modern spirit with which they had become imbued. It is, in Heaney's terms, an Antaean place visited by a Herculean sensibility. Yeats is the great poet in whose work this debate had been most dramatically staged. His folk Ireland and his occult worlds were constantly coalescing to form an alternative to the modern world of eighteenth-century Anglo-Irish enlightenment and its degenerate offspring, the modern secular world of the twentieth century. He too was intent on achieving an act of repossession out of a series of dispossessions. The territory of Ireland and the realm of magic were dissolved into one another in an attempt to assert an originary and blessed quality that had disappeared in a world without the aura of memory, without the charisma of the spiritual. This is all part of the traditional debate between the metropolitan and the regional community, with the latter now claiming that it possesses a form of knowledge not subordinate but superior to the rational knowledge produced by the metropolis. Regions, thus conceived, regard themselves and are regarded as the habitat of the instinctual, the irrational, or the nonrational. The attractions of this form of the debate were too much for Yeats. He sought to sacralize the territory of Ireland in order to ratify his notion of the Irish as an autonomous and antimodern community. This is the most powerful form of conservative nationalism, partly because it is based on a critique of the colonial power as a degenerate version of civilization. To that extent, it served Yeats well; the political situation in Europe in the first three decades of this century encouraged such views, although it did not often see such poetry elicited by them.

Since then, poetry in Ireland has, in its more remarkable manifestations, sought to reconstitute the Yeatsian version of culture. Yeats found all his versions of origin were complicit with violence. So too, from a quite different version, does Thomas Kinsella. Heaney rewrites the issue by attributing to his version of origin this pure emptiness. When the emptiness speaks, it speaks of violent death, but is distinct from it. The act of poetry is a Herculean effort to lift off from the old Antaeus-like hugging of the holy and violent ground into the realm of air and fire, the zone of vision, not merely the dry air of rational enlightenment. Heaney's later poetry is full of subtle slicings that confirm this distinction. He does not move from the regional to the metropolitan. The quizzical relationship between these two is of interest to him; but it is too limiting. He wants the powers of earth to give him sufficient liftoff to carry him into the regions of the air. In *The Haw Lantern*, there is a poem called "Mud Vision" about an "appearance"—of a sort frequent in Ireland, although usually in the form of the Virgin—that transforms a ruined gable wall into a great mud rose window. The enchantment stays for a while; then it disappears and the media begin their explanations. The community gives its trust to these and betrays itself.

Just like that, we forgot that the vision was ours,
Our one chance to know the incomparable
And dive to a future. What might have been origin
We dissipated in news. The clarified place
Had retrieved neither us nor itself—except
You could say we survived. So say that, and watch us
Who had our chance to be mud-men, convinced and
                                        estranged,
Figure in our own eyes for the eyes of the world.

That is only the most recent of a number of missed visionary opportunities. The poem "Exposure" (in *North*) is another notable example; in that instance, the poet misses the "comet's pulsing rose" because he had been listening to the rational or rationalizing explanations of his friends, attempting to account for the political crisis and for Heaney's ascribed or proscribed role within it. Listen to reason and you'll miss the vision, especially the vision that belongs to the air but is constituted of the material of the earth.

One has to be careful, therefore, with Heaney's invocations, in *Station Island* and elsewhere, of his mentors—whether Carleton or Joyce, Wordsworth or Dante or the name not mentioned, the emptiness at the heart of the list: Yeats. In effect, he is asking them for no specific guidance; he is really asking them to let him go, let him be free. The Irish mentors in these poems, Joyce especially, talk like Heaney. They are occasions for self-endorsement, to go ahead "and fill the element / with signatures on your own frequency." Immediately after the Joycean encounter that closes the central sequence in *Station Island*, Heaney takes his own advice and becomes Sweeney, the legendary Irish king who was changed into a bird and is famous for his madness and his poetry. (It was Flann O'Brien who had most memorably commemorated Sweeney before Heaney's version, *Sweeney Astray*, 1983.) The cleric who had changed Sweeney into a bird played, unwittingly, the stern role of a Heaney mentor. He rebuked him into poetry by releasing him from the ground of history, from the imprisonment threatened by the competing allegiances of Irish experience:

> he opened my path to a kingdom
> of such scope and neuter allegiance
> my emptiness reigns at its whim.

That is Heaney's way of making history, especially Irish political and literary history, consort with that pure emptiness, that blank and fictive center that is the heart of his desire. An allegiance that is neuter is a fidelity

without an object of faith commensurate with its strength. As Sweeney
Redivivus, Heaney looks for it in moments when the given, that which is
there, is suddenly released from its congealment in the actual. A cave painting of a drinking deer is meditated on

> until the long dumbfounded
> spirit broke cover
> to raise a dust
> in the font of exhaustion.

Heaney's ultimate home is not Station Island, or the island of Ireland, but,
as he titles it in *The Haw Lantern*, "The Disappearing Island." In this poem
the imagined situation is that of a band of wandering Irish monks, voyaging
in the western seas and making camp on an island that disappears as they
light their fire. (The old tales mention such islands that turned out to be
whales, sea monsters.) The final stanza restores to us memories of Heaney's
earlier explorations of that boundary between the actual and the visionary.
"Water and ground in their extremity" (from "The Peninsula," in *Door into
the Dark*) is one version of it; another is registered in the recurrent images of
eye, needle, notch, the infinitesimally small opening through which the actual flows, as through an isthmus, into the visionary. For that to happen, the
fidelity must be there; but it must be given to a vision and in such a manner
that it is the actual that becomes the product rather than the precondition
of the vision.

> The land sustaining us seemed to hold firm
> Only when we embraced it *in extremis*.
> All I believe that happened there was vision.

Perhaps it is this probing, exact and exacting measurement of the fictive
distance between actualities and their representation that so attracts audiences and readers to Heaney's work. He gives the double impression that
nothing gets lost in the translation of the world into poetry, and that it is
only through the poetry that the world to which it refers comes fully into
existence. He so narrows the discrepancy between world and word, so win-
ningly lends a tongue to emptiness, that the effect is genial. His is an earth
that speaks directly and in recognition to the body. It is without even the
vestige of alienation. At the root of every word there is a tentacular hand-
shake between the speaker and the thing spoken of. In "A Postcard from
Iceland" (in *The Haw Lantern*), we learn that the word "lukewarm," describing the temperature of the water from a spring, derives from the old Icelandic
word *luk*, meaning "hand." Heaney characteristically shares this knowledge

with his reader by making it more intimate, by making hand into "palm" and by telling us we knew it already. Of course we did; but never this way.

> And you would want to know (but you know
> already)
> How usual that waft and pressure felt
> When the innerpalm of water found my palm.

Here the reader is acknowledged as a lover in a world that is "usual" and yet, as in love, extraordinarily perceived.

Heaney's *New Selected Poems, 1966–1987* does not include this poem, but then there are very few indeed from the last three volumes that I would have had the heart to exclude. The work gets more and more Herculean, but the Antaean root does not snap. In *The Place of Writing*, the inaugural Richard Ellmann Lectures in Modern Literature delivered at Emory University, Heaney broods on the question of place and writing, with Yeats finally taking here a priority never assigned him in Heaney's own poetry. Heaney's reading of Yeats is also a reading of himself, particularly what he calls Yeats's "desire for foundedness" and the accompanying "fear of unfoundedness which might lurk beneath it." Heaney is exploring his own recent preoccupation with an origin that is empty, because writing reveals its absence, and yet is actual because writing envisions its presence. Yeats's tower is transposed into the poems; for Heaney these themselves become buildings, stanzas return to their origin by becoming rooms, and the verbal architecture of the poem locates itself in a space that is also a place. The actuality of place queries the insubstantiality of space; but space is what place becomes in vision. This affirmation and denial are an operatic affair in Yeats. The music is Wagnerian, the libretto Nietzschean. Heaney loves the Götterdämmerung atmosphere, but his admiration is more pronounced than his affection. He prefers what his contemporaries, such as Kinsella, Montague, Mahon, and Muldoon, do when they refuse the limited destiny of place and go in search of "the problematic place of the writer." In Ireland, where the place has been invested with such political energy, this is a difficult problem. In one sense, it is the struggle to become a writer rather than an Irish writer. You can't be one without the other; yet to be too self-consciously Irish might rob one of the freedom to be a writer, an author. These poets have to authorize their Irishness by giving primacy to *authority*; only then will the place of Ireland become real. Otherwise it is merely a stereotype, a place that is given, not found.

Moments of Misremembrance:
A Poem and Its Audiences

JOHN R. BOLY

Each utterance, whether simple or complex, opposes an inseparable pair. Someone speaks. Someone else (even if it be the initial speaker, some other facet of his or her being) listens. As a worldly science, criticism cherishes this drama of master and slave. A subspecies of rhetoric, criticism considers how the speaker renders an intended meaning and how the listener can more accurately decode its content. Occasionally, though, a text dissents from this familiar bondage by recalling that the image of the speaker is derivative. Until opened and read, a text has no voice. And what voice it has attains an image only through an act of construction, by a reader. Yet who is this reader? Criticism routinely ducks the issue through the subterfuge of myth: The reader is a lowest common denominator, a residue of correct stereotypes, someone who gets it right. Ordinary experience, though, indicates something quite different. The reader is a speculative image, that is, made up from refractions and cast upon a void. The reader is thus an event. The reader is whatever happens when the text projects an image on the inconceivable enigma that confronts it: an audience that anyone may join and each of whose members consists of a volatile, continuously mutating array of personalities. And it is this audience, or more precisely, its variable response to the image imposed upon it, that in turn constructs a version of the speaker. But the image of the audience, even if entirely implicit, comes first. Far from serving as an origin (paternal, all-seeing, stable), the speaker is a derivative, a surmise cast from what is itself adrift.

Seamus Heaney never forgets the priority of his audience. That elusive entity, its form and lot, is the focal point of his poetry. Yet caution is necessary here, lest a venerable myth be replaced with a more intransigent one. Paradoxically, the image of the audience can be approached only belatedly, as an inference from its own inference. Because the poetic audience is typically implied rather than presented, its image must be pieced together retrospectively, from the profile of the speaker, even though the audience both precedes and constructs that image. Accordingly, Heaney's texts propose a strange path for criticism, one that supersedes rhetoric with lexeography. Literally *a writing of a reading,* the lexeographic disentangles the implicit from the reactive by studying speaker/audience as a matched, unstable, continuously evolving pair. It begins, as does rhetoric, with a master image, the genius loci of a presiding intent. But rather than offering up all subsequent inquiry to the appeasement of this image, lexeography balances it with a necessary other, its implied respondent. Even more important, rather than relegating this respondent to a lustrous meekness, lexeography takes the imputation in earnest: as the writing of a reading, it *acts out* the role assigned to the audience, thoroughly, exhaustively, even perversely. That acting opens an unexplored critical itinerary. For no sooner does the audience take on an imputed part than it discovers, by acting out its role, that the prior image of the speaker has changed as well. And because speaker and audience are inseparably linked, their misshaping is continuous, erratic.

An immediate consequence of this misshaping is a different sense of poetic voice. When Heaney described the title poem, "Death of a Naturalist," as an early work in which he found his voice, the remark seems like an endorsement of rhetoric: the voice is what establishes a link between stable images, of speaker and audience. Yet the poem does not suggest a link but a diaspora. It begins, "All year the flax-dam festered in the heart / Of the townland." The "All year" belongs to the promiscuous simultaneity of *illud tempus,* mythic time. This is not the deceptive composure of a moment, but all the unrelated and incalculable impulses of an entire lifetime. Accumulative, it brings together a recollecting narrator, an ebullient idolater of frogspawn, a child terrified of the frog kings, and a nameless, helpless infant. Nor do matters stand otherwise with the audience. Addressed to the inhabitants of the townland, the poem asserts an absolute democratic right. It accepts anyone who can read. To be all-embracing, however, is to be all-negating. Permitted to be anyone, we become no one. Thus Heaney's voice severs its connection with a defined imagery of either speaker or audience. A contest between protean mysteries, it marks a certain cast: whether as dramatis personae, desperate conjecture, or deceptive simulacrum.

"Death of a Naturalist" serves as a reminder that what we meet in a poem is not an image, but a persona. Taken from the name of the mask worn by ancient actors, a persona is that which is sounded-through. Certainly it has an evident image. Yet this image is but one characteristic and by no means the most important. For example, a persona remains mute until an actor, a human subject, dons its guise. Thus the persona is a concealment as well as a disclosure, and its apparent image offers ample opportunity for provocation, cunning, and deceit. Moreover, custom often demanded that the mask have no opening for the eyes, save for two tiny holes drilled toward its top. So just as the persona hid the actor from the audience, it also hid the audience from the actor. Still, one visible opening had to be permitted, a slit for the actor's mouth, so that sounds could pass. The resulting asymmetry is highly important. While the persona imposes its visible image at the cost of blindness, it offers to refine and develop that image (to permit the actor to think, change, and act) by splitting itself asunder. Through this required opening, a rift in its image, the persona begins to play a complex part. It sets the stage for an intricate drama within its fourfold cast: a hidden subject, a conjectured audience, a concealing image, a fatal rift.

Both rhetoric and lexeography start with the same question: What is the image assumed by the persona? But while for rhetoric this image serves as a rule to which all else is subordinate, for lexeography it is an early move in an unrelenting dialogue. The initial speaker in "Death of a Naturalist," like the narrator of Joyce's "Araby," suggests a retrospective figure, older, seasoned, embittered. He deliberately refrains from any contemporary self-portrayal and instead proposes an earlier representation, himself as a boy of five or six. So the audience must make its way from a proffered image to an occluded source. How is this child father to the man? Seeking an answer to the inevitable question about the origin of life, the little boy chances upon the revelation of the frogspawn. The tiny eggs promise to tell him whence he has come and whither he is going. Yet such knowledge of destiny is gathered at a terrible price. The frogspawn are stolen from the flax-dam. Promethean in nature, the child's discovery is a windfall that nonetheless demands retribution. It is to avert this fate that the poem is conceived as a confession. By disclosing the theft of a little boy, the narrator hopes to avert the dire consequences of his past.

If the persona is cast as penitent, then the audience becomes the confessor. Forgive me, reader, for I have sinned. And so we arrive at the first pair in the lexeographic drama: penitent/confessor. To inquire as to the duties of the confessor in fact poses a more important question: What advantages does the persona gain by casting the audience in this way? Readers do not enter the text as a tabula rasa, blank screens with no inscriptions of their own. Rather, readers enter the text as fugitives from a hostile world: a place where each nameless one must endure the insult of being insignificant, powerless, expendable. Yet all this disappears in the moment of reading! Magically (without *apparent* effort, that is, through a hidden mechanism), the audience is raised to a position of importance and respect. The confessor is a standard of community mores, a keeper of deepest intimacies, a judge whose verdicts may not be appealed. As if in a fairy tale, the abject reader suddenly discovers that he or she is the long-lost and rightful heir.

The reader, of course, has no right whatsoever to this role. Yet who might decline so alluring an offer? As in any decent seduction, the first job is to hook the mark. The sole function of the persona's initial move is to entice the audience into taking a part, *whatever that part might be.*

But the thrill of this newfound status is brief. Actor and audience, the adversaries of any lexeographic contest, are held in the poise of a genteel antagonism. As confessor, the audience must ascertain the true nature of the offense. And given the human propensity to cunning and self-deception, that task can be difficult. Is it really so terrible to plunder a few jarfuls of frogspawn? The pond contains an abundance, they serve no useful purpose, and the biblical imperative enjoins Adam to subjugate nature. Or is such a "confession" the ploy of a hypocrite who diverts attention to a lesser offense? On closer examination, the text suggests that the announced crime is but a prelude to another theft, one not of knowledge but of sight.

> Then one hot day when fields were rank
> With cowdung in the grass the angry frogs
> Invaded the flax-dam; I ducked through hedges
> To a coarse croaking I had not heard
> Before. The air was thick with a bass chorus.
> Right down the dam gross-bellied frogs were cocked
> On sods; their loose necks pulsed like sails. Some hopped:
> The slap and plop were obscene threats. Some sat
> Poised like mud grenades, their blunt heads farting.
>
> (*DN* 6)

The little boy, intent upon his quest for origins, stumbles upon quite a different revelation. Drawn by unusual noises, he wanders into the primal scene, the parents in bed. Because of its intolerable disclosure, that one begins in no more than the brute fact of an inglorious coupling (oblivious, arbitrary, trite), this is an aboriginal trauma that must be repressed. Yet, repression, despite its misleading name, is an honest recorder. It preserves each crucial detail and asks only that the language of anxiety be translated to one of triviality. Thus the frog trauma faithfully bears a child's essential impressions: the ridiculous noise of bodies pressed together, the curious folds of skin, the awkward and erratic movements. To seal matters, the child is not seen before he flees in terror: "I sickened, turned, and ran." There is no intervening discourse, no propitiatory myth, not even the odd solace of punishment to stand between the little and the awful truth, "Right down the dam. . . ."

In effect the audience is asked to overcome a paralyzing blindness: to see what the child has seen yet cannot bear. This request opens an immensely gratifying prospect for the audience: to play the decoder, to retrieve truth from the devious clutches of repression, to trivialize the traumatic. But before the audience can pursue this role at any length, a difficulty arises. Whereas the trauma is endured by the child, it is narrated by the adult. Does the later narrator share the repressive blindness, or is this only a pretense? The question is unanswerable. Yet that does not matter because even its possibility is determinative. By putting an earlier image of himself on display, the persona shifts from penitent to exhibitionist. And in doing so he in turn transforms the audience from confessor to voyeur. Through this subtle shift, then, the lexeographics enters a further phase. Having engaged the audience, the persona proceeds to cast it in a quite compromising role. The child accidentally stumbles upon the scene. The narrator, shielded by repression, can at least claim to be innocent of its true nature. Yet the onlooking audience has not only recreated each sordid detail but indulged in a shameless fantasy of power.

Unexpectedly, the audience is brought face to face with that most insufferable of perversions, its own normality. Readers take for granted the privilege of an absolute detachment. Uninvolved themselves, they feel free to penetrate the disguises of others, to pin down the truth lurking behind the mask. Thus the persona can easily lure the audience into a reprehensible part, for the gap between reader and voyeur is so slight as to court nonexistence. Unlike some of his other poems in which Heaney casts the narrator as a voyeur ("Punishment," "Bog Queen," "The Grauballe Man"), in "Death of a Naturalist" he exposes the unmentionable link between critic and criminal. The plane of the text may as well be a bedroom window: the reader an onlooker cloaked in shadow, and the persona a hapless performer on some specular altar. Quite early on, then, the lexeography confronts the reader with the appalling deviancy of reading itself. Yet even this outrageous an affront does not go far enough. What is it the voyeur strives to behold? Tormented by deception, the audience seeks some indisputable certainty, a fixed point in a world of deceit. Yet the voyeur's quest can never reach further than that enticing declivity that leads back to the persona itself, the rift in the mask through which the mocking image withdraws again into the polymorphous actor. With a thoroughness bordering on the prescient, the lexeography not only reveals a criminal normality but illustrates its comic desperation.

How can the audience elude this latest stigma? One might simply turn the page, or even close the book. But then the persona would win. Such flight leaves the audience imprisoned forever in the last assigned part. Lexeography (Jacob and the Angel; Odysseus and the Cyclops) is a struggle for a name, which is to say a return to the ancient combat to see who will be the master and who the slave. The antagonists contend across the rift of the image. Not until one flees from that abyss does the master become a potent namer, the slave a castrated victim. Once underway there is no turning back.

If it is impossible for the audience to reject an assigned role (since to reject is actually to accept), then the next tactic is to assume the assigned part, yet to enact it so assiduously that it turns into something else. For example, to play the voyeur *to the hilt* is to become a scientist: taking meticulous notes at a striptease. To achieve such a metamorphosis the audience need only ask, What secret desire could impel the persona/exhibitionist to such exposure? The innocent question opens a vast topic. It has become a truism that we live in a narcissistic age. The romantic ego supposedly dwells in a prison of its own reflections, immured in an intransigent imagery of itself. Heaney's peculiar genius, however, is to understand the demise of this myth. For the modern heirs to romanticism, the problem is not to escape or transcend the obsessive mirror of the ego, but to achieve any such reflection at all. So diverse and antagonistic are the forces warring within an ego-image that its identity and even existence are readily cast into doubt. In Heaney's adaptation of the myth of Narcissus, the shepherd boy's serene pool becomes an abandoned well, or Atlantic sinkhole, or treacherous bog. The ego, that is, no longer finds itself reflected in a docile Wordsworthian nature. Rather, it must trace its features within an alien realm of terrifying dissolutions and ghastly returns. At any instant the identity that seems so confident and assured might sink into the morass, and some unspeakable image of the bog might emerge. It is in the death of the Narcissus myth, then, that the audience may find an answer to its question about desire. The exhibitionist persona is driven to capture and hold an audience's gaze, at whatever cost, so as to avoid a fate of chaotic dissolution. The ego, by itself, is no longer capable of sustaining its tremulous image. It now needs the strength of a collective gaze, the force of an audience, to hold an image in place.

Of course, a scientist requires ample evidence. What would happen were the postnarcissistic ego to lose its self-image? As chance would have it, this is the condition figured in the poem's opening passage.

> All year the flax-dam festered in the heart
> Of the townland; green and heavy headed
> Flax had rotted there, weighted down by huge sods.
> Daily it sweltered in the punishing sun.
> Bubbles gargled delicately, bluebottles
> Wove a strong gauze of sound around the smell.
> There were dragon-flies, spotted butterflies,
> But best of all was the warm thick slobber
> Of frogspawn that grew like clotted water

> In the shade of the banks. Here, every spring
> I would fill. . . .
>
> (*DN* 5)

In a poem obsessed with beginnings, the flax-dam is the unthinkable abyss of the aperture itself, the pure rift around which no image has yet formed. Like a paralyzed body left out in the sun, the subject can neither express nor protect itself. Without an ego to focus and direct its energies, its limbs are like bowed stems, weighted down with a heaviness that makes movement impossible. What impulses exist only mimic the erratic buzzing of insects. Prior to the emergence of a central ego, the subject exists as a stifled cry, barely a gap, a choked passageway that cannot even scream its despair.

Or at least, that is what the passage intimates. It is worth noting, though, that this primal remembrance is also an act of misremembrance. The "I," formal marker of a presiding identity, does not enter the text until the eleventh line. Yet the syntactic ruse cannot quite conceal the problem of how it is possible to have a memory when there is no one to do the remembering. Prior to the emergence of an ego, there is only a drift of impressions. These cannot assume a specific aspect (ebullient/melancholy; exciting/dull) until grasped from a specific site. Thus the awful paralysis figured in the poem's beginning is a foundation myth, a lie, and an impossibility all at once. As the ground of the ego's ascendancy, this hellish condition insinuates the violent bias of a presiding consciousness into a realm where supposedly there is no ego at all.

At this juncture the audience has achieved a modest triumph: the stigma of voyeurism has been transmuted, via analysis, into the respectability of scientific rigor. Yet the turns of lexeography are relentless. For just as the audience shifts its role, so does the persona. The exhibitionist is merely the image of an aftereffect. Clearly the ego had to be delivered from the flax-dam well before the reader came along. (Any discourse entails an image of the entity who would wield it, even if this be the image of one-not-yet-having-an-image, the *imago ignota*.) So there must have been a prior gaze, some midwife who rescued the infant from the rushes by conferring a primordial identity. Further, there must have been a terrible betrayal. Otherwise the persona would not need to seek the support of a supplemental gaze. Hence the audience cannot enjoy its triumph for long before it must return to the text that, in aptly oracular fashion, offers a response if not an answer to each question put.

> Here, every spring
> I would fill jampotfuls of the jellied
> Specks to range on window-sills at home,

On shelves at school, and wait and watch until
The fattening dots burst into nimble-
Swimming tadpoles. Miss Walls would tell us how
The daddy frog was called a bullfrog
And how he croaked and how the mammy frog
Laid hundreds of little eggs and this was
Frogspawn. You could tell the weather by frogs too
For they were yellow in the sun and brown
In rain.

A demiurge within the microcosm of the self, Miss Walls separates order from chaos, ego from subject. Her very name designates the condition of identity: the means to circumscribe an image so that it is itself, *and nothing else*. Here is the primordial power that brought the persona into being by solidifying an initial space around the aperture. Through Miss Walls the little boy emerges from the confusion of infancy and attains his first self-reflection, a center to which all other impressions are subordinate. Small wonder that with the abandon of childhood he falls utterly in love, laying at the goddess's feet the being she has so graciously bestowed.

Yet even before the audience's eyes, a complex drama unfolds. For a time the boy is ecstatic with his newfound deliverance. The coda about telling the weather is more than childish prattle. Miss Walls not only defines but limits in advance the acceptable bounds of existence. But absolute passion readily yields to its opposite. The recollecting narrator does not share the child's enthusiasm. Indeed, the direct address of "You could tell" marks an ironic division: the audience can accept the image of a gullible boy, or that of a later, distrustful, even embittered narrator. Why the fall from grace? The flax-dam is a spawning chaos, yet it is only through its tumult and disarray, the polymorphous perversity of the subject, that the ego can change and grow. Miss Walls, however, cuts off access to this source. No sooner does the daddy frog commence its procreative activity than she sees to it that he "croaks," passes away. An avatar of the flax-dam's ebullient renewal, the daddy frog suffers a terrible fate: he is relegated not to insignificance but to nonsignifying. Left beyond the pale, he becomes a permanently inoperative function. So in accepting the reassuring identity conferred by Miss Walls, the little boy also suffers the initial pass of the gelding knife. He is given a stable image yet denied any capacity to change it. Like the wriggling tadpoles he is a captive being, forever undeveloped, forever the same.

But the gap between innocent victim and embittered eunuch is perhaps too extreme. There must be an intermediary part, or even several, that convey the persona from its initial role to the one played by the poem's embittered narrator. Cut off from the flax-dam, the little boy had to find a substitute for its creative powers. Because Miss Walls suppressed this initial origin, it is only natural that she should take its place. Thus her fascinating and mysterious body comes to replace the demonic energy of the flax-dam. Yet there is a bizarre asymmetry here. Whereas the child can return to the terrifying scene of the actual origin anytime he likes, the safe and reassuring substitute is forbidden ground. It is this anomaly that drives the little boy to create a corrective fetish. Like everyone else, he needs not only a secure ego image but the space in which he can extend its limits through freedom and play. Because Miss Walls promises and yet withholds such a space, he must devise a substitute for her: in effect, a substitute for a substitute. Paradoxically, this activity takes him back to the flax-dam. His cherished kitchen jars offer a surrogate for the body of Miss Walls, just as the ecstatic tadpoles suggest simulacra of himself. Whereas she is modestly covered, the jars display an exultant nakedness. Whereas she is inaccessible, the jars bestow a blissful Eden on their carefree denizens. Anytime the little boy likes he can not only hold their transparent surfaces but even reach into their welcoming depths. As the meticulous observer of a covert drama, then, the audience gradually unearths a bizarre ritual. Bereft of a recreative origin, the child becomes the votary of an awful cult. Each spring, driven by the cruelty of the castrating goddess, he restores the fetish that comforts the hurt of his terrible wound.

For a while the ritual is innocent or, to put it another way, explicit. Yet before long the energies of the denied origin, the forsaken flax-dam, assert their ancient right. The tadpoles eventually die, and to replenish his store the little boy must empty the kitchen jars. Through this emblematic act of inversion, the powers of the flax-dam reclaim him as their own. He holds no longer an insignia of his victimization (the passive receptacle that mimics his wound) but rather an instrument of aggression, a means to penetrate and rule. The withheld phallus is restored. Miraculously, he holds the scepter of power and judgment in his hands. Yet the scripts that might ensue from the use of this reclaimed power are too crude and explicit. Even in the mind's solitary theater, the taboos against his contemplated revenge (object-rape, mutilation, murder) are too strong. Hence the unspeakable fantasy undergoes a more complex displacement, through which it becomes at once more subtle and, as if to compensate, more spectacular. Instead of wielding the avenging phallus himself, its power is shifted to the surrogate tadpoles. And instead of remaining a single entity, it becomes the collective force of an apocalyptic band. The audience arrives in time for the finale of the resulting drama. Out of the bog crawl the slime kings, their grotesque heads swollen with malice and pulsing with demonic life. Hideous, invincible, they shadow the body of the treacherous Miss Walls.

How quickly all this happens. One of the miracles of displacement is its capacity to perform contradictory tasks. In the same instant, a scene is necessitated and disowned. The visionary finale of the frog kings is certainly the most charged passage of the poem. It mingles erotic fascination with ecstatic revenge. Yet where is this apocalyptic drama actually performed? It occurs in one place and one place only: the imagination of the audience. The narrator, after all, has a perfect alibi. He need only express amazement at the discovery (or more likely, imputation: the familiar crime of "reading into") of such a plot. So once again the audience finds itself caught in the serpentine coils of lexeography. It is our hands that hold the inverted jar, and our desire that unleashes the avenging horde. What began as analytic pursuit, then, turns into complicity. When it reaches the climax of the carefully traced drama, the audience finds it has been tricked onstage, that it, not the actors, is the one making a scene. As the persona cunningly shifts, from childish enthusiast to bereft victim, compulsive fetishist, and retributive avatar, the audience is steadily drawn into the performance. The previously indicted voyeur (whose release was only provisional, pending trial) is turned into an accessory, or worse, a provocateur.

Nonetheless, even this most insolent of charges may be played out: the accomplice *(a complice)* is woven together with a partner, into a complex. Threaded together, persona and audience configure a single text. Their intimacy is fatal, in that it cannot be escaped. As we have learned, the one who would flee is already constituted, in advance, by the other who survives. If there is any respite, it must be in death, which in terms of reading means total exposure. The final violence of the accomplice is to expose, with the fury of an intimate, the hiddenness of the other. And what more merciless exposure than the master narrative of the therapist? Thus by a logic as subtle as it is inevitable, the audience plays out its rage against Heaney's devious persona by turning from accomplice into healer. If someone is so tormented as to dupe us into such licentious conjurings, then clearly it is a case of serious illness. Thus the therapist's narrative encloses a threat, rechristens wonder as banality, by leaving nothing unsaid. (Note, the exact nature of the master narrative is incidental; it need only be semicredible.) For example, the talisman might be assembled as follows:

The little boy is plucked from infantile chaos by the adult who gives him his first role in the life of the community. Unfortunately, he assumes that this role entitles him not only to a modest social status but to an impossible bliss. Miss Walls is the hapless object of this delusion. Because he lacks the courage either to present his demand or to accuse her, he fashions a substitute for his lost bliss: the fetish of the kitchen jars. Yet this ritual still leaves him oppressed with self-loathing for his cowardice, so he takes refuge in the apocalyptic vision of the avenging frog kings. His later retelling of this episode is a clear case of neurotic ambivalence. The story permits the narrator to objectify and thus discard a proscribed fantasy. At the same time, however, it also perpetuates his retributive rage by casting the audience in the role of Miss Walls (the assigner of images) and cleverly manipulating / seducing it into complicity.

How gratifying to wield such a masterful device. The loose ends are tied, the persona affixed to an image, and the audience permitted at last to elude the coils of lexeography by settling into a final role that is admirable, correct. Yet there is a problem with this finality, the death wish so reluctantly deferred by orthodox criticism. What could be more fatal to reading than truth? Once found, the aperture closes, the persona rigidifies to a death mask, and there is only an uncontesting emptiness behind. Further, there remains an even more vexatious doubt. What if the role of therapist has been plotted all along, as a trap? Might not a postnarcissistic narrator, willing to risk any cost to secure a sustaining gaze, calculatedly incite an audience into playing the one part from which there is no alternative or appeal, that of normalizer and healer? Perhaps the last move in the lexeographic game is the coup de grâce of a brilliant seduction, as ultimate conquest collides with final bondage.

Still, our entrapment is self-imposed. A spiteful audience / accomplice can silence the persona by fixing it to a static image. Yet as a cofunction of the same text, the audience can do so only by silencing itself. If we are to continue our own inquiring existence (the announced goal, but also the real nemesis of orthodox criticism), then we must tolerate the further provocations of the persona. The clue to this possibility is dropped on the threshold of trauma when the narrator recalls, "I ducked through hedges. . . ." The upright "I" suggests both enduring cenotaph and devious slit. It ducks. In constant anticipation of a forthcoming blow, it cannot occupy the space it held but an instant before. It commits only to an abstention from itself. With the impunity of a moving target the "I" bobs up and down in a treacherous yet buoyant medium. If it returns at all, it is through hedges, a cunning straddle, the ingenious tactic of betting against itself. Thus far in the lexeography the audience has played at predator and tried to track this entity to its final image. But what if that is an elementary, albeit perennial, mistake? If the "I" is not an identity but an opening, then the audience might follow a performance rather than an image. In that event lexeography would enact no longer a struggle unto death but the modulations of an incessant exchange.

Yet to follow this path is to awaken an ancient fear. In effect the lexeography brings the audience itself before the flax-dam. The text ungoverned by any permanent image is like the subject prior to the advent of the ego, a prolific but helpless and incoherent flux. In terms of reading, the equivalent of this experience would be all that responsible criticism dreads: extravagant impressions, unfettered associations, voluptuous caprice.

Unchecked by any presiding center, reading must surely drift into a solipsistic and incommunicable reverie. Thus the lexeography at this point confronts interpretation with its deepest fear, a repudiation of itself as a progressive, rational, and thus compelling (coercive) endeavor.

But how warranted is this fear? "Death of a Naturalist" suggests that such anxiety may result from a primordial misremembrance. As already noted, it is impossible to have a pure subject, the chaos of the flax-dam, without an attendant ego, because there can be no apprehended experience without a focal point. Consequently there can be no experience of the flax-dam, *except from the vantage of someone who has already left it.* Any recollection of this always prior condition, then, is an act of misremembrance: a mythification designed to shore up the ego's status and centrality. One of the most fascinating features of "Death of a Naturalist" is its intimation that the audience may be able, if not to circumvent, then at least to trace this misremembrance. Prior to his fatal vision, the little boy is drawn to the flax-dam by a strange sound, "To a coarse croaking that I had not heard / Before." The strangeness is itself strange. Since he recalls no surprise at Miss Walls's version of the event, he had probably heard the frogs before. Furthermore, given his familiarity with the flax-dam, it would have been difficult not to notice something so obstreperous. So why the note of strangeness? We can guess that it is not the noise itself that is shocking, but the experience of hearing it *after* Miss Walls's narrative. She claims to speak the truth of origin. Yet the frog chorus divulges a whole cacophony she has left out; in other words, Miss Walls is a fraud. The real origin is not a properly inflected syllable, but an outrageous and licentious din. By itself this commotion is perfectly harmless. But when discovered as the priority from which the myths of the townland—the ego's ciphers of identity and limit—must be forged, its effect is annihilating.

The flax-dam festers in the heart of the townland, an origin as incurable wound. Curiously, its tremendous recreative energy springs from its limited scope. The human ensemble of tongue, lips, throat, and palate can produce only a small range of differentiable sounds. Yet from this limited repertoire all the myriad and variable words of a language must be formed. Language is thus alive with an intense, dissident buzz of possibilities. Like the bluebottles and butterflies, each of its elements is in constant motion and undergoing continuous metamorphosis. As the primordial stuff from which the persona has to shape itself and its world, the flax-dam interposes a radical and permanent instability.

Although a poem illustrates a decision, there is no rule to say that an audience must accept it. The narrator in "Death of a Naturalist" tries to save an ego image from the terrors of the flax-dam. But what if this scene of origin is taken as a place not of paralysis and decay but of growth and change? The narrator dreads a world without identity in which each particular melts wantonly into every other. Yet that is not what the little boy found. He discovers only that borders are porous. He weaves a path through the hedges around the flax-dam. He leans over its banks to scoop up the frogspawn. And just as he can enter the frogs' world, so they may return to his. Gradually, he finds that each bounded image leads back to the mysteries of the persona's aperture, the place where varied possibilities meet, engage, and transform one another.

Reading Heaney is a matter of outliving a universal but empty threat. The audience itself must dare to come face to face with the great slime kings. If it does, the regenerative scene so artfully denied by the narrator's misremembrance might be discovered anew, in its comic aspect. The frog chorus echoes an ancient laughter. As monsters they are ludicrous, comically bellowing and harmlessly sliding across one another. They are great, but in the sense of being pregnant with new life, a burden of otherness. Lords of misrule, the frog kings are threshold guardians who might serve as guides through the purgatories of the past.

"Inscribed in Sheets": Seamus Heaney's Scribal Matrix

RAND BRANDES

In 1989 Stephen Spender wrote Seamus Heaney requesting that he contribute a poem to *David Hockney's Alphabet* (1991), a collaborative project
whose proceeds would go to the AIDS Crisis Trust. To produce what looks
like a postmodern illuminated manuscript, each contributing writer was
given a letter of the alphabet illustrated by Hockney to use as an inspiration
for his or her text; Heaney received the letter *G*. The result of this request is
Heaney's poem, "G as in Gaelic," which begins; "*Guh Guh* / Like breath
being shunted. / The sound of the Gaelic / word for voice— / written as
guth." In addition to reconfirming Heaney's commitment to social causes
(as with UNICEF and Amnesty International), Heaney's poem "about"
the nature of language in relation to the word and the world embodies one
of the most significant and distinctive aspects of his writing—his fascination
with the physicality of the writing process, the materials of the trade, and
the inscribed word or the word as *word*. I have labeled this fascination the
scribal in Heaney's poetry in order to suggest Heaney's cultural, aesthetic,
and ascetic connections with the ancient monastic scribes of Ireland, represented by figures such as Moling in Heaney's *Sweeney Astray*.

The scribal is both a matrix of tropic reference points and a function, a
mode of production, an event, and a decentering activity. Heaney has looked
to the realm of the scribe throughout his career, including recent poems
such as "Tollund" (1994), which refers to the road of the "Scribe." The
scribal appears in many of Heaney's most important poems and at crucial
places within these poems themselves. The scribal has also become more
prevalent in Heaney's work as he begins to write in a metapoetic mode that
is more sophisticated than that of his manifesto "Digging." After a brief
discussion of the theoretical framework and the cultural and historical referents of the scribal and the scribal function, I will trace the scribal through
Heaney's work, concentrating on *Sweeney Astray, Station Island,* and *The Haw
Lantern*—three volumes clearly illuminated by the scribal Heaney.

47

I

Like the "assiduous illuminator himself bowed to his desk in a corner" who appears in Seamus Heaney's early poem "Cloistered" (*Stations* 20), the figure of the scribe has always inhabited the margins of Heaney's poetry. One senses the presence of the scribe in Heaney's work whenever one encounters allusions to writing (the physical act of writing), to the word as word, or in references to the instruments and the materials of writing, as in several of Heaney's "school poems," such as "The Master" (*SI* 110). Heaney has commented in regard to "The Master": "I love all of those things, those school images. . . . we must not underestimate the primal, phenomenological, biological, whatever it is, that gives pleasure to writing."[1] The scribe also appears in relation to Heaney's numerous references to inscriptions—the historically recent inscriptions of the sculptor or lithographer or the more ancient inscriptions of the Viking scrimshawist, the Egyptian scribe's hieroglyphs, or the shamanistic cave drawings of Lascaux.

Heaney's work as a translator of Dante, *Buile Suibhne,* and *Beowulf* and his exposure to Timothy O'Neill's *Irish Hand* (1984) and Frances Yates's *Giordano Bruno and the Hermetic Tradition* (1964) are apparent literary sources for the increased presence of the scribe in his work. In terms of Heaney's metapoetics, the scribe is a trope, or constellation of tropes, under which the contemporary poet can contemplate the art of writing, where "good poetry reminds you that writing is writing," and can reconsider what it means to be an author in a poststructuralist age that contemplates his death.[2] Although scribal tropes—the figure of the scribe, his craft, his illuminated text, and his inscriptions—occasionally appear in Heaney's earlier volumes, in his later works (*Sweeney Astray, Station Island,* and *The Haw Lantern*) they become central tropes.

In addition to forming a significant undercurrent in Heaney's imagery and metapoetics, the scribal tropes also provide a profitable method for discussing particular aesthetic and ideological characteristics of Heaney's poetry in general. Certainly, what I see as the "scribal function" in Heaney's poetry is not representative of the radical or the avant garde in Irish poetry as embodied in the writings of Paul Muldoon or Ciaran Carson.[3] The scribe rejects pop culture and believes in the continuity of history and tradition; he turns to the past, listening for voices that attract his conservative tendencies—tendencies that resemble those of Nietzsche's cultural conservationist, the antiquarian historian.[4] The scribal function in Heaney's poetry reflects what Blake Morrison rejects as the "safe" side of Heaney's work.[5] However, the scribal in Heaney's writing is more culturally conservative than poetically conventional. The scribal signifies what Seamus Deane refers to as Heaney's "desire for absolute, radical certainty."[6]

The scribal function in Heaney's verse also underscores the traditional religious responsibilities of the scribes as "professional interpreters of the Law" *(OED)* in Jewish history and as monastic transcribers in Irish history. Even though the scribal tropes remind the reader of Heaney's Catholic origins and of the importance of monastic scribes to Irish history, the scribe, as constructed here, is not directly related to Heaney's Catholicism. The scribal tropes are more than Catholic anchors in Heaney's verse; the tropes emphasize the loss or absence of these religious foundations. The scribal tropes recall the memory of the Catholic faith and not the faith itself. In this regard, the scribal is not to be associated with the Irish Catholic's sense of "guilt" in which Heaney's "attitude to paternity and authority is apologetic";[7] the scribal, from the perspective of Heaney as Northern Irish Catholic, is that of iconographer and preservationist—beyond belief, but not beyond politics. Consequently, the scribal construct may also take on political associations as a result of its denominational affiliations. This essay, however, will target the scribal, not the tribal, dimensions of Heaney's poetry.[8]

In the scribe's sphere, print is memory (*GT* 57), and like his Greek and Roman precursors, the scribe attempts to chisel "'the world's order into stone'" (*GT* 55). The poet in his scribal mode is a maker and not a creator. By conceiving of the poet as scribe, the poet reduces the egocentricism that accompanies the ownership of the text; the scribe, like Sweeney in "Sweeney Redivivus," has "a deep suspicion of one's own reputation and excellence."[9] In other words, the scribal corresponds to the sense of humility one finds, whether one believes it or not, in Heaney's poetry. The poet inscribes his name on a text not as sole creator, but in the awareness that he is only part of a larger literary and historical activity, as poststructuralist critics Pierre Macherey[10] and Michel Foucault,[11] among others, have argued. The poet's ambivalence toward notoriety finds some symbolic relief in the figure of the scribe.

The scribe who writes with Auden's "'strict and adult pen'" (*GT* 114) is the poet who has a "distrust of happiness" and who appreciates "the deep pleasure in a mournful litany."[12] In this regard the scribe closely resembles a pilgrim whose penitence is the physical act of writing. In the scriptorium the scribe composes his soul through writing.

A historical parallel to Heaney's idea of writing as penitence is found in Francis John Byrne's introduction to Timothy O'Neill's *Irish Hand,* in which Byrne says "even Saints . . . continued to practice the craft of penmanship as a spiritual exercise."[13] Correspondingly, in his essay "The God in the Tree," Heaney briefly alludes to a type of Celtic Christian "penitential verse" that springs from "the tensions of asceticism" (*Pr* 183). The scribal corresponds to Heaney's "reading" of "the government of the tongue" that is "full of monastic and ascetic strictness" (*GT* 96). For the scribe as well as for the poet, the tension produced by disciplined writing is generative, as in Heaney's analysis of Hopkins, whose "use of language is disciplined by a philological and rhetorical passion" (*Pr* 85). The formal and intellectual constraints of the text can be, when seen from the perspective of the scribal poet, sources of inspiration and liberation. The scribal function in Heaney's poetry, then, appears in his "predisposition" and "prejudice . . . toward poetry that contains and practices force within a confined area."[14]

The poet in his scribal form is a laborer. His is the labor of "a conscious push of the deliberating intelligence" (*Pr* 85); it is similar to the type of labor Heaney associates with Yeats in "The Makings of a Music." Heaney argues that if "instead of surrendering to the drift of the original generating rhythm," the poet seeks to discipline it, to "harness its energies," the poet will produce "a music not unlike Yeats'" (*Pr* 61). For Yeats, to write is to work, and to work, according to Heaney in "Shelf Life," "is to move a certain mass / through a certain distance" (*SI* 22). The "mass" is the original rhythm of the poem that the poet discovers, and the "distance" is the space between the preverbal utterance and the written text. The discipline of the scribal poet is also that of David Jones's *"disciplinae"* in *The Anathémata,* who asserts that "in a sense all *disciplinae* are warnings: 'This is the way to make the thing, that way won't do at all.'"[15]

Heaney also realizes that this scribal discipline can be disabling. The social, moral, aesthetic, and linguistic laws can function as nets; they can govern the tongue into servitude. In "Englands of the Mind," Heaney employs the image of the scribe in "the scholar's cell" in his criticism of Geoffrey Hill's work: "The poet is not a wanderer but a clerk or perhaps an illuminator or one of a guild of masters. . . ." (*Pr* 152). In analyzing the scribal qualities of Hill's poetry, Heaney argues that the act of writing is not penitential but pernicious. The labor is laborious not rapturous. The scribe must avoid becoming too mainstream, too rigid, too orthodox, or too Latinate. The poet as scribe must guard against unknowingly becoming a spokesman for the dominant party line. In contrast, he must be true to the physical, passionate, individual self. The poet, then, must be the passionate scribe; he must "cultivate a work-lust" without reducing the art to anguished erudition (*SI* 93).

Although other modern and contemporary Irish poets such as Austin Clarke, John Montague, and Thomas Kinsella have been in positions similar to that of Heaney in which they too could have drawn upon scribal tropes or perceived their resemblance to the scribe, the figure of the poet as scribe has not influenced their writing to the extent that it has Heaney's. Austin Clarke in his poem "Secrecy" does rely upon scribal imagery to describe a lover's desire: "Had we been only lovers from a book / That holy men, who had a hand in heaven, / Illuminated" (47). Still, Clarke's illumination is momentary and the romantic scribe disappears in his work. Thomas Kinsella most closely approaches Heaney's awareness of the metapoetic potential of the scribe. Like Heaney, Kinsella has also translated a major work of Irish literature, *The Táin*, into English. Consequently, it is not surprising to find the brooding Kinsella envisioning himself as a medieval scribe in his poem "Wyncote, Pennsylvania: A Gloss."[16] The poem's dramatic situation is introduced by "A mocking-bird on a branch / outside the window, where I write." As a storm approaches, the poet / scribe's "papers seem luminous," and he vows that "over them I will take / ever more painstaking care." Kinsella's poem is a gloss written on the edge of the text. This gloss replicates the ending of one of the "Monastic Poems" translated by Kinsella in *The New Oxford Book of Irish Verse*. The poem, "Pangur Ban," ends with the scribal voice's declaration: "Bringing darkness into light / is the work that I do best."[17] The scribal illuminator clearly resembles the poet at work. Yet, Kinsella, unlike Heaney, has not kept in touch with the scribe or the medieval illuminator. Though many poets eventually incorporate references to the act of writing or the instruments of writing into their verse, as Edna Longley mentions, few have relied upon these images to the extent to which Heaney has.[18] Nonetheless, many critics primarily associate Heaney not with a disciplined scribe's text, but with Sweeney's turbulent travels.

In an interview with Bel Mooney, Heaney comments in regard to his position to "the whole northern thing": "I suppose a lot of self-censorship goes on. So the idea of a freed self becomes very attractive."[19] The censored self falls within the disciplined scribal realm of "moral utterance" (*GT* 100), while the "freed self" occupies the space of lyric utterance—the space of Sweeney from Heaney's *Sweeney Astray* and "Sweeney Redivivus." In many ways, Sweeney is the scribe's nemesis. Sweeney seems to be the spirit of the margins, of liberation, of individuality, and of forgetfulness. He appears to be the outlaw, the exiled poet lost in a moment of cultural and spiritual crisis—in other words, the perfect analogue for the Northern Irish poet Heaney. However, only in retrospect, when Heaney moved to Wicklow in 1972, does this analogy fit Heaney's actual more centralized situation. While Sweeney fades symbolically into the background, the scribe asserts himself with confidence in Heaney's later works.

When Heaney imagistically moves out of the topography of the bog and into the inscriptions of the book, the figure of the medieval scribe occupies the space where myth and history, the individual and the communal, the visionary and the laborer, and the sacred and the profane converge and diverge. The scribe replaces the archaeologist as the poet's most implicit analogue. The scribe does not stand at the threshold; he *is* the Janus-like threshold through which the primitive, unconscious, private and unarticulated discoveries of the poet slip into postmodern, conscious, public, and inscribed utterances. Like Heaney's description of Yeats, the poet as scribe is someone "who is spoken through" (*GT* 149). Heaney's scribe is the postmodern writer perched at the terminal, meditating upon the word-processed ghost-writing as it flashes into offscreen space. The scriptorium becomes Heaney's new "image-cellar," "dream-bank," "word-hoard" or "truth cave" (*GT* 163) over which Hermes keeps watch.

II

Since his first acclaimed poem, "Digging," Seamus Heaney has considered writing as work. The pen that replaces the spade becomes the poet's tool. The limpid analogy, which reduces "physical labor to a metaphor for cultural labor,"[20] is one source of the poem's enchantment. The poet as digger obviously foreshadows the poet as archaeologist. In between these two metapoetic tropes Heaney also uses the diviner, the thatcher, and the smith (among other) figures as analogues for the poet. Each figure's trade requires crafts and techniques that appear transferable to the work of the poet. The digger, diviner, and archaeologist are representative of a writing process in which the object of their search precedes them in both time and space. They *discover* their desired artifact, and in this way the writing process itself becomes its own end. The smith and thatcher, in contrast, produce their artifacts. The poem becomes a product and to a certain extent relinquishes its claims of originality. The scribe is an amalgamation of the poet as discoverer and the poet as producer. In this form, he is similar to Lévi-Strauss's *bricoleur;* he is a "do-it-yourself-man" who constructs his works from discovered pieces. The scribe's pieces are also similar to David Jones's "fragmented bits," "pieces of stuffs," or "things that are yours to use because they happen to be lying about the place or site or lying within the orbit of your 'tradition.'"[21] Heaney's tropes for the writing process and the poem rely heavily upon the notion of writing as labor and the poem as discovered artifact.

Heaney's early poems also abound in images that refer to the act of writing or the written word. In addition to the "inked up" berries of "Blackberry Picking," the "soft printed slabs" of butter in "Churning Day," and the "inky putty" of "Turkeys Observed" in *Death of a Naturalist*, "The Diviner" holds the hazel stick "by the arms of the 'V'" (*Pr* 26). The image of the *V* is actualized in the letter's transformation into a stick and the stick's transformation into a letter. The letter's visual appearance on the page, the *V*, draws attention to the poem's self-conscious construction in print. The scribe transcribes the world into letters and letters into the world. The poems take on the qualities of a rebus. Drawings replace words and letters in a visual riddle—a talismanic puzzle. Heaney also uses this technique in the "black *O*" of "Broagh" (*WO* 27). The letter *O* is the image of perfect closure and wholeness and the image of imprisonment and isolation. To the scribe it would appear as the Ouroboros of the illuminated text—as a symbol of the self-consuming act of writing. The seventeenth-century scribe David O'Durgenan captures this feeling of mortality in his gloss:

> It's a pity, O little white book
> The day will come, for sure,
> When over your page it will be said
> The hand that wrote it is dead. [22]

In *North* the allusions to the act of writing, letters, and the possible etymological fecundity of language take a more primitive orientation. The scribe's interest in writing focuses on the ancient and prehistoric inscriptions (lost languages and opaque ideograms) that are written into the world and transcribed in the poem. Even though the poet's language in *North* echoes the early word poems, as in *"moss"* and *"bawn"* from "Belderg" (*N* 14), the scribal tropes include cave drawings, scrimshaw, calligraphy, Braille, hieroglyphics, scribblings, and longhands.

The more literary terms, such as "dictions," "latins," and "consonants" (*N* 28), join with the other scribal allusions to produce a self-reflexive metalinguistic substratum in *North*. In "Belderg," for example, the "first plough-marks, / the stone-age fields, the tomb" (13) provide prehistoric reference points for the central scribal trope in the poem "North":

> It said, "Lie down
> in the word-hoard, burrow
> the coil and gleam
> of your furrowed brain.["]

(20)

Heaney's "word-hoard"—which recalls David Jones's "word-hoard"[23] —is imagistically connected to the "first plough-marks" of "Belderg." The prehistoric ploughed furrow looks to the origins of poetry as Heaney sees them: "The poet as ploughman, if you like, and the suggestive etymology of the word 'verse.'. . . 'Verse' comes from the Latin *versus* which could mean a line of poetry but could also mean the turn that a ploughman made at the head of the field as he finished one furrow and faced back into another" (*Pr* 65). The ploughed furrow links not only the poet and the ploughman but also the poet and the scribe. A riddle written by a medieval scribe makes this connection clear:

> An iron point
> In artful wanderings cuts a fair design,
> And leaves long, twisted furrows like a plough. . . . [24]

As he writes, the scribe's "iron point" turns the wax on his tablet over like a plough turning over the earth. The scribe actually inscribes the text; he cuts into the wax. The "furrow" created by the pen becomes the fertile line growing out of the "furrowed brain."

In *North*, the figure of scribe also assumes a slightly more archaic form in the figure of the engraver or scrimshawist in "Viking Dublin: Trial Pieces." The "small outline" that "was incised, a cage / or trellis to conjure in" (21) on bone graphically joins "Viking Dublin: Trial Pieces" to "North." The ploughed furrow of the scribe corresponds to the "incised" image that is cut into the bone.

The primitive incised line, which could be magical, is the forerunner to the scribe's inscription, which appears in the fourth section of the poem:

> That enters my longhand,
> turns cursive, unscarfing
> a zoomorphic wake,
> a worm of thought
>
> I follow into the mud.
>
> (23)

The poet takes over the "incised" "outline" and "calligraphy" and transcribes them into the poem. The "zoomorphic wake" is the collection of beasts living in the illuminated margins of the text. The scrimshawist's talisman becomes the "interlacing[s']" "worm" of the scribe's textual decoration. These interlacing beasts and foliage are the scribe's trial piece, as the poem is the poet's.

In *Field Work* the barn appropriately becomes the poet's scriptorium: "But this barn is an ideal place to write" (45). It is here that the poet practices his "tentative art" (22) and sings his "grace notes" (30). Reworking an earlier image from "North," one of *Field Work*'s most preeminent scribal tropes is the plough-pen, field-text analogy that begins the "Glanmore Sonnets." In the first sonnet "Vowels ploughed into other: opened ground"; "the turned-up acres breathe"; "Now the good life could be to cross a field / And art a paradigm of earth new from the lathe / Of ploughs" (33).

The scribal trope of the plough is more fully developed in the second of the "Glanmore Sonnets," which concludes, "Vowels ploughed into other, opened ground, / Each verse returning like the plough turned around" (34). The couplet obviously mimics the returning verse, while the line repeated from the first sonnet establishes a closing echo. Here the "verse" is the "turn that a ploughman" made, while the furrow is the "line of poetry" (*Pr* 65). The page is the scribe's field. The pen must stay in the sonnet's range; it must respect its margins even while looking for the "other(ness)" of the margins' "hiding places." The scribe maintains control of the poet's formal structures.

The scribe assumes his role as the transcriber in *Field Work* in Heaney's translation of the Ugolino passage from Dante's *Inferno*. The inscription becomes transcription; the translator, transcriber. In a 1988 interview Heaney describes the notion of translation "as taking it [the original] over. Taking it over in two senses—in the slightly imperial sense and in the original etymological sense of carrying a thing across."[25] The scribe as transcriber takes on a political as well as poetical dimension. The poet discovers a text in the other language and through transcription, through "hearing" the preceding text, brings it into current discourse. As Heaney says of the politics of art: "In the deep, deep sense that's the politics of art: that you make current what is undercurrent."[26] The Dante translation that ends *Field Work* is the pen-ultimate "scribal performance" before the publication of his first major translation, *Sweeney Astray*. In *Sweeney Astray*, the poet clearly assumes his role as the "assiduous illuminator."

In the last scene of *Sweeney Astray*, the cleric, Moling, informs Sweeney: "You shall leave the history of your adventures with us," and commands Sweeney "to return to me every evening so that I may record your story" (79). The disciplined voice of Moling is not merely the oppressive voice of Christianity; it is the voice of the medieval scribe—the scribe who is as necessary to the narrative as Sweeney himself. Moling occupies the space where myth and history merge; the individual utterance becomes manuscript and enters the public discourse of history. Heaney the man and poet encourages (and critics have been quick to reinforce) the primary association of Sweeney with the poet. Even though Moling, the passionate scribe, is a marginal voice in the text, he still most closely approaches the voice of Heaney the poet. Of course, all of the voices in *Sweeney Astray* are initially "other" and outside the poet in the preceding Irish text, but as Heaney the poet states in the introduction to the volume, some poems in *Sweeney Astray* have been invested "with a more subjective tone than they possess in Irish." Since *Sweeney Astray* is a translation or for the scribe a transcription, the connection between Heaney the poet and Moling the scribe is substantial. Moling is the passionate scribe conscientiously, yet subjectively, recording and recoding Sweeney's narrative from his own religious and cultural matrix.

Heaney's work with *Sweeney Astray* further intensified his awareness of the correspondence between the poet and the scribe. It confirms the idea that the scribe resembles the more conservative communal aspects of the poet. The monkish scribe lives in an established community (not exiled like Sweeney); the scribe is the medieval cleric writing either from dictation or another text in the austere darkness of the scriptorium; in the general sense, the scribe takes dictation like a court reporter making public records. Still, the scribe, as the poet Heaney constructs him and as he appears in Moling, is not completely detached from his preceding text, but transcribes it passionately and devotedly. Since the *Sweeney Astray* text precedes Heaney, he discovers it (and does not create it); he transcribes it, and he labors over it like Moling. Heaney is only the author of the text to a limited degree.

The poet in *Field Work* resurfaces from Dante's *Inferno* only to discover the "moonlit stones" of *Station Island*'s opening poem, "The Underground" (13). In "The Underground," the poet suggests that the first panel of the *Station Island* triptych will involve "Retracing the path back." Retracing is not to recall, but to rediscover a previously written self; in the first section, the poet continually imagines "I felt I had come on myself." Despite the few obviously optimistic poems, the first section of *Station Island* offers a bleak and stony landscape where the crimes committed against humanity and Nature are recorded with bitterness and moral indignation. The voice of the "jaggy, salty, punitive" stone in "Granite Chip" (21) echoes the tough-minded voice that the poet imagines advising him in "Stone from Delphi": *"that I may escape the miasma of spilled blood / govern the tongue, fear the god / until he speaks in my untrammeled mouth"* (24). The resistant voice of the stone resembles that of the disciplined scribe. The poet in this instance imagines that he must, in his role as scribe, not be the "creative" source of the poem but the conduit through which the poem travels.

Sweeney finally reappears in the last poem of the first section in "The King of the Ditchbacks" where the poet recounts his interaction with Sweeney from the same perspective as the scribe Moling. The poem is dedicated to John Montague, who has also translated parts of the *Buile Suibhne*. The dedication reminds the reader that Sweeney has been appropriated by other writers, that Sweeney's kingdom is a literary territory that has been raided before, and that more than one scribe has worked on the text. Heaney the poet recognizes that Sweeney, though possibly an aspect of the poet, is ultimately "other" than himself. The poem's voice is that of the scribe who "spent" time "obsessively in that upstairs room bringing myself close to him" (57). Sweeney as text does not "move" towards the poet; the poet must transcribe his way to Sweeney. By transcribing Sweeney's narrative, the poet has prepared himself for recording the stories of the ghosts he meets in the *Station Island* sequence.

The poet as pilgrim occupies the foreground of the sequence; however, the poet as passionate scribe drifts in the background, fulfilling his duty by recording the various voices' stories. Supporting this duty are the exacting codes of aesthetic and spiritual discipline that are announced with the first poem's "bell-notes." As Heaney comments in "Envies and Identifications: Dante and the Modern Poet": "Yet the choice of Lough Derg as a locus for the poem did, in fact, represent a solidarity with orthodox ways and obedient attitudes, and that very solidarity and obedience were what had to be challenged."[27] The bell-notes demarcate the sacred space of the *Station Island* sequence; territory is transformed into an aural field defined by sound. The poet touches upon this possibility in the third poem of the sequence when the poet thinks of "walking round / and round a space utterly empty, / utterly a source, like the idea of sound" (*SI* 68). Writing maintains the silence while filling the space. The scribe must commit memory to print; he must "witness" (*GT* xvi).

After recording / inscribing the story of the "perfect, clean, unthinkable victim" (80) in section VII, section VIII merges the familiar figure of the archaeologist in Heaney's poetry with that of the scribe: "I came to and there at the bed's stone hub / was my archaeologist, very like himself, / with his scribe's face smiling its straight-lipped smile" (81). The scribal activities of the archaeologist interweave the scribe's recovery of the text with the archaeologist's recovery of historical artifacts.

The third section of the *Station Island* triptych, "Sweeney Redivivus," celebrates the holy church of Sweeney reconstructed. Although Heaney the poet clearly has in mind T. S. Eliot's "mythic method," where the past and present coalesce in the body of the poem, Heaney also told the present author that (in the Sweeney section) he was recalling the epilogue to Ted Hughes's *Gaudete*. Though Heaney explicitly identifies with Sweeney in this section (as he did in *Sweeney Astray*), in some of the poems Heaney unquestionably assumes the detached posture of the scribe. However, in other contexts, as in the poem "The Scribes," Heaney regards the scribe as his critical or poetical nemesis. Although the scribal aspects of the poet and the writing process are often repressed in the "Sweeney Redivivus" section, the scribal tropes form one of the section's most significant conceptual configurations; they are emblematic of the poet's frustrated attempts to deny the centrality of his work. Sweeney attempts to transform the scribe into an outlaw only to realize that he is the scribe's dream / nightmare—a scribal fiction.

Heaney comments in a personal interview that he had once considered calling the "Sweeney Redivivus" section the "Sweeney Glosses" with the idea that "a gloss is on the edge." Thus, the section opens with "The First Gloss," of which Heaney says, "I did not think at the time, but I can see that I saw immediately that it was the same as 'Digging,' 'Digging Redivivus.'" The pen remains a pen and is not transformed into the metaphoric spade.

The poet's labor is the scribal labor; the text is the cryptogenic field of action. "The First Gloss" immediately supports the duplicity of its self-reflexive metapoetic title. This minimalist creation myth or political allegory asserts its significance by flexing its marginal power so that when one physically sees the abrupt four-line poem, the margins dominate the text itself. The "gloss" is the intertextual or interlinear subtext that may verify or falsify the text. Heaney acknowledges his awareness of the conceptual potential of the poem's images when he comments that he was "conscious of 'subscribe,'. . . 'justified line,' 'margin'. . . as terms of the trade—of printing and writing, but also conscious of the whole idea of getting out of the main line." This is the first gloss on the edge of the *Station Island* manuscript.

The historical documents of "The First Kingdom" produced by the scribe reappear in the poem "The Cleric" where Heaney reconstructs the scene between Sweeney and St. Ronan from the opening of *Sweeney Astray.* The arch tone of the poem hints at contrived antagonism between the scribal Ronan and Sweeney, through whom the poet speaks: "I heard new words prayed at cows" and "found his sign" (107). The cleric is as much a part of Heaney's poetic stances as is Sweeney in this poem. Of course, Ronan is the imperialist in saint's clothing. The dialectic between Sweeney and Ronan is confirmed in the poem's closing confession made by Sweeney:

> Give him his due, in the end
> he opened my path to a kingdom
> of such scope and neuter allegiance
> my emptiness reigns at its whim.
>
> (107–8)

Again the poet explores the point-counterpoint structure of the disciplined life and the life of disengagement. Sweeney wants a life outside the text, an unwritten life, but the mere existence of the cleric painfully reminds him that his life and freedom only have significance in that they exist in opposition to Ronan's repressive discourse.

The assiduous illuminator and passionate scribe move toward the thematic and tropologic center of the poet's text in "The Master" and "The Scribes." Heaney associates the generative ethical and moral qualities of the scribe with the disciplined apprenticeship of the young writer in school. The main figure in the poem "The Master" is reminiscent of Master Murphy from "Cloistered" and the "Station Island" sequence. The poet's objective correlative for the development of moral values and literary skills are the scribe's toil and tools. Although Neil Corcoran logically speculates that the Master is Yeats,[28] Heaney says that he had Czeslaw Milosz in mind when writing the poem. As "a wonderful hero of the intelligence, intellect, and principle," the Polish poet comes to signify the simple, basic rules of integrity and obedience. The "master" is related to the laboring Yeats and the disciplined Hopkins of *Preoccupations,* and to the pilgrim, archaeologist, and scrimshawist of the earlier poems.

The scribal tropes that have structured some of Heaney's most significant works culminate in "The Master." When the master opens "his book of withholding / a page at a time" the deliberateness of the gesture reflects the solemnity of the imagined moment (110). The master is judge and guide—the book is the constructed, written self. The book's contents are "just the old rules / we all had inscribed on our slates," but they are cut into the memory and then rediscovered there. The poem's scribal tropes expand to include allusions to writing in stone and to public discourse. The "quarrymen's hammers and wedges" inscribe the "old rules" and "maxims" into stone. In the ancient stone inscriptions, the poet links the rules of writing with the beginning of civilization itself. The "quarrymen's" tools are the ancient scribe's tools, the prehistoric poet's tools. The poet works to chisel "'order into stone'" (*GT* 55). In "The Master" the scribal tropes argue for the cultural and political centrality of poetry and the poet by offering images of continuity, stability, and verity.

In opposition to the affirmative associations of the scribe in "The Master," in "The Scribes" Heaney the poet uses the scribe as a thematic as well as tropologic analogue for the oppressive characteristics of a culturally inscribed pedantry and dogmatism. As in other poems, Heaney imagines in "The Scribes" that he is the marginal Sweeney living at the cultural edge of the text. Heaney asserts that the poem "was very much about literary life." The scribal sphere, then, is directly equated with literary sphere—the scribal text becomes the fabricated life of the poet. Heaney admits also that he appropriated some of the images of the scribe from Timothy O'Neill's *Irish Hand,* an engaging study of the history of calligraphy in Ireland. Heaney's primary sources for the poem are two selections of marginalia, written by medieval Irish scribes, which Francis John Byrne quotes in the introduction to *The Irish Hand.* The poem's initial reference to the "holly tree / they rendered down for ink" comes from the closing quotation of the Byrne introduction:

> A steady stream of wisdom springs
> from my well-coloured neat fair hand;
> on the page it pours its draught
> of ink of the green-skinned holly.[29]

In "The Scribes" Heaney focuses on the holly "ink" as an image of the scribe's abuse of and encroachment upon nature and perhaps lyric poetry.

Heaney also concentrates on the scribes' innately angry dispositions. Byrne quotes several translated medieval passages that describe the scribes' pains: "Let me not be blamed for the script, for the ink is bad, and the vellum defective, and the day is dark."[30] Heaney glosses this passage in "The Scribes" in his references to the "hush of the scriptorium," "old dry glut inside their quills," "the day was dark," and "the vellum bland."

Although the assemblage of marginalia in *The Irish Hand* provides an original medieval source for Heaney's images, the fact that he had already been thinking in terms of the scribe is important here. The original manuscript's elegance, presented in *The Irish Hand*, moves into the margins: "Above my lined booklet / The trilling birds chant to me."[31] The scribe's perfect lines are the score upon which the poet composes. Nonetheless, Sweeney flies from these linear bars into "On the Road," the final poem in *Station Island.*

Even though the poet identifies with the free self, the countercultural and antitextual self—Sweeney—in "On the Road," the scribal function produces an essentially orthodox and intertextual work. The poet driving down the road in "On the Road" is the quintessential modern man, reminiscent of Montague's driver in *The Rough Field,* which Heaney reviewed in 1973, and of Zbigniew Herbert's modern man returning from Lascaux, cited in Heaney's "Atlas of Civilization" (*GT* 59). The poet's chronological trajectory is clearly toward the prehistoric. The Christian pilgrim of *Station Island* reappears in the "rich young man" while the White Goddess of Robert Graves flashes by in her traditional colors: "earth-red," "white" and "black" (119). The metaphor of the soul rising from the congregation in "black-letter Latin" (120), stresses the scribe's attention to the actual rubric as it appears on the page. The scribal Latin is left behind for what resembles Bede's warrior hall with a "small east window" that he "once squeezed through" (120).

When Sweeney rests in his stone nest, "the cleft / of that churchyard wall" in the "hard-breasted / votive granite," the scribal intertextuality of the poem surfaces (120). In the margins of this passage one reads Robin Flower's version of "The Difference": "All birds build nests; so, like the rest, / we call the tit's wee lodge a nest."[32] Sweeney's "cleft" also resembles David Jones's "laughless Megaron" in *The Anathémata.* Jones provides the relevant note to his phrase when describing the "'laughless rock' at pre-Hellenic Eleusis where the modelled cult-object in its stone cist within the cleft of the rock, represented the female generative physiognomy."[33] Heaney's stone "cleft," though a primitive image, assumes a more contemporary textual fertility.

Without being aware of the scribe's presence, one would assume that at the end of "On the Road" Heaney is simply referring to the actual cave drawings that he found in Dordogne. However, if one explores the primitive pagan inscriptions—the "drinking deer" "cut into rock," whose "incised outline" strains "at a dried up source"—from the scribal perspective, other more central, conservative, and ecclesiastic referents appear (121). The cave that Sweeney and the poet enter is certainly the primogenital womb, Christ's tomb, and the hermit's cell, in addition to representing the actual caves of Lascaux. Several of the poem's closing stanzas parallel passages in David Jones's *Anathémata*. The "oaten, sun-warmed cliff" echoes Jones's "Two thousand lents again / since the first barley mow."[34] The image of the deer itself is reflected in Jones's "And see how they run, the juxtaposed forms, brighting the vaults of Lascaux."[35] The "font of exhaustion" from "On the Road" is also prefigured in Jones's closing to *The Anathémata:* "He by whom the welling *fontes* / are from his paradise-font mandated."[36] Sweeney's flight to the margins of Western civilization is actually a flight to its Judaeo-Christian core.

The "font of exhaustion" is emblematic of the poet's sense of aesthetic and spiritual exhaustion. Nonetheless, the "font"—which appears again in "Clearances"—is the baptismal font. In Catholicism, the blessing of the font is part of the liturgy for Holy Saturday. Although Jones also refers to this ritual,[37] Heaney as scribe surely was associating the font with either the liturgy itself or with Ps. 42, which is sung as part of the Holy Saturday blessing of the font: "As the hind longs for the running waters, / so my soul longs for you, O God." Again Jones could be an intermediary text in "the bleat of the spent stag / toward the river-course" and in "his desiderate cry: / SITIO [I thirst]."[38]

Even though Heaney the poet strives to transcend culture and history by using images with pre-Christian or counter-Christian associations, as in the pagan deer, the longing for regeneration and cleansing follows an orthodox Catholic pattern. Like the South American poet Vallejo, to whom Heaney refers in his essay on translation, Heaney's own language and tropes are "vestigially Catholic and persistently elemental."[39] The scribal poet, the assiduous illuminator, binds the poet to the central forces of his culture. The cultural inscriptions remain cut into the poet's grain, even when he goes against it.

The poet's subterranean quest into the prehistoric chamber of the Lascaux cave drawings on Holy Saturday ended with the poet's Easter prayer for purification and regeneration. Heaney the poet responds to the Eliot-like drought not by immersing himself in water—as did Ted Hughes in *River*. Instead, he, as mentioned in a 1988 interview, "found—at the end of *Station Island* and through *The Haw Lantern*—that one of the genuinely generative images I had was of the dry place. And throughout *The Haw Lantern* these images were happily assembled but weren't desperately hunted for—

images of a definite space which is both empty and full of potential. . . . It's a sense of a node that is completely clear where emptiness and potential stream in opposite directions."[40]

The scribe of the Egyptian gods, the divinity of wisdom, and according to myth the inventor of the system of hieroglyphics, Thoth, in the form of Hermes, guides the poet through the unfamiliar abstract landscapes of *The Haw Lantern*. Thoth is the most ancient source of the Neoplatonic and hermetic dimensions of the volume. The magical or occult possibilities of signs, the inscribed ideogram, letter, or word, are linked to Thoth through Hermes, who appears in "The Stone Verdict." The scribe's presence is intensely felt in the poems about writing such as "Alphabets," in the poems that use the parable or fable form of the Eastern European poets, in the scribal tropes of "Clearances," and in the omnipresence of Hermes, Hermes Trismegistus, or Thoth.

The opening poem of *The Haw Lantern*, "Alphabets," is the quintessential scribal rebus. It appears as if all of Heaney's previous allusions to writing, words as words, inscriptions, writing tools, terms of the publishing trade, and intertextual imperatives were assembled into one poem. "Alphabets" also develops chronologically in exact reversal of "On the Road." The latter poem traces the autobiographical journey of the poet back to the past, while "Alphabets" traces the poet's life as a writer forward—one might even say into death. In "Alphabets" the poet equates learning to write with learning to write poetry. The poet's increased dexterity and experiential knowledge correspond to the poet's improved craftsmanship and literary erudition. The poet as scribe becomes in "Alphabets" what he has always been—the teacher. The scribe drops his pen to "write aloud"[41] in "Alphabets."

At the beginning of "Alphabets" the shadow puppet made by the father is a ghostly refraction of the deer in "On the Road." This inscription is magically alive. For the young writer, the act of writing remains a mystery at school, where he makes the forked stick that they call a Y (1). The innocence of the tone diverts us from connecting this Y to Heaney's earlier V in "The Diviner" and O in *Field Work*. The epistemological realm of the letter is preceded by the phenomenological realm of the stick. When writing on the "slate" the young writer learns "there is a right / Way to hold a pen and a wrong way." The moral development of the young writer, his sense of right and wrong, corresponds to the mastering of his tools. The right and wrong way to "hold the pen" or "to write" suggests the possibility of transgression or punishment. Thus, the young writer must develop control and discipline if his work is to be "Marked correct with a little leaning hoe." This "hoe" is not the spade "Digging," but it does carry some of the scholarly weight of the earlier image. The first section of the poem ends with one of the poem's dominant images: "A globe in the window tilts like a coloured

O." In this line, the poet has reduced the world to a simple letter, an *O*. But the *O* is not a void, a nihilistic hole empty of meaning; it is the "empty space" full of potential. The world becomes the alchemist's mystical orb, and the student of writing resembles the student of magic.

When the student leaves the rigorous confines of the "Latin form" in the second section of "Alphabets" (2), he discovers the "new calligraphy that felt like home" of ancient Irish texts. In the medieval Irish illuminated manuscripts the poet finds the world rendered not in the wisdom and beauty of the narrative or lyric, but in the texts' actual graphic splendor. The world is inscribed on the page in the scribe's and illuminator's decorative lettering. Here the apprentice writer comes upon the beauty of the ancient Irish "Aisling" and the woman of the poet's dream "in her snooded garment and bare feet." In the following stanza the poet leaves the lushness of the grove and the temptation to write the undisciplined line. The poet assumes the role of translator who must follow "rules that hardened the farther they reached north." As a transcriber (of Dante, of Sweeney), the poet locks himself in his cell:

> He learns this other writing. He is the scribe
> Who drove a team of quills on his white field.
> Round his cell door the blackbirds dart and dab.
> Then self-denial, fasting, the pure cold.

The "pure cold" is the "chastising cold" of "The Scribes"; the "field" is the "opened ground" of the "Glanmore Sonnets." Heaney the poet in this instance openly identifies himself with the scribe as a result of the freedom provided by the poem's literalness. Explicitly writing about the writer as writer in the act of writing momentarily releases the repressed scribe in Heaney's work. The scribe is no longer a threatening figure; he is the prototype for the postmodern poet confronting the necromantic potential of the text.

The third section of "Alphabets" describes the maturing writer's sense of the incantatory potential of writing. The first stanza's heavy reliance on Shakespeare—especially the "wooden O" from the prologue to *Henry V*—and to Robert Graves is offset by the humorous tone of "He alludes." Shakespeare's "wooden O" is the ark that rides out the tempest, while the *O* becomes the moonlit womb of *The White Goddess*. The writer in the poem, who distrusts the feeling of being at the center of the globe—even of his own constructed globe—calls on his memory to remind him of the passing of time, the transience of all humans and of their monuments. The past is gone; the "sheaves," "harvest," and "potato pits" can never be recovered. The poem's tone strikes a melancholy and elegiac note: "All gone, with the omega that kept / Watch above each door, the good luck horse-shoe" (2–3). The poem's pitch is momentarily nostalgic. The simple, rural, and totemistic life of the poet and of the world is lost.

Through the foggy field of despair, the disillusioned writer hears a music in his deep inner ear.[42] The moment of epiphany comes in the "shape-note language, absolute on air / As Constantine's sky-lettered IN HOC SIGNO." The "shape-note language," or "Fa, So, La" music from North Carolina, is pure sound clearly vocalized without words. The song possesses an incantatory capacity. The reference to Constantine's skywriting not only alludes to Christian miracles of transformation, but also, in the suggestion of Yeats's Byzantium, prepares the way for the "necromancer" of the subsequent stanza.

The allusion to the magician, who would suspend "A figure of the world" from his ceiling so that he could see the entire cosmos before him "And 'not just single things,'" is quoted from Frances A. Yates's book, *Giordano Bruno and the Hermetic Tradition*. Yates quotes a passage from Marsilio Ficino's *Opera Omnia* (1576). Yates describes Ficino's idea that someone will construct

> on the domed ceiling of the innermost cubicle of his house, where he mostly lives and sleeps, such a figure with the colours in it. And when he comes out of his house he will perceive, not so much the spectacle of individual things, but the figure of the universe and its colours.[43]

Yates's interpretation of the passage is helpful:

> These various forms of the "figure of the world" are thus artistic objects which are to be used magically for their talismanic virtue. . . . By arranging the figure of the world and its celestial images with knowledge and skill, the Magus controls the influences of the stars. Just as Hermes Trismegistus arranged the images in the City of Adocentyn. . . . [44]
> . . .The man who stares at the figure of the world on his bedroom ceiling, imprinting it and its dominating colours of the planets on memory, when he comes out of his house and sees innumerable individual things is able to unify these through the images of a higher reality which he has within.[45]

The reference to Ficino then refers to the poet's awareness that writing is a way not only to order the world but also to discover symmetry that is perhaps already there. As Heaney states, "Art is not an inferior reflection of some ordained heavenly system but a rehearsal of it in earthly terms; art does not trace the given map of a better reality but improvises an inspired sketch of it" (*GT* 94). In the hermetic tradition the adept sees through the shadow world into the world of ideal forms. Thus, the poet looks to the "shape-note language," "Constantine," and Ficino as emblems of a beauty and order that transcend time.

In the following stanza the "astronaut" literally sees the world as an *O*, without magic. The young writer has traveled physically, spiritually, and intellectually far from his home. The weightlessness of the astronaut is the weightlessness of the postmodern poet. Here the poet, who is encouraged to fly away in the *Station Island* sequence, arrives. Free-floating in space, the poet is completely cut off from the gravities that held him down and writes in a condition similar to the one Heaney associates with Milosz: "the weightlessness of impersonal despair for the humanist venture."[46]

Thus, the poem's time-warp ending that sends the poet back to a moment in his childhood reflects his final desire for the permanence and weight of the inscription. The plasterer, who writes "our name there / With his trowel point, letter by strange letter," reminds the poet of his scribal origins. The oghamlike inscription appears in an earlier Heaney poem from *Stations*, "Sinking the Shaft," where the poet describes a water pump "set on a pediment inscribed by the points of their trowels, I suppose we thought it could never be toppled" (8). Again the inscribing trowels are associated with the passage of time. They are not so much attempts to chisel order into stone, as they are attempts to resist time; as Heaney says of Mandelstam: "the poet had come to realize that a manuscript was more durable than a man" (*GT* 75). Like the medieval scribe's marginalia, the inscription embodies the message that "The hand that wrote it is dead." From one perspective, "Alphabets" is a slightly self-indulgent literary composition; from another, it is a powerful reconstruction of the poet's life as writer. The scribe is both monk and magician, the manuscript both methodical and mystical.

The poet's "pre-reflective stare" of "Alphabets" is left behind for the self-conscious gaze of the poet in "From the Frontier of Writing." At the allegorical "frontier" the poet writes to fill "that space" when "everything is pure interrogation" (6). The interrogated poet of "The Frontier of Writing" anticipates the "scrutinized" poet of *The Haw Lantern* (7). In the volume's title poem the "data" sought is moral and ethical and not political. As at the end of "Exposure," the poet accepts the likelihood that poetry will not bring about significant change in Ireland or in the world. Thus in *The Haw Lantern*, the poet searches for a simple, clear text "not having to blind them with illumination." The illuminating light is neither the poet's visionary blaze nor the poem's ornamental marginal "illumination[s]." The "assiduous illuminator" adopts the posture of rhetorician; Heaney the poet assumes a more antagonistic relationship with his readers than he had in earlier poems. Still he realizes that he too must pass the test that will "clear you." Diogenes is the poet's self-selected critic, the figure of scribal responsibility.

The scribal tropes that shaped "Alphabets" reappear in the inscribed and inscribing "lithographs" of "The Stone Grinder" (8). The lithographer's prints, however, cannot mark the politically sublime boundaries on "Parable Island." If "Parable Island" is Ireland, then the allusion to the "missionary scribes" (perhaps informed by O'Neill's *Irish Hand*) complements the scribal tropes informing Heaney's previous work (11).

The third section of "Parable Island" examines those who fight "for the right to set 'the island story'" straight (11). The glosses of the scribe reappear as the archaeologists' (mis)reading of the Irish landscape as they "gloss the glosses." The debate in this section is between the historical materialists (perhaps Marxists) and the mythologists (nostalgic Gravesians). To the poet, both groups are myopic; the skeptic and the believer, by claiming the truth, repeat the pattern of possession, transgression, and revenge that has plagued the island.

The poem "The Stone Verdict," which was to be the title of the volume, directly alludes to Hermes. Neil Corcoran has commented upon Hermes in relation to hermeneutics and to hermetics.[47] Although the classical and Neoplatonic associations of Hermes are significant—god of the "stone heap" and of the arts—a more important association is that of Hermes with his Egyptian prototype, Thoth. As the scribe of the gods, Thoth was occasionally depicted as being present when the living entered the land of the dead.[48] Symbolically, his role was that of judge with the evidence inscribed in front of him. Iconographically, then, Hermes is linked to the judge as well as to the "judgment." It is the silence of the judge "in the ultimate court" that will acquit the poet whose slate should be clean. The "blabbed out" sentence confirms the poet's guilt—his "giving into" political edicts. In a way, the logocentric poet desires a wordless death. Thoth as Hermes stands like Janus between the old and the new, the living and the dead, the exoteric and esoteric. He is the stone threshold of silence. Ultimately, it is the scribal function of the poet that must deliver the verdict—a verdict upon himself.

Although scribal tropes appear in "From the Republic of Conscience" and "From the Land of the Unspoken," the volume's sonnet sequence "Clearances" relies most heavily upon their metonymic power. Heaney the poet immediately uses a scribal trope to end the sequence's prologue where he entreats the memory of his mother to teach him "to listen, / To strike it rich behind the linear black" (24). In a scribelike pose the poet "listen[s]" for the original call. It is the scribe who sees the wealth in the "linear black" verse—the wealth being the aesthetic and spiritual beauty of the "line" as it is worked out.

The fifth and sixth sonnets in the sequence look directly to the scribe and his inscriptions for their associative affect. Sonnet 5 was published separately as "The Cool that Came Off Sheets."[49] The "sheets" obviously rely upon their correspondence to sheets of paper. The "cool" that comes from the sheets is the "cool" that comes from writing. As the poet and mother ritualistically fold the sheets, the poet describes the action "In moves where I was x and she was o / Inscribed in sheets she'd sewn from ripped-out flour sacks" (29). In a moment of lost identity, the writer and mother become inscriptions that are folded into or written down in the sheets. Even though the letters moved with the childish simplicity of tick-tack-toe, their real energy lies in their totemistic presence. The letters resemble magical symbols in an alchemical rebus that connects the living and the dead.

The "inscribed sheets" remind one of the incised deer in "On the Road" and of Ps. 42. The scene in the sixth sonnet of "Clearances," published separately as "During Holy Week,"[50] is that of the Holy Saturday Easter liturgy that influenced the earlier poem. The personal moment is actually an intertextual moment when the poet and mother "would follow the text / And rubrics for the blessing of the font" (30). The poet and mother literally meet in the "rubrics." The poet's longing for his deceased mother echoes the Psalmist longing for God: *"As the hind longs for the streams, so my soul. . . ."* The mother does not supplant God, but the poet's and "psalmist's outcry" converge in the poem. The "font" has been blessed; the mother has been recalled.

In the deeply ingrained manner of the scribe, Heaney closes *The Haw Lantern* with "The Riddle." The riddle ends what is essentially the self-conscious poet's journey into an unfamiliar realm of poetic discourse. The riddle (one of the most ancient and magical verse forms) was also a popular form among medieval scribes. Enclosed in the scriptorium, in the logo-center of the community, and living in words and by words, the riddle opens the door to a realm where writing cannot follow. Of course the riddle has an answer; yet that solution remains unwritten. The riddle is not a conundrum; the puzzle can be solved. Thus, the man who "carried water in a riddle" carries his own regeneration in the linguistic construct. For the scribe, who perhaps is trapped in the prison house of language, the riddle written in the margins addresses the audience and establishes a dialogic exchange with the reader. It is the reader then who must close the book on the scribe—the scribe who knows that "the hand that wrote it is dead."

Notes

1. On 28 February 1988, in Swarthmore, Pennsylvania, Seamus Heaney talked to the author about issues related to writing *as* writing. This recorded conversation is the source of this quotation and others in the text.

2. Heaney comments that he has "made no conscious effort" to address poststructuralist concepts; however, "if you're within earshot of that language, it begins to affect you like a drip-treatment." He then mentions Barthes. See Roland Barthes, *Image, Music, Text*, trans. Stephen Heath (New York: Hill and Wang, 1977), 142–48.

3. In relation to the "scribal function" in Heaney's poetry, I have in mind Foucault's "author function." See Michel Foucault, *The Foucault Reader* ed. Paul Rabinow (New York: Pantheon, 1984), 108.

4. Friedrich Nietzsche, *Untimely Meditations*, trans. R. J. Hollindale (Cambridge: Cambridge University Press, 1983), 72–77.

5. Blake Morrison, *Seamus Heaney* (London: Methuen, 1982), 12.

6. Seamus Deane, *Celtic Revivals* (Winston-Salem, N.C.: Wake Forest University Press, 1985), 174. The conservative and disciplined aspect of the scribal in Heaney's poetry also relates to Terence Brown's assertion that Heaney's poetry occasionally lacks "emotional range and drama" and to what Douglas Dunn suggests is Heaney's inability to "let go." See Harold Bloom, ed. *Seamus Heaney* (New York: Chelsea House, 1986), 35, 157.

7. Deane, *Celtic Revivals*, 175.

8. Tony Curtis, "A More Social Voice: *Field Work*," in *The Art of Seamus Heaney*, ed. Tony Curtis (Bridgend, U.K.: Poetry Wales Press, 1985), 100.

9. Neil Corcoran, *Seamus Heaney* (London: Faber and Faber, 1986), 180.

10. See Pierre Macherey, *A Theory of Literary Production*, trans. Geoffrey Wall (London: Routledge and Kegan Paul, 1978), 66–68.

11. See Foucault, *Foucault Reader*, 101–2.

12. Heaney, interview by Frank Kinahan, *Critical Inquiry*, Spring 1982, 409.

13. See Timothy O'Neill, *The Irish Hand* (Mountrath: The Dolmen Press, 1984), xiii.

14. Heaney, interview by author.

15. David Jones, *The Anathémata* (New York: Viking, 1965), 34.

16. Thomas Kinsella, *Poems, 1956–1973* (Winston-Salem, N.C.: Wake Forest University Press, 1979), 192.

17. Thomas Kinsella, ed., *The New Oxford Book of Irish Verse* (Oxford: Oxford University Press, 1986), 31.

18. Edna Longley has touched upon the metapoetic nature of Heaney's verse: "Every poet worth his salt imprints his poetry with a subtext about poetry itself—as does Heaney. . . ." See Edna Longley, "*North*: 'Inner Emigré' or 'Artful Voyeur'?" in Curtis, *The Art of Seamus Heaney*, 87.

19. Heaney, interview by Bel Mooney, *Sunday Times*, 11 October 1984.

20. David Lloyd, "Pap for the Dispossessed," *Boundary 2* 13, nos. 2–3 (1985): 326.

21. Jones, *Anathémata*, 34.

22. Quoted in O'Neill, *Irish Hand*, 88.

23. Jones, *Anathémata*, 42.

24. Donald Jackson, *The Story of Writing* (New York: Taplinger, 1981), 72.

25. Seamus Heaney, interview by author.

26. Seamus Heaney, interview by Michael P. Toner, *Irish Edition* (Philadelphia), June 1986.

27. Seamus Heaney, "Envies and Identifications: Dante and the Modern Poet," *Irish University Review* 15, no. 1 (1985): 19.

28. Corcoran, *Seamus Heaney*, 174.

29. O'Neill, *Irish Hand*, xxvii.

30. Ibid., xxvi.

31. Ibid.

32. John Montague, ed., *The Book of Irish Verse* (New York: Macmillan, 1974), 112.

33. Jones, *Anathémata*, 56.
34. Ibid., 58.
35. Ibid., 60.
36. Ibid., 235.
37. Ibid., 234.
38. Ibid., 237.
39. Seamus Heaney, "The Impact of Translation," *Yale Review* 76, no. 1 (1986): 12.
40. Seamus Heaney, interview by author.
41. Roland Barthes, *The Pleasure of the Text*, trans. Richard Miller (New York: Hill and Wang, 1977), 66.
42. Heaney mentions that when he was in North Carolina, he thought the idea of "shape note" music was "beautiful" and continues, "I thought of the poem as being a shape note silence—as you read it you can hear it on the inner ear."
43. Francis A. Yates, *Giordano Bruno and the Hermetic Tradition* (Chicago: University of Chicago Press, 1964), 75.
44. Ibid.
45. Ibid., 76.
46. Seamus Heaney, interview by author.
47. Neil Corcoran, review of *The Haw Lantern* by Seamus Heaney, *Times Literary Supplement*, 26 June 1987, 681.
48. Jackson, *Story of Writing*, 23.
49. Seamus Heaney, "The Cool that Came Off Sheets," *Salmagundi*, Spring-Summer 1987, 42.
50. Seamus Heaney, "During Holy Week," *Salmagundi*, Spring-Summer 1987, 43.

Works Cited

Barthes, Roland. *Image, Music, Text*. Translated by Stephen Heath. New York: Hill and Wang, 1977.

———. *The Pleasure of the Text*. Trans. Richard Miller. New York: Hill and Wang, 1977.

Bloom, Harold, ed. *Seamus Heaney*. New York: Chelsea House, 1986.

Clarke, Austin. *The Collected Poems of Austin Clarke*. New York: Macmillan, 1936.

Corcoran, Neil. Review of *The Haw Lantern*, by Seamus Heaney. *Times Literary Supplement*, 26 June 1987, 681–82.

———. *Seamus Heaney*. London: Faber and Faber, 1986.

Curtis, Tony. "A More Social Voice: Field Work." In *The Art of Seamus Heaney*, edited by Tony Curtis, 100–127. Bridgend: Poetry Wales Press, 1985.

Deane, Seamus. *Celtic Revivals*. Winston-Salem, N.C.: Wake Forest University Press, 1985.

Donoghue, Denis. *We Irish*. New York: Knopf, 1986.

Foucault, Michel. *The Foucault Reader*. Edited by Paul Rabinow. New York: Pantheon, 1984.

Glob, P. V. *The Bog People*. Translated by Rupert Bruce-Mitford. London: Faber and Faber, 1969.

Heaney, Seamus. "Atlas of Civilization." *Parnassus* 14, no. 1 (1987): 17–32.

———. "The Cool that Came Off Sheets." *Salmagundi*, Spring-Summer 1987, 42.

————. "During Holy Week." *Salmagundi,* Spring-Summer 1987, 43.

————. "Envies and Identifications: Dante and the Modern Poet." *Irish University Review* 15, no. 1 (1985): 5–19.

————. "G as in Gaelic." In *Hockney's Alphabet,* edited by Stephen Spender. New York: Random House, 1991.

————. "The Impact of Translation." *The Yale Review* 76, no. 1 (1986): 1–14.

————. Interview. *Salmagundi,* Fall 1988.

————. Interview by author. 28 February 1988.

————. Interview by Bel Mooney. *The Sunday Times* (Dublin), 11 October 1984.

————. Interview by Frank Kinahan. *Critical Inquiry,* Spring 1982, 406–14.

————. Interview by Michael P. Toner. *Irish Edition* (Philadelphia), June 1986.

————. Review of *The Rough Field,* by John Montague. *The Listener,* 26 April 1973, 550–51.

————. *Stations.* Belfast: Ulsterman Publications, 1975.

————. "Tollund." *The New Yorker* 70, no. 31 (3 October 1994): 92.

Jackson, Donald. *The Story of Writing.* New York: Taplinger, 1981.

Jones, David. *The Anathémata.* New York: Viking, 1965.

Kinsella, Thomas. *Poems, 1956–1973.* Winston-Salem, N.C.: Wake Forest University Press, 1979.

————, ed. *The New Oxford Book of Irish Verse.* Oxford: Oxford University Press, 1986.

Lloyd, David. "'Pap for the Dispossessed.'" *Boundary 2* 13, nos. 2–3 (1985): 319–42.

Longley, Edna. "*North:* 'Inner Emigré' or 'Artful Voyeur'?" In *The Art of Seamus Heaney,* edited by Tony Curtis, 65–95. Bridgend: Poetry Wales Press, 1985.

Macherey, Pierre. *A Theory of Literary Production.* Translated by Geoffrey Wall. London: Routledge and Kegan Paul, 1978.

Montague, John, ed. *The Book of Irish Verse.* New York: Macmillan, 1974.

Morrison, Blake. *Seamus Heaney.* London: Methuen, 1982.

Nietzsche, Friedrich. *Untimely Meditations.* Translated by R. J. Hollingdale. Cambridge: Cambridge University Press, 1983.

O'Neill, Timothy. *The Irish Hand.* Mountrath: The Dolmen Press, 1984.

Yates, Francis A. *Giordano Bruno and the Hermetic Tradition.* Chicago: The University of Chicago Press, 1964.

Seamus Heaney's
Anti-Transcendental Corncrake

JONATHAN ALLISON

The corncrake is a bird that winters in Africa and until quite recently was a familiar summer bird in Ireland, nesting in rough dead grass, bog meadows, and cornfields.[1] Although it can be found in England (indeed in much of Europe) and is featured in D. H. Lawrence's story, "The Overtone," it is most common in Ireland and western Scotland.[2] It is an ungainly flier, dangling its feet behind as it moves, has a distinctive harsh call, often rendered as "crex crex" (which is also the Latin name of the bird), and is elusive and secretive. When frightened, it is as likely to run away as fly away, and thus has a reputation for being grounded: "It is only when hard pressed that it rises from the ground."[3] The corncrake has been the subject of numerous literary treatments and has proven especially interesting to Irish poets since the 1960s since the bird's survival is now under threat from modern agricultural methods, particularly from the cutting of grass for silage early in the summer, during the corncrake's nesting season.[4] As Angela Bourke puts it in a recent short story: "The machinery's wiping them out and people are starting to get all nostalgic about them."[5]

Its call sadly beautiful, the corncrake has sometimes been seen in Irish poetry as an aspect of an idyllic pastoral setting; for example, in William A. Byrne's poem "Bog-Lands," the call of the crake embodies the beautiful remoteness of the turf-cutters' lives: "No morning bells have we to wake / Us with their monotone, / But windy calls of quail and crake / Unto our beds are blown."[6] In the song "Lullaby of London" Shane McGowan of the London-Irish folk-rock band The Pogues detaches himself from precisely this kind of pastoral myth, and in so doing shows how the crake has sometimes been taken to represent a pre-industrial idyllic landscape:

> Though there is no lonesome corncrake's cry
> Of sorrow and delight
> You can hear the cars

> And the shouts from bars
> And the laughter and the fights.

For Polly Devlin, the song of the corncrake, like the sound of horses' hooves
and the smell of flax, is evocative of rural Ulster during her childhood in the
fifties: "Those smells, those sounds, are part of a way of life that has totally
vanished."[7] For John Hewitt, who titled one of his collections *The Day of the
Corncrake,* the crake's call represented a prewar Ulster before the introduction of silage and the combine harvester had changed farming conditions
and broken the long tradition of mowing with the scythe, along with the
various folk traditions that he associated with rural life in the Glens of Antrim;
in "The Swathe Uncut" (1943) he pictures the mowers with scythes in the
hayfield, and as they cut the hay, the small animals and birds who live there
scatter: the hare is "the last at bay, / for even the corncrake, blind in his
dismay, / had found the narrow safety of the drain." He alludes to the
ancient superstition that the last swathe should be hung in a prominent
place to ensure the success of the next harvest: "the spirit of the corn that
should be slain / if the saved seed will have the strength to live."[8] The
corncrake lives very near to the spirit of the corn.

Despite these appropriations of the crake as à version of pastoral or as
a symbol of vanishing agricultural and social practices, the bird has traditionally been portrayed as ungainly, with a hoarse and ugly call, as in the
Circe section of *Ulysses,* where Joyce imagines "Elijah's voice, harsh as a
corncrake's," which "jars on high."[9] For D. H. Lawrence, in "End of Another Home Holiday," the bird's call is "a hoarse, insistent request,"[10] and
Estyn Evans, in his account of the landscape of South Down, claims that
the crake's call is a typical sound of the Mourne district, and that the crake
is more common in Ireland than in England (Lawrence notwithstanding):
"To the English visitor the only unfamiliar summer sound will be the harsh
cry of the corncrake."[11] Francis Ledwidge's poem "The Death of Ailill"
begins, "When there was heard no more the war's loud sound, / And only
the rough corn-crake filled the hours."[12] In "Dawn Shoot" Seamus Heaney
speaks of the bird as a soldier guarding his territory: "A corncrake challenged / Unexpectedly like a hoarse sentry" (*DN* 29). Given the threatened
extinction of the bird, it is perhaps fitting that it should be seen as a sentry,
as one besieged and ratcheting hoarsely in defense of its place.[13]

Henry Hart argues that in Heaney's earlier poem "Nostalgia in the
Afternoon," published in 1959, the bird's call represents the loss of Edenic
childhood innocence and is contrasted with the cuckoo's "smooth music":

> Times when the cuckoo curled lobes of smooth music
> Over sunny acres of hay coloured sound

> And larks were spilling light pebbles of all
> Sand falling, stumbling, tinkling,
> Sound torn ragged and open with a corn-crake's
> Jagged-edge noise,
> Rasping backwards and forwards
> As metal through gravel.[14]

In the poem, which clearly shows the influence of both the jagged edge of Hopkins and the smooth music of Dylan Thomas, the crake's violent, metallic tune actually tears or rips the fabric of sound, undermining the harmonies of lark and cuckoo, and can be seen as the voice of postlapsarian experience, challenging the light felicities of the Edenic cuckoo. As such, it is similar to the threatening slime kings of "Death of a Naturalist," who embody grotesquely the life of reproduction and the body, and challenge the young naturalist's benign and innocent conception of nature (*DN* 15–16). As Hart notes, the poem might be called "Death of a Pastoralist."[15]

Although the corncrake's call might be thought of as a spondaic sound, ("crake crake"), several recent poets have heard it as an iambic foot—its song an epic, iambic poem. Perhaps this is because of its almost mechanical regularity. In Ciaran Carson's antipastoral poem "The New Estate," the poet urges his mother to "Forget the corncrake's elegy" and speaks of the "rusty iambics" of its call, the word "rusty" suggesting something metallic and harsh.[16] Seamus Heaney has described in "Glanmore Sonnet, III" the corncrake in consort with the cuckoo: "it was all crepuscular and iambic."[17]
In "Song for a Corncrake," Richard Murphy asks of the bird:

> Why draft an epic on a myth of doom
> In staunchly-nailed iambics
> Launched nightly near my room?
> Since all you need to say is *crex*
> Give us lyrics,
> Little bridegroom.

> (90)

The reference is to the incessant, repetitive, and therefore "epic" song of the mating male. By requesting lyrics, he wishes that its poem be much shorter, for it keeps him awake all night, and he wants it to shut up.[18]

We may wonder why poets consider the bird a poet if its voice is so harsh and even ugly. The answer lies in the fact that some poets feel that the crake's rough music appropriately represents the poetic voices of contemporary poetry who evade the conventionally beautiful in order to express the rough textures of their experience and the harshness of their age. For the early Heaney, the presiding genius of his poetry was "the guttural muse" of the Irish language itself, and of the nonstandard English of rural County Derry—a muse whose throaty voice might be likened to the call of the crake. For example, in his poem "Traditions" he writes, "Our guttural muse / was bulled long ago / by the alliterative tradition," which refers to the conquest of the Irish language by the English language, and of the Gaelic poetic tradition by the alliterative tradition of Anglo-Saxon poetry (*WO* 31). The hoarse sound of the corncrake represents both guttural muse and, in its repetitive alliterative call—"crake crake"—the Anglo-Saxon poetic tradition; as such it represents a blend of both English literary tradition and native Irish experience. In this way it comes to represent Heaney's own poetic voice, which finds its origins both in English literary tradition (he lists Marlowe, Webster, Hopkins, and Ted Hughes among his early influences) and in the experience of Catholic farmers in rural Ulster. The bird breeds and summers in rural Ireland and is a part of that traditional life which John Hewitt evokes in a poem like "The Swathe Uncut" and which Heaney gives a voice to in many of his early poems. Heaney comes closest to recognizing an affiliation between the crake's unbeautiful call and his own poetic voice in the 1972 poem, "Serenades":

> The Irish nightingale
> Is a sedge-warbler,
> A little bird with a big voice
> Kicking up a racket all night.
>
> (*WO* 62)

Unlike the "immortal" English nightingale, which seduced Keats into an illusion of transcendence with its "plaintive anthem," its "high requiem," the Irish nightingale's voice is strikingly unbeautiful, the harshness of its call is suggested by the alliteration of that last line, "Kicking up a racket all night."[19] Its call is "Not what you'd expect / From the musical nation," Heaney writes and adds that he has not even heard one. Instead he knows only the crow, the bat, and the corncrake:

> My serenades have been
> The broken voice of a crow
> In a draught or a dream,
> The wheeze of bats
>
> Or the ack-ack
> Of the tramp corncrake
> Lost in a no man's land
> Between combines and chemicals.
>
> (*WO* 62)

The so-called musical nation (Ireland) is represented not by a lyrical voice but by the noisy warbler; thus Heaney identifies Irishness with the hoarse and broken voices of the antipastoral crow, bat and crake.[20] It is implied that the English poetic tradition is associated with the lyrical and apparently transcendent nightingale. It is as though the broken voices are those of creatures who, like Thomas Hardy's "darkling thrush" with its "blast-beruffled plume," have suffered with humans and are thus anti-transcendental revisions of an English romanticism that imagined a world of song beyond human suffering.[21] In a 1925 note to his poem "To The Rose upon the Rood of Time," Yeats distinguished between his rose symbol and the quality of Intellectual Beauty as represented by Shelley and Spenser in that he imagined his rose as "suffering with man," whereas they envisaged it as "seen from afar."[22] Heaney's broken voices also suffer with us and are implicitly opposed to the Shelleyan "blithe spirit," the sublime "Scorner of the ground." One cannot say of the corncrake what Shelley says of his sky-lark: that "Shadow of annoyance / Never came near thee."[23] Heaney claims to have been nourished, educated, and serenaded by these unpastoral voices, with which he identifies. He expresses sympathy for the crake, a "tramp" because he runs along the ground and because the double pincer of mechanical harvester and agricultural chemicals has deracinated it. He is again defensive (as in "Dawn Shoot"), his call rendered as "ack-ack," which captures the alliterative guttural of the bird and which likens it to the antiaircraft fire of World War II, an appropriate comparison for this bird of the ground, whose song has repeatedly been thought of as metallic and mechanical. These broken voices are the singing masters of the poet, part of the unprettified rural landscape of his childhood. The fact that the crow's "broken voice" is suggestive of a postpubescent male voice, recently initiated into sexual awareness, underlines the association of the crow and the crake with the human body, not with the self-erasing spirit world of Keats's tender night. It also suggests, I think appropriately, that Heaney's poetic is rooted not merely in a vision of self-transcendence but in a continuous awareness of bodily and sexual processes.[24]

It is possible to consider Heaney's interest in the crake in light of his fascination with the harsh qualities of Northern Irish speech and of Northern speech generally.[25] Observing the connection between his admiration for Hopkins's alliterative poetry and the regional characteristics of the Northern Irish accent, Heaney has written that "the Ulster accent is generally a staccato consonantal one. Our tongue strikes the tangent of the consonant rather more than it rolls the circle of the vowel" (*Pr* 45). He quotes W. R. Rodgers's poem, which argues that Ulster people are

> an abrupt people,
> who like the spiky consonants of speech

and think the soft ones cissy; who dig
the k and t in orchestra, detect sin
in sinfonia, get a kick out of
tin-cans, fricatives, fornication, staccato-talk,
anything that gives or takes attack
like Micks, Teagues, tinker's gets, Vatican.

                                                    (*Pr* 44–45)

Clearly, there is a resemblance between the "spiky consonants" of the corncrake's "ack-ack" and the "staccato-talk" alluded to here, as though the crake's call is intoned through a strong Ulster accent and a distinctively Northern sensibility. There is also something of the broken voice of the crake in Heaney's depiction of the voice of David Hammond, the singer, in the poem "The Singer's House," where he speaks of "a hint of the clip of the pick / In your winnowing climb and attack"—those "k" rhymes suggesting the picklike accents of Hammond's throaty, Woodbine-smoking voice, the consonantal staccato that Rodgers identifies with Ulster speech and that is not dissimilar from the corncrake's ratcheting (*FW* 27). Also, the elegiac portrait of Sean Armstrong, Heaney's friend killed in Ulster by "a pointblank teatime bullet" includes a description of his voice that suggests the aggressive, earthbound ratcheting of our antiromantic bird: "It was independent, rattling, nontranscendent Ulster," which again bears some resemblance to the voice of Hammond and perhaps to Heaney's poetic voice, his guttural Muse mixed with the alliterative tradition, which relishes the "consonantal staccato" typical of Ulster speech and of the crake itself ("A Postcard from North Antrim," *FW* 20). The call of the corncrake, therefore, is laden with connotations of Ulster speech and identity and is a nontranscendental reply to the airy transcendence of those birds adored by the English romantic tradition, although it invites comparison with Hardy's thrush, which, like the crake, has suffered.

In 1974 Heaney wrote that from the summer of 1969, when the crisis in Ulster was reaching a boiling point—with civil rights demonstrations being suppressed by force—"the problems of poetry moved from being simply a matter of achieving the satisfactory verbal icon to being a search for images and symbols adequate to our predicament," which he likens to Yeats's "emblems of adversity" (*Pr* 56). There are numerous such emblems or "semaphores of hurt" in *Wintering Out*, including the speechless boy raised in a hen coop, the human fetus discovered in fishermen's nets, and the shore woman caught between aggressive porpoises and a boorish husband (*WO* 66, 70, 71). The tramp corncrake is also an emblem of adversity, although the primary reason for the bird's marginalization is the ecological destruction that "combines and chemicals" (those agents of Ulster capitalism) are doing to the landscape and wildlife. But the crake might also be considered a symbol of Ulster's Catholics, marginalized and intimidated by Unionist hegemony, or of the poet himself, who sees himself in a later poem as secretive and birdlike, "taking protective colouring from bole and bark" ("Exposure," *N* 73). And after all, Heaney's most infamous bird-on-the-run, the king of the ditchbacks, Sweeney Astray, is a figure of the poet himself.

In an early uncollected poem ("Corncrake"), Heaney more explicitly deploys the crake as an image of Ulster Catholicism:

> In the wet catacombs of the grass
> A loner with a breaking note
> Prays tenebrae.
>
> He is the mendicant of these dark acres
> And makes his own responses:
> Solace and reproach, his nightly office.
>
> My window's open for the cool
> So he takes advantage.
> All night his beads go ratcheting.

In its appropriation of the bird as a Christian, the poem recalls "The Corncrake" by the Belfast-born Victorian, James Cousins, in which the call of the crake is heard as a lament for the dead ("Ache! Ache!") and as prophecy of the Resurrection ("Wake! Wake!").[26] Heaney's bird is devout but less evangelical in tendency as he prays in darkness, in the damp ground, which is his catacombs, the "breaking note" of his call an echo of the broken voice of "Serenades." "All night his beads go ratcheting" as he fingers his rosary. Playfully, the voice of the corncrake—shy, marginalized, threatened, unlyrical, obsessive—calls to mind the devotions of Catholic Ulster, and Heaney's poem demonstrates how the poet appropriated the outcast bird as a symbol of the minority in Northern Ireland on the eve of the establishment of the Northern Ireland Civil Rights Association.

What has this all to do with Heaney's more recent poetry, his parables, visions and lightenings of the spirit? At a time when there is increased concern about the survival of the corncrake (Irish Wildbird Conservancy workers heard only 60 birds in northwest Donegal in 1991, compared to 220 in 1988),[27] Heaney employs the bird's call again in "Casting and Gathering," a poem in *Seeing Things*, in which "like a speeded-up corncrake, / A sharp ratcheting went on and on / Cutting across the stillness as another / Fisherman gathered line-lengths off his reel" (13). In describing the crake's call as a "ratcheting," he steals from his own 1967 poem, "Corncrake," but also suggests (again) the metallic or mechanical sound of the bird, which several writers have previously noted.[28] The poet remembers a river, on each side of which he heard different sounds: on the left bank a fisherman cast his line, "a green silk tapered cast / Went whispering through the air." On the right bank he heard the crake of the fishing reel, as the fisherman reeled in the line. The speaker is "still standing there, awake and dreamy," as though in a state of negative capability or conscious vision; he construes the crake sound as an attitude of curmudgeonly aggression or misanthropic defensiveness: "'You are not worth tuppence, / But neither is anybody. Watch it! Be severe.'" Here the crake represents severity, control, aggression. The casting sound, on the other hand, says: "'Go with it! Give and swerve. / You are everything you feel beside the river.'" It says you should be open, generous, free-flowing. The poet is clearly attracted to both voices ("I love hushed air. I love contrariness"), and he cannot be said to choose definitively between them: the voices go on talking; the fishermen keep on casting and gathering. Here then a continuous dialectical process is envisioned, which embodies two fundamentally different attitudes to experience, both of which are considered valid and persuasive. The casting and gathering, we must imagine, continue ad infinitum, as inevitably and persistently as Yeats's primary and antithetical gyres. Heaney's serenades are no longer merely those songs of experience, the "broken voices" of crow and crake, but include the *unbroken*, whole, swishing voices of the "silk tapered cast," the innocent, "entirely free" sound, which represents that openness to a vision of transcendence, buoyancy and "lightening" that marks so much of his recent poetry.

In the 1959 poem, "Nostalgia in the Afternoon," Heaney identifies two bird calls, which might represent the voices of Hopkins and Dylan Thomas— the crake's "jagged edge noise" and the smooth music of the cuckoo. Hart finds here the competing voices of innocence and experience, and we can see a similar dialectic in "Casting and Gathering," in which the smooth music of the cast line rivals and is challenged by the rattle of the reel.[29] Such a confrontation echoes other antithetical myths in Heaney's work (Hercules and Antaeus; the fecund darkness and the main of light; Ireland and England) and points to the continuance in his poetry of the thirst for transcendent vision challenged by the vicissitudes of historical experience; or, to borrow a metaphor of Auden's, which Heaney himself discussed in his essay "Sounding Auden," the dialectic in "Casting and Gathering" exemplifies Heaney's continuing preoccupation with the tension between the free-flowing Ariel ("poetry's enchantment") and the sterner voice of Prospero, "whose covenant is with 'truth' rather than 'beauty'" (*GT* 110). I do not suggest an identification of Prospero with the modest crake, merely a similarity on the basis that, for Heaney, both represent severity and control.

In "Corncrake," Heaney deployed the bird as a symbol of the besieged minority community in Northern Ireland shortly before the outbreak of the "troubles" in the late sixties. In "Serenades," he expressed an ecological consciousness of the bird as victim of modern agricultural techniques, marginalized in an antipastoral landscape of "combines and chemicals," while also constructing the crake as an emblem of the poet's "guttural muse," rooted in the Ulster landscape but also alluding to the "alliterative tradition" in its repetitive call. The bird's crepuscular call is closest to conventional idyllic pastoral in "Glanmore Sonnets," but in "Casting and Gathering" the call is mediated through the mechanism of the reel and has become an integral part of the poet's dialectical voice.

Notes

1. I wish to thank the following for providing information about the corncrake: Chris Agee, Anne Allison, Angela Bourke, Ciaran Carson, Rachel Giese, Jack and Marie-Claude Gillespie, Brendan Glass, John Stewart, and John Thompson.

2. Gordon D'Arcy, *The Guide to the Birds of Ireland* (Dublin: Irish Wildlife Publications, 1981), 74. Estyn Evans, *Irish Heritage* (Dundalk: Dundalgan Press, 1978), 80. Finlay J. MacDonald, *The Corncrake and the Lysander* (London: MacDonald, 1985), 25.

3. Rev. C. A. Johns and J. A. Owen, eds. *British Birds in Their Haunts* (London: Routledge; New York: Dutton, 1910), 228.

4. D'Arcy, *Guide to the Birds*, 74. Sean MacConnell, "Survey shows continuing decline of corncrake," *Irish Times*, 26 July 1991, 12. Christine Newman, "Birdwatchers out for the count," *Irish Times*, 6 January 1992.

5. Angela Bourke, "Nesting." *Krino* 12 (Winter 1991): 23. The bird's increasing rarity in Ireland adds to the sentimental value recently placed upon it, although it has traditionally been thought of as a "blessed bird" in the north of Scotland and as a leader of other birds: the Greeks, like the French, believed the corncrake to be the chieftain of quails, hence the French appellation, "Roi des cailles." See Rev. Charles Swainson, *Provincial Names and Folk Lore of British Birds* (London: English Dialect Society, 1885), 177.

6. Padraic Colum, *An Anthology of Irish Verse* (New York: Liveright, 1948), 166.

7. John Quinn, ed., *A Portrait of the Artist as a Young Girl* (London: Methuen & RTE), 44.

8. John Hewitt. *The Selected John Hewitt*, ed. Alan Warner (Belfast: Blackstaff, 1988), 59.

9. James Joyce, *Ulysses: A Critical and Synoptic Edition*, ed. Hans Walter Gabler, 2 vols. (New York: Garland, 1984), 2:1099.

10. D. H. Lawrence, *The Complete Poems of D. H. Lawrence*. Ed. Vivian de Sola Pinto and Warren Roberts (New York: Viking, 1964), 1:64.

11. Evans, *Irish Heritage*, 80.

12. In Kathleen Hoagland, *1000 Years of Irish Poetry* (Old Greenwich, Conn.: Devin-Adair, 1975), 701.

13. Although the eighteenth-century Irish poem, "The Yellow Bittern" (in Thomas MacDonagh's translation) describes the crake as gregarious and "common," Norman Dugdale's 1978 poem "Corncrake in October" expresses the contemporary perception of the crake as shy and threatened. See John Montague, ed., *The Book of Irish Verse* (New York: Macmillan, 1977), 184 and Norman Dugdale, *Corncrake in October* (Belfast: Blackstaff, 1978), 37.

14. Quoted in Henry Hart, *Seamus Heaney: Poet of Contrary Progression* (Syracuse, N.Y.: Syracuse University Press, 1992), 17.

15. Ibid., 22.

16. Ciaran Carson, *The New Estate and Other Poems* (Winston-Salem, N.C.: Wake Forest University Press, 1989), 69.

17. Heaney's use of the word "crepuscular" echoes the use of that word in a profile of the bird provided by Bob Scott and Don Forrest, but Heaney may be directly invoking Richard Murphy's "Song for a Corncrake," in which he portrays the bird as a "Crepuscular, archaic politician." See Richard Murphy, *New Selected Poems* (London: Faber, 1989), 90.

18. As one British ornithologist put it, "its incessant cry in the evenings is monotonous, if not wearisome." See Johns and Owen, *British Birds*, 228. The bird is also portrayed as a poet in the Gaelic poem translated by Frank O'Connor as "May," in which "The corncrake drones, a bustling bard." See Frank O'Connor, *Kings, Lords and Commons* (Dublin: Gill and Macmillan, 1959), 18.

19. John Keats, "Ode to a Nightingale," in *The Norton Anthology of English Literature: The Major Authors*, ed. M. H. Abrams (New York: Norton, 1987), 1845.

20. In an uncollected early poem, "Rookery," Heaney writes of the rooks' "guttural chat," a trope that associates the birds' harsh cawing with his own "guttural muse."

21. Thomas Hardy, "The Darkling Thrush," in Abrams, *Norton Anthology*, 2210–11.

22. W. B. Yeats, *The Collected Poems of W. B. Yeats*, ed. Richard J. Finneran (New York: Macmillan, 1989), 453.

23. Percy Bysshe Shelley, "To a Sky-Lark," in Abrams, *Norton Anthology*, 1783.

24. Traditionally, the crake's call has had sexual connotations, being associated with courtship, as Richard Murphy's poem might suggest. See Murphy, *New Selected Poems*, 90. According to Wright, the dialectical expression "To listen the craik in the corn" means "to carry on courtship by night in the open air"—an occasion dramatized by Lawrence in his story "The Overtone," in which the sexually frustrated husband's desire finds expression in the song of the corncrake. See Joseph Wright, ed., *The English Dialect Dictionary* (London: Henry Frowde; New York: Putnam's, 1897), 768 and D. H. Lawrence, *The Complete Short Stories of D. H. Lawrence* (New York: Viking, 1961), 3:749.

25. In a BBC interview Heaney speculated that there is an invisible frontier in Britain, north of which people express dismay and annoyance with the word "och," south of which they use the softer sound "aw." He included Northern Ireland in the first category. Seamus Heaney, "Desert Island Discs," interview by Sue Lawley, BBC Radio, 19 November 1989.

26. Hoagland, *1000 Years of Irish Poetry*, 632.

27. MacConnell, "Survey," 12.

28. Estyn Evans in *Irish Heritage* has described a mechanical device known as a "corncrake": "a home-made device once familiar in the north was the crow-scarer or 'corn-crake' a noisy instrument made on the principle of the watchman's rattle or—to give a modern instance—the gas rattle of the A.R.P. services" (94). Heaney's fishing reel is like the crow-scarer as much as it is like the bird.

29. Hart, *Seamus Heaney*, 17

Works Cited

Abrams, M. H. ed. *The Norton Anthology of English Literature: The Major Authors*. Fifth Edition. New York: Norton, 1987.

Bourke, Angela. "Nesting." *Krino* 12 (Winter 1991): 23–25.

Carson, Ciaran. *The New Estate and Other Poems.* Winston-Salem, N.C.: Wake Forest University Press, 1989.

Colum, Padraic. *An Anthology of Irish Verse.* New York: Liveright, 1948.

D'Arcy, Gordon. *The Guide to the Birds of Ireland.* Dublin: Irish Wildlife Publications, 1981.

Dugdale, Norman. *Corncrake in October.* Belfast: Blackstaff, 1978.

Evans, Estyn. *Irish Heritage.* Dundalk: Dundalgan Press, 1958.

——. *Mourne Country: Landscape and Life in South Down.* Dundalk: Dundalgan Press, 1951.

Hart, Henry. *Seamus Heaney: Poet of Contrary Progressions.* Syracuse, N.Y.: Syracuse University Press, 1992.

Heaney, Seamus. "Corncrake." *Listener,* 2 November 1967, 573.

——. "Desert Island Discs." Interview by Sue Lawley. BBC Radio, 19 November 1989.

——. "Rookery." *Listener,* 29 September 1966, 475.

Hewitt, John. *The Selected John Hewitt.* Edited by Alan Warner. Belfast: Blackstaff, 1988.

Hoagland, Kathleen. *1000 Years of Irish Poetry.* Eighth Edition. Old Greenwich, Conn.: Devin-Adair, 1975.

Johns, Rev. C. A., and J. A. Owen, eds. *British Birds in Their Haunts.* London: Routledge; New York: Dutton, 1910.

Joyce, James. *Ulysses: A Critical and Synoptic Edition.* Edited by Hans Walter Gabler. Vol. 2. New York: Garland, 1984.

Lawrence, D. H. *The Complete Poems of D. H. Lawrence.* Edited by Vivian de Sola Pinto and Warren Roberts. Vol. 1. New York: Viking, 1964.

——. *The Complete Short Stories of D. H. Lawrence.* Vol. 3. New York: Viking, 1961.

MacConnell, Sean. "Survey shows continuing decline of corncrake." *Irish Times,* 26 July 1991, 12.

Macdonald, Finlay J. *The Corncrake and the Lysander.* London: Macdonald, 1985.

MacGowan, Shane. "Lullaby of London." *If I Should Fall from Grace with God.* By the Pogues. WEA Records, 1987; Stiff Records, 1988.

Montague, John, ed. *The Book of Irish Verse.* New York: Macmillan, 1977.

Murphy, Richard. *New Selected Poems.* London: Faber, 1989.

Newman, Christine. "Birdwatchers out for the count." *Irish Times,* 6 January 1992.

O'Connor, Frank. *Kings, Lords and Commons.* Dublin: Gill and Macmillan, 1959.

Quinn, John, ed. *A Portrait of the Artist as a Young Girl.* London: Methuen & RTE, n.d.

Scott, Bob, and Don Forrest. *The Birdwatcher's Key.* New York: Frederick Warne, 1976.

Swainson, Rev. Charles. *Provincial Names and Folk Lore of British Birds.* London: English Dialect Society, 1885.

Wright, Joseph, ed. *The English Dialect Dictionary.* London: Henry Frowde; New York: Putnam's, 1897.

Yeats, W. B. *The Collected Poems of W. B. Yeats.* Edited by Richard J. Finneran. New York: Macmillan, 1989.

Fusions in
Heaney's *North*

DAVID LLOYD

In Part I of *North*, Seamus Heaney develops a mythical, cultural, and historical perspective on Northern Ireland: the reader experiences a consciousness moving freely and rapidly through many cultures and a vast time scale. The poems of Part II then delve into autobiographical and political material, presenting a specific speaker (Heaney himself) reacting to events in specific places and times: St. Columb's College in 1951; Belfast in 1962; and Madrid in the summer of 1969, to give a sampling. But this dichotomy between mythical and autobiographical content, between a wide-ranging historical perspective and a perspective anchored in highly specific contemporary times and locations, is not absolute. The poems of *North*, Part I, in fact, fuse mythic and historic "matter"[1] with contemporary, autobiographical content, to help create what Jay Parini terms "a unique species of political poetry."[2]

Heaney fuses ancient impulse and present reality in Part I of *North* primarily by merging his voice and sensibility with figures from mythology, literary texts, or historical periods. His contemporary, English poet Geoffrey Hill, uses a similar technique in the poem sequence *Mercian Hymns*. Like Hill, Heaney analyzes and critiques his country's political and social life by showing how archaic elements of history and myth underpin and partially direct the consciousness of contemporary individuals. In *Mercian Hymns*, Hill undertakes a single fusion: he merges elements of his life and consciousness—mostly from his childhood years in the English midlands—with elements from the historical and imagined life of Offa, the eighth-century king of Mercia.[3] Heaney, on the other hand, undertakes multiple fusions with mythic figures such as Antaeus, historical figures such as the Vikings and the bog people of Denmark, and literary figures such as Hamlet. These fusions are perhaps most evident in three poems from *North*, Part I: "Antaeus," "Hercules and Antaeus," and "Viking Dublin: Trial Pieces."

In "Antaeus," the first poem of Part I, the speaker anticipates the arrival of

Hercules, journeying to obtain the golden apples of the Hesperides, his twelfth labor. Antaeus's boast conveys confidence that he can defeat whatever invader might arrive:

> Let each new hero come
> Seeking the golden apples and Atlas,
> He must wrestle with me before he pass
> Into that realm of fame
>
> Among sky-born and royal:
>
> (*N* 12)

This persona merges the giant wrestler and cave dweller of Greek mythology with attributes readers of *Death of a Naturalist* and *Door Into the Dark* associate with Heaney's early poetry: a profound connection with the physical, natural world, a "hankering for the underground side of things" (*Pr* 21). Like the mythical cave-dweller Antaeus, Heaney the twentieth-century poet draws inspiration and even magical power from the earth, as he makes clear in "Mossbawn," a Radio Talk published in *Preoccupations:*

> I always remember the pleasure I had in digging the black earth in our garden and finding, a foot below the surface, a pale seam of sand. . . . So I find it altogether appropriate that an old superstition ratifies this hankering for the underground side of things. It is a superstition associated with the Heaney name. In Gaelic times, the family were involved with ecclesiastical affairs in the diocese of Derry, and had some kind of rights to the stewardship of a monastic site at Banagher in the north of the county. There is a . . . belief that sand lifted from the ground at Banagher has beneficent, even magical, properties, if it is lifted from the site by one of the Heaney family name (*Pr* 20–21)

As the first poem of Part I, "Antaeus" announces several themes picked up by later poems. The synchronic presence of contemporary and ancient or mythic sensibilities, which suggests that modern humanity harbors ancient and ongoing impulses, prepares the reader for the Viking and bog poems, which achieve a similar effect of simultaneity. Other subjects and concerns introduced or suggested include violent struggle, potential or actual dispossession, and regeneration. While the thematic concerns of "Antaeus" generate echoes through *North*, the poem's main effect is to begin Part I with a focus on the mythic and the ancient.

The last poem of Part I, "Hercules and Antaeus," relates—by means of a third-person rather than a first-person narrative—the final battle between those two mythological figures. In the Greek myth Hercules kills Antaeus by holding him off the ground, away from his source of regeneration. In

Heaney's poem, however, Antaeus is not killed: he is elevated from the earth, becoming "a sleeping giant / pap for the dispossessed." While "pap" suggests weak nourishment for a dispossessed people, the fact that Antaeus is sleeping implies his eventual awakening. Hercules' privileged birth (as Zeus's son, he is "Sky-born," which puns on "high born"), unsavory strength (he is called "snake-choker" and "dung-heaver"), base material ambition (his mind is "big with golden apples"), and assured success in life (his future is "hung with trophies") characterize him for the reader as a dangerous, arrogant and unsympathetic enemy. It is with the dispossessed, sleeping Antaeus that the reader sympathizes.[4]

In "Hercules and Antaeus," Heaney describes Hercules' intelligence as

> a spur of light,
> a blue prong graiping [Antaeus]
> out of his element
> into a dream of loss.
>
> (52)

The word "graiping"—the only verb in the poem not in current use—creates a sudden shift of diction, providing an entrance into Heaney's technique of layering analogous political or cultural struggles in a number of *North*'s poems. An old Norse word for "griping" or "grasping," "graiping" recalls the Viking invasions of Ireland and their linguistic legacy, a major motif of Part I of *Wintering Out*, Heaney's third collection (see "Anahorish," "Toome," "Broagh," and "Traditions," in particular).

Two stanzas later the speaker prophesies the death of three figures richly suggestive of further analogies to the mythic struggle between Antaeus and Hercules: "Balor will die / and Byrthnoth and Sitting Bull." Although these names are gathered from vastly different historical periods and cultures, they relate in the context of the poem's wider political dimension. "Balor" refers to the giant (or "fomor") of Celtic mythology known as "Balor of the baleful eye," defeated by his grandson Lugh during the second battle of Moytura. It took four men to lift Balor's eyelid, the exposed eye then killing all on whom it glanced.[5] "Byrthnoth," the second name, refers to the Anglo-Saxon leader memorialized in the Old English poem, "The Battle of Maldon," for resisting (unsuccessfully) Viking invaders in 991. In that poem, Byrthnoth—like Balor a giant man—is blamed by the poem's author for adhering to the heroic code of his culture when he allows the Vikings to cross the Blackwater River for a fair fight. The Anglo-Saxon warriors are defeated and Byrthnoth beheaded. Sitting Bull, the last figure named, is the famous chief of the Dakota Sioux Indians who masterminded General

Custer's defeat at the Battle of Little Big Horn but who was eventually driven with his tribe off their land into exile in Canada. Later, he was killed by soldiers of the United States Army.[6]

These three figures—mythologized in legend or folklore—are national military heroes who, in different contexts, fought invading enemies to retain their lands and preserve their cultures, only to face ultimate defeat. Heaney fashioned this list with an eye to chronological progression and cultural plurality: the giant heroes belong to Greek, Celtic, Anglo-Saxon, and Native American history and legend. Thus the Antaeus persona works on numerous levels in these two framing poems. The first Antaeus poem conveys Heaney's profound personal and creative connection to the physical world, "the underground side of things." But "Hercules and Antaeus" adds to that connection a wide-ranging exploration of political struggle and cultural violence, demonstrating Heaney's "awareness that poetry was a force, almost a mode of power, certainly a mode of resistance."[7]

"Viking Dublin: Trial Pieces," like the two Antaeus poems, creates complex interactions between the ancient and the modern, the personal and the political, in part by fusing Heaney's contemporary sensibility with the consciousness and preoccupations of an unknown Viking artist and of Shakespeare's Hamlet. Viking artists used bones from deer or other large animals to carve "trial pieces," preliminary designs for larger projects.[8] Usually very small, trial pieces could themselves be, despite their preliminary nature, intricate artistic creations, depicting real or mythological elements of Viking culture. They show correspondences to the artistic style of the Celtic monasticism of that period, often depicting elaborate real and imagined creatures:[9]

> the craft's mystery
> improvised on bone:
> foliage, bestiaries,
>
> interlacings elaborate
> as the netted routes
> of ancestry and trade.

> (*N* 21, 22)

The title, "Trial Pieces: Viking Dublin," suggests that the poem's six parts are trial pieces made of words, incorporating real and mythological elements from Ireland's Viking past. This sense of a cultural heritage, a body of knowledge, and a vocation shared with the Viking artist is further highlighted by Heaney's pun on the word "line" as the means of composition for artist *and* poet: "the line amazes itself / eluding the hand / that fed it."

Both the Viking artist and the contemporary poet create "a cage / or trellis to conjure in": for the Viking, the cage is the outline incised on bone, the artist's work area; for Heaney, the cage is the poem itself. Some of the Viking trial pieces, such as the four-sided Dungarvan piece in the National Museum of Ireland collection, actually look like elaborately designed cages (see plate). Others convey the sense of a cage through their elaborate design. The very word "cage" suggests the containing of a powerful and independent—even dangerous—entity, while "conjure" emphasizes the magic and mystery Heaney associates with poetry. In his essay "Feeling Into Words," Heaney asserts that writing poetry constitutes an act of "divination" (*Pr* 41). While the merged persona of "Antaeus" highlights the poet's connection to the natural world and to the political struggles of indigenous peoples, this merged persona allows Heaney to explore the ways historical and cultural forces shape an artist's craft and vocation. The speaker's felt link to the Viking artist is traced back not only through their similarities as artists but also through complex, wide-ranging cultural and historical associations, the "netted routes / of ancestry and trade" that spread through the whole of northern Europe during the Viking era.

Part IV of "Viking Dublin: Trial Pieces" provides a far more explicit fusion, this time of the speaker and Shakespeare's Hamlet:

> I am Hamlet the Dane,
> skull-handler, parablist,
> smeller of rot
>
> in the state, infused
> with its poisons,
> pinioned by ghosts
> and affections,
>
> murders and pieties,
> coming to consciousness
> by jumping in graves,
> dithering, blathering.
>
>   (23)

The fact that Hamlet is a Dane connects that literary figure to the Viking concerns of *North* in general and to "Trial Pieces: Viking Dublin" in particular. The Hamlet/Heaney persona who comes "to consciousness / by jumping in graves" also points ahead to Heaney's imaginative and mythic

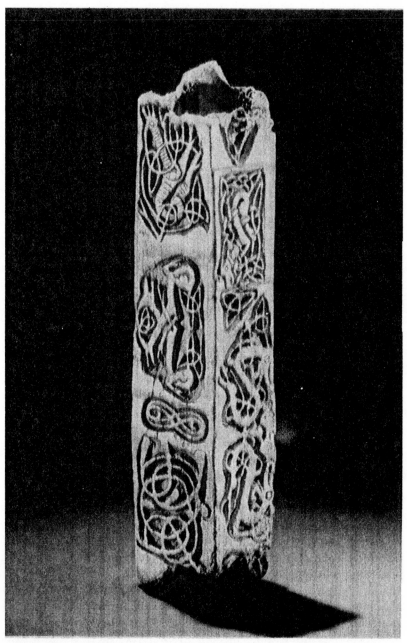

Bone Trial piece, Dungarvan, County Waterford. Rept. with permission of Boltin
Picture Library, Croton-on-Hudson.

exploration of bodies exhumed from Danish bogs—the "bog poems" sequence—bringing the poet to a greater consciousness of the ancient origins
of ritual revenge and sectarian atrocity.

"Skull-handler," Heaney's kenning phrase for Hamlet, is particularly
rich with implications for other poems of *North*, in part through its linking
with Heaney's own skull handling in bog poems such as "Come to the
Bower" ("I unwrap skins and see / The pot of the skull"), or in "Strange
Fruit" ("Here is the girl's head like an exhumed gourd"). It also resonates
with Celtic representations of the severed human head, iconographically
central to the Irish pagan religion (*Pr* 59), and with contemporary political
implications, for this image is often taken to represent the six counties of
Ulster severed from the body of the Irish nation (as in "A Severed Head,"
Part IV of John Montague's poem sequence *The Rough Field*).

The "Hamlet" persona becomes, in fact, a particularly resonant focal
point for recurring concerns of *North*: Europe's Dark Ages, political and
personal paralysis or indecision, assassination, familial loyalties, intellectual and artistic consciousness, the impingement of the past on the present
in the form of vengeful ghosts, and the hoped-for redemptive capabilities of
art. Heaney's merging with Hamlet embodies a dilemma faced by writers
from postcolonial cultures such as Ireland: can one experience loyalty and
love for the language and literature of the conquering nation?[10] Heaney's
fusion with Hamlet in "Trial Pieces" signifies his absorption of English literature and its tradition, a condition brought on by the conquering of Ireland and the dismantling of its cultural infrastructure. All the above concerns are central to Heaney's apprehension of the political and religious
divisions in his home country, as presented in *North*. "Dithering, blather-
ing"—the final line of this section of "Viking Dublin: Trial Pieces"—foreshadows the diction and tone of *North*, Part II, where Heaney expresses
much anguish (often in a tone of bitter irony) over his own ambivalence in
the face of difficult political choices.

As the reader moves from Part I of *North* to Part II, he or she emerges
from the dark passages and echo chambers of Irish and European myth
and cultural history to the too-bright light of contemporary reality in Northern Ireland, a surfacing complementary to the motif of burial and resurfac-
ing that resonates through *North*. That emergence is prepared for in Part I
by Heaney's fusions: despite the reader's immersion in ancient cultural
"matter"—figures from Greek mythology, the burial chambers of the Boyne
(in "Funeral Rites"), the artifacts of Viking Dublin—he or she never loses
connection with the present and the poet's own consciousness of the personal and political dilemmas of contemporary Northern Ireland. In this
way Heaney widens the mythological and historical context of contemporary sectarian conflict, making the private public, and the personal political.

Notes

1. David Jones uses this term to describe a nation's accumulated mythic, historical, and cultural elements. See David Jones, preface to *The Anathémata*. (London: Faber and Faber, 1955), 16–17.

2. Jay Parini, "The Ground Possessed." *The Southern Review* 16 (1980): 100.

3. For a discussion of Hill's treatment of the merging of personal and public history, see my article, "The Public and Private Realms of Geoffrey Hill's *Mercian Hymns*." In *World, Self, Poem: Essays on Contemporary Poetry*, ed. Leonard M. Trawick (Kent, Ohio: Kent State University Press, 1990).

4. Heaney's treatment of Antaeus brings to mind David Jones's long poem "The Sleeping Lord," published one year previous to *North*. That poem incorporates the Welsh myth that King Arthur, sleeping in a cave in Wales since his defeat by Mordred, will eventually awaken to free his people from their oppressors. Heaney and Jones share a fascination with defeat, burial, and regeneration—a paradigm central to the bog poems of *North*.

5. In an essay first published in the *Education Times* (1973), Heaney refers to the strong impression this story made on him as a child: "But the real imaginative mark was made with a story of Dagda, a dream of harp music and light, confronting and defeating Balor of the Evil Eye on the dark fortress of Tory Island" (*Pr* 23).

6. When Byrthnoth's remains were discovered and identified in 1769, no head was found with the bones, and the discoverers estimated that Byrthnoth must have been 6 foot 9 inches in height: "It was observed that the collar-bone had been nearly cut through, as by a battle-axe or two-handed sword." See E. V. Gordon, *The Battle of Maldon* (Manchester, U.K.: Manchester University Press, 1976), 21.

7. James Randall, "An Interview with Seamus Heaney." *Ploughshares* 5, no. 3 (1979): 20.

8. Liam de Paor, "The Christian Triumph: The Golden Age," in Frank G. Mitchell et al., eds., *Treasures of Irish Art, 1500 B.C. – 1500 A.D.*. (New York: The Metropolitan Museum of Art and Alfred A. Knopf, 1977) 103.

9. Maire de Paor. "The Viking Impact." in Mitchell et al., *Treasures*, 149.

10. When confronting this issue in his prose pieces, Heaney has acknowledged a great ambivalence: while his educational immersion in English literature shaped his poetic technique to a considerable degree (see "Belfast," *Pr* 28–37), he saw that education as an alien enterprise: "The literary language, the civilized utterance from the classic canon of English poetry, was a kind of force-feeding. It did not delight us by reflecting our experience; it did not re-echo our own speech in formal and surprising arrangements" (from "Mossbawn," *Pr* 26).

Works Cited

de Paor, Liam. "The Christian Triumph: The Golden Age." In *Treasures of Irish Art, 1500 B.C.. – 1500 A.D.*, edited by Frank G. Mitchell et al. New York: The Metropolitan Museum of Art and Alfred A. Knopf, 1977.

de Paor, Maire. "The Viking Impact." In *Treasures of Irish Art, 1500 B.C.. – 1500 A.D.*, edited by Frank G. Mitchell et al. New York: The Metropolitan Museum of Art and Alfred A. Knopf, 1977.

Gordon, E. V. Introduction to *The Battle of Maldon*. Manchester, U.K.: Manchester University Press, 1976.

Hooker, Jeremy. *Poetry of Place.* Manchester, U.K.: Carcanet Press, 1982.

Jones, David. Preface to *The Anathémata.* London: Faber and Faber, 1955.

Lloyd, David. "The Public and Private Realms of Geoffrey Hill's *Mercian Hymns.*" In *World, Self, Poem: Essays on Contemporary Poetry,* edited by Leonard M. Trawick. Kent, Ohio: Kent State University Press, 1990.

Parini, Jay. "The Ground Possessed." *The Southern Review* 16 (1980): 100–123.

Randall, James. "An Interview with Seamus Heaney." *Ploughshares* 5, no. 3 (1979): 7–22.

Violence and the Sacred
in Seamus Heaney's *North*

CHARLES L. O'NEILL

Published in 1975, Seamus Heaney's *North* remains the most complex and problematic work of art provoked by the renewal of sectarian conflict in Northern Ireland. It has been praised for putting that conflict in a larger mythological perspective as well as criticized for appearing to impute to it a fatalistic historical determinism.[1] By bringing the violence of the past in touch with that of the present, the poems of *North* draw Iron Age, Viking, and modern Irish societies together in a lyric sequence that aspires to mythic resonance. Examining Heaney's myth of "North," a myth that mixes violence, revenge, human sacrifice, and religion, in light of the ideas of nature and culture proposed by the critical theorist, René Girard, may illuminate and extend the images and intuitions Heaney's sequence develops. "Violence," Girard has written, in terms that bring the poems of *North* to mind, "is the heart and secret soul of the sacred."[2]

Dillon Johnston, in *Irish Poetry After Joyce,* declares that in *North,* "Heaney constructs a hemispheric myth, inherent in the Viking foundations of Dublin, of man's homicidal nature, which is as inexplicable as nature's unconscious processes from which it is derived."[3] At the same time, however, that Heaney was constructing his myth, other writers and thinkers, such as Konrad Lorenz, the natural scientist, Walter Burkert, the historian of Greek religion, and René Girard, the literary critic, were investigating "man's homicidal nature" in an effort to make it explicit. It is the work of Girard that best explicates and endorses the image of man that Heaney implies in *North.*

In *Violent Origins,* a collaborative effort by Girard, Burkert, and Jonathan Z. Smith that treats the origins of culture, the core of Girard's complex theory is explained this way:

> Violence . . . is endemic to human society, and there is no solution to this problem except for the answer that religion gives. Since that answer is given in the rituals of killing and their rationalizations as "sacrifice," the solution

91

that religion provides is also an act of violence. Violence, then, is the manifestation of the Sacred in its dual mode of (1) the terror of uncontrolled killing, and (2) controlled rituals of sacrifice. (6–7)[4]

What has erupted in Northern Ireland since 1969 is a cycle of "uncontrolled killing." What has been lacking are any "controlled rituals of sacrifice," whether religious, political, or imaginative, to bring that violence to
an end. In his *Children of Wrath: Political Violence in Northern Ireland*, Michael
MacDonald writes that, as of 1986, "So pervasive and permanent has violence become that it serves less to change than to define Northern Ireland."[5] The poems of *North* embody this bleak perception.

That search for adequate "images and symbols" to treat this social catastrophe came into focus when he read P. V. Glob's *Bog People*. In it, Heaney
found descriptions and photographs of Iron Age men and women of Northern Europe sacrificed, according to Glob, to a mother goddess. Glob wrote,

Heaney began his career as a pastoral poet, his first three books evoking the landscapes and immemorial customs of the Northern Irish country-
side in which he was raised. The violence that escalated in 1969 between
Catholic and Protestant factions had serious imaginative consequences for
Heaney's work. "From that moment," he wrote, "the problems of poetry
moved from being simply a matter of achieving the satisfactory verbal icon
to being a search for images and symbols adequate to our predicament" (*Pr*
56).

> The Tollund man and many of the other bog men, after their brief time as
> god and husband of the goddess . . . fulfilled the final demand of religion.
> They were sacrificed and placed in the sacred bogs; and consummated by
> their death the rites which ensured for the peasant community luck and fer-
> tility in the coming year.[6]

In an interview, Heaney stated what the book meant to his work:

> The Tollund Man seemed to me like an ancestor almost, one of my old
> uncles, one of those moustached archaic faces you used to meet all over the
> Irish countryside. . . . And the sacrificial element, the territorial religious
> element, the whole mythological field surrounding these images was very
> potent. So I tried, not explicitly, to make a connection between the sacrifi-
> cial, ritual, religious element in the violence of contemporary Ireland and
> this terrible sacrificial religious thing in *The Bog People*. [7]

The first result of Heaney's reading of Glob was the poem "The Tollund
Man," published in his 1972 collection *Wintering Out;* it was the poem that

opened the world of "North" for him. In it, Heaney prays to the Iron Age victim as a modern saint, asking him to "make germinate" the bodies of victims of sectarian violence. The poem concludes,

> Out there in Jutland
> In the old man-killing parishes
> I will feel lost,
> Unhappy and at home.

> (*WO* 48)

The "parishes" of "North"—Jutland, Iceland, Norway, Northern England, and Ireland—are, to Heaney, "religious" districts distinguished chiefly by "man-killing": murder and concomitant revenge, the inexorable circle of reciprocal violence. And here the poet is "unhappy and at home."

In *Things Hidden Since the Foundations of the World*, Girard claims that "Religion is nothing other than this immense effort to keep the peace," and he continues in terms that recall Heaney's response to Glob's descriptions and photographs:

> *The sacred is violence*, but if religious man worships violence it is only insofar as the worship of violence is to bring peace; religion is entirely concerned with peace, but the means it has of bringing it about are never free of sacrificial violence.[8]

Heaney has noted: "And just how persistent the barbaric attitudes are, not only in the slaughter but in the psyche, I discovered . . . after I had fulfilled the vow [to visit the Tollund Man] and gone to Jutland" (*Pr* 59).

For both Glob and Girard, such "barbaric attitudes" are regarded as religious by those who offer ritual sacrifices. Girard claims that "The signifier is the victim. The signified constitutes all actual and potential meaning the community confers on to the victim and, through its intermediacy, on to all things."[9] For Glob's Iron Age communities, the sacrifice of a chosen victim ensured "luck and fertility." "There is no difficulty," Girard continues,

> in explaining why ritual is repeated. Driven by sacred terror and wishing to continue life under the sign of the reconciliatory victim, men attempt to reproduce and represent this sign; this attempt consists first of all in the search for victims who seem capable of bringing about the primordial epiphany. . . . [10]

The poems of *North* are "consecrated" to understanding and reenacting this "primordial epiphany."

Heaney's myth of "North" is developed in a sequence of lyric poems

that blend violence and the sacred to suggest man's homicidal nature. With
"The Tollund Man," this sequence consists of "Funeral Rites," "North,"
"Viking Dublin: Trial Pieces," "Bone Dreams," "Come to the Bower," "Bog
Queen," "The Grauballe Man," "Punishment," and "Kinship," ten poems employing the same two-beat line and quatrain stanza, 167 quatrains
in all. Heaney has commented on the formal unity of this sequence, noting
"those thin small quatrain poems, they're kind of drills or augers for turning in and they are narrow and long and deep." [11]
  In the poem "Kinship" (*N* 40–45) Heaney writes,

> Kinned by hieroglyphic
> peat on a spreadfield
> to the strangled victim,
> the love-nest in the bracken,
>
> I step through origins. . . .

The poems of the sequence attempt to dig deeply for the "origins" of such
communal sacrificial violence. But, as Girard claims,

> The community is both attracted and repelled by its own origins. It feels the
> constant need to reexperience them, albeit in veiled and transfigured form.
> By means of rites the community manages to cajole and subdue the forces of
> destruction. But the true nature and real function of these forces will always
> elude its grasp, precisely because the source of the evil is the community
> itself.[12]

That evil is, he states, "the very real (though often hidden) hostilities that *all
the members of the community feel for one another.*"[13]
  "North" (*N* 19–20), the title poem of the sequence, dramatizes Heaney's
quest for this "originary" violence. It begins thus:

> I returned to a long strand,
> the hammered shod of a bay,
> and found only the secular
> powers of the Atlantic thundering.
>
> (19)

But those "secular powers" are soon replaced in Heaney's imagination by
"fabulous raiders"—the Vikings—whose "ocean-deafened voices / . . . lifted
again / in violence and epiphany." To the poet, "The longship's swimming
tongue / was buoyant with hindsight—"; it recalls

> thick-witted couplings and revenges

> the hatreds and behindbacks
> of the althing, lies and women,
> exhaustions nominated peace,
> memory incubating the spilled blood.

(20)

If "memory"—here subjective individual vision as well as collective unconscious—"incubates" "spilled blood," the poem's "sacred powers" are im-
plicated in violence and revenge. "Violence," Girard writes, "strikes men as
an epiphany,"[14] and this recognition provides the poem's epiphanic injunc-
tion as the voice of the violent past enjoins the modern poet to "'Lie down
/ in the word-hoard,'" and there, "in the coil and gleam / of your furrowed
brain" (20), the poet will find the words and images of the past that precisely define the catastrophic present moment.

In the next poem, "Viking Dublin: Trial Pieces" (*N* 21–24), Heaney
describes the founders of that city as "neighbourly, scoretaking / killers . . .
/ hoarders of grudges and gain." And he invokes them:

> Old fathers, be with us.
> Old cunning assessors
> of feud and of sites
> for ambush or town.

(24)

Joyce's Stephen Dedalus had invoked his "Old father, old artificer" to stand
by him while he "forge[d] in the smithy of my soul the uncreated conscience of my race."[15] Heaney's poem subverts Joyce's Dedalian enterprise
by suggesting that the conscience Joyce hoped to create had in fact been
created long ago: a conscience defined by "scoretaking" killings and perpetual feud. And instead of fashioning wings for their heirs, the "Old fathers" of Ireland,

> With a butcher's aplomb
> they spread out your lungs
> and made you warm wings
> for your shoulders.

(24)

As this sequence suggests, it is through his personal fascination with
violence and the sacrificial victim that the poet himself has acquired consciousness, if not conscience. He writes,

> I am Hamlet the Dane,
> skull-handler, parablist,
> smeller of rot
>
> in the state, infused
> with its poisons,
> pinioned by ghosts
> and affections,
>
> murders and pieties,
> coming to consciousness
> by jumping in graves. . . .

(23)

"Hamlet," Girard claims, "is both revolted against [sic] the mimetic contagion of revenge, eroticism, fashion, philosophy, etc., and eager to become its victim in order finally to become what other men think he already is or ought to be."[16] In his use of *Hamlet,* the premier revenge tragedy, Heaney suggests not only a personal correlative but also a national one: Northern Ireland today is another Denmark, a kingdom poisoned by violence and revenge. Girard poses the question, "Why does the spirit of revenge, whenever it breaks out, constitute such an intolerable menace?" And he suggests,

> Perhaps because the only satisfactory revenge for spilt blood is spilling the blood of the killer; and in the blood feud there is no clear distinction between the act for which the killer is being punished and the punishment itself. Vengeance professes to be an act of reprisal. . . . Vengeance . . . is an interminable, infinitely repetitive process. Every time it turns up in some part of the community, it threatens to involve the whole social body.[17]

"The Grauballe Man" (*N* 35–36), another of Glob's bog people, becomes for Heaney the victim of a modern revenge killing, whose "chin is a visor / raised above the vent / of his slashed throat."[18] Heaney sees him "perfected in my memory" (36), where he is

> hung in the scales
> with beauty and atrocity:
> with the Dying Gaul
> too strictly compassed
>
> on his shield,
> with the actual weight

of each hooded victim,
slashed and dumped.

(36)

The Grauballe Man, the Dying Gaul, the modern casualty of Ulster's troubles—all are, for the poet, victims of societies in crisis. Girard notes that

The mechanism of reciprocal violence can be described as a vicious circle. Once a community enters the circle, it is unable to extricate itself. We can define this circle in terms of vengeance and reprisals. . . . As long as a working capital of accumulated hatred and suspicion exists at the center of the community, it will continue to increase no matter what men do. Each person prepares himself for the probable aggression of his neighbors and interprets his neighbor's preparations as confirmations of the latter's aggressiveness.[19]

In *Children of Wrath,* Michael MacDonald suggests that violence is so deeply rooted in Northern Ireland because of the "lack of a consensual social order" and that "with the two communities set in opposition, intense conflict is built into the social order."[20]

According to Girard, the usual way for a community to escape the circle of violence is to select a scapegoat as a ritual sacrifice. "The function of ritual," he writes, "is to 'purify' violence; that is, to 'trick' violence into spending itself on victims whose death will provoke no reprisals."[21] "Ritual," in other words, "is nothing more than the exercise of 'good' violence."[22] Heaney's poem "Punishment" (*N* 37–38) describes an incident of ritual scapegoating.[23]

Once again the poem is based on a description in Glob, this time of the exhumed body of a young girl. Although the girl is, for Glob, a guiltless sacrifice to the goddess of fertility, Heaney's victim is a "Little adulteress" (38)—someone who has "collaborated" (sexually) with the enemy. In Girard's terms, such a victim makes an "ideal" scapegoat—the member of a group who has transgressed a social taboo, making him/her at the same time both an insider and an outsider. Girard writes,

Reinforcement of the community is identical with the strengthening of socio-religious transcendence. But such reinforcement demands a flawless scapegoat mechanism, completely unanimous agreement that the victim is guilty.[24]

And he states that "the system consists of whitening the community by blackening the scapegoat."[25]

Heaney addresses the young girl as "My poor scapegoat": he recognizes

in her both the sacrificial victim, whose Iron Age death was supposed to
have brought fecundity to the community, and the modern collaborator,
whose "punishment" helps to reinforce a sense of group identity that continued violence may have undermined. Girard writes,

> At the instant the scapegoat is selected, through a nonconscious process of
> mimetic suggestion, (s)he obviously appears as the all-powerful cause of all
> trouble in a community that is itself nothing but trouble. The roles are re-
> versed. The victimizers see themselves as the passive victims of their own
> victim, and they see their victim as supremely active, eminently capable of
> destroying them. The scapegoat always appears to be a more powerful agent,
> a more powerful cause than (s)he really is.[26]

Heaney vividly describes his scapegoat:

> her shaved head
> like a stubble of black corn,
> her blindfold a soiled bandage,
> her noose a ring
>
> to store
> the memories of love.
> Little adulteress,
> before they punished you
>
> you were flaxen-haired,
> undernourished, and your
> tar-black face was beautiful.

(37–38)

His personal response, however, is complex:

> My poor scapegoat,
>
> I almost love you
> but would have cast, I know,
> the stones of silence.

(38)

He is, in other words, one of the victimizers, the "artful voyeur" of both
Iron Age sacrifice and modern atrocity. He concludes:

> I who have stood dumb
> when your betraying sisters,

cauled in tar,
wept by the railings,

who would connive
in civilized outrage
yet understand the exact
and tribal, intimate revenge.

(38)

From Girard's perspective, Heaney is exactly right in stressing his personal complicity in the rites of tribal revenge: "All are drawn unwittingly into the structure of violent reciprocity."[27] But the scapegoat of "Punishment" can satisfy only one segment of the warring factions; no matter how many similar scapegoats are selected and "sacrificed" in Northern Ireland (collaborators, unarmed "suspects," British soldiers), none can end the circle of violence. In *Children of Wrath*, Michael MacDonald claims that the "failure of institutional solutions . . . stresses that the problem is more than individual 'terrorists'; the problem is a social order that renders 'terrorism' entirely commonplace."[28]

Heaney's poem "Kinship" (40–45) concludes with skepticism about the possibility of ever ending the circle of violence. In it, the poet calls on the Roman historian Tacitus to

observe how I make my grove
on an old crannog
piled by the fearful dead:

a desolate peace.

(45)

It appears that for Heaney, as well as for Girard, peace is the gift of violence. "Primitive religion," Girard writes, "is no 'cult of violence' in the contemporary sense of the phrase. Violence is venerated insofar as it offers men what little peace they can ever expect. Non-violence appears as the gratuitous gift of violence."[29] The poet concludes by asking Tacitus, as the impartial spirit of history, to

Come back to this
"island of the ocean"
where nothing will suffice.
Read the inhumed faces

of casualty and victim;
report us fairly,

> how we slaughter
> for the common good
>
> and shave the heads
> of the notorious,
> how the goddess swallows
> our love and terror.
>
> (45)

For Heaney, as for Girard, the archaic processes of the past return to dominate the present, and politics, institutions, and individual actions are subsumed by the recurrent and murderous compulsions inherent in man's basic nature. We are reduced to feeling, in Tacitus's words, "a mysterious terror and an ignorance full of piety as to what that may be which men only behold to die."[30]

As Girard notes,

> Death is the ultimate violence that can be inflicted on a living being. It is therefore the extreme of maleficence. With death a contagious sort of violence is let loose on the community, and the living must take steps to protect themselves against it. So they quarantine death. . . . Above all, they have recourse to funeral rites, which (like all other rites) are dedicated to the purgation and expulsion of maleficent violence.[31]

Heaney's poem "Funeral Rites" (*N*15–18) begins with a personal memory: "I shouldered a kind of manhood / stepping in to lift the coffins / of dead relations" (15). But familial piety soon gives way before a larger historical pattern:

> Now as news comes in
> of each neighbourly murder
> we pine for ceremony,
> customary rhythms:
>
> the temperate footsteps
> of a cortège, winding past
> each blinded home.
>
> (16)

In this environment, murder is domesticated, and there is no "ceremony" that can serve to allay its contagion. The homes the funeral procession passes are "blinded" both by their mourning and their complicity in the circle of violence. "Quiet as a serpent / in its grassy boulevard," Heaney continues,

> the procession drags its tail
> out of the Gap of the North
> as its head already enters
> the megalithic doorway.
>
> (17)

As the community enters the "megalithic doorway" of violence and the sacred, they find the unity Girard indicates when he says that "the best men can hope for in their quest for nonviolence is the unanimity-minus-one of the surrogate victim."[32] Heaney writes,

> When they have put the stone
> back in its mouth
> we will drive north again
> past Strang and Carling fjords,
>
> the cud of memory
> allayed for once, arbitration
> of the feud placated,
> imagining those under the hill
>
> disposed like Gunnar
> who lay beautiful
> inside his burial mound,
> though dead by violence
>
> and unavenged.
>
> (17–18)

"Gunnar"—one of the heroes of the Icelandic *Njal's Saga*—is the surrogate victim whose death will supposedly allay the circle of reciprocal violence. Heaney imagines a modern ritual action that binds the myths of the past and the realities of the present. The victim will be buried "unavenged" by a community awakened to its own complicity in the circle of violence. "To leave violence behind," writes Girard, "it is necessary to give up the idea of retribution."[33] The poem concludes with an image of the victim as poet:

> Men said that he was chanting
> verses about honour
> and that four lights burned
>
> in corners of the chamber:
> which opened then, as he turned

with a joyful face
to look at the moon.

(18)

"All religious rituals," Girard notes, "spring from the surrogate victim, and all the great institutions of mankind, both secular and religious, spring from ritual."[34] He continues:

> The surrogate victim, as founder of the rite, appears as the ideal educator of humanity, in the etymological sense of *e-ducatio*, a leading out. The rite gradually leads men away from the sacred; it permits them to escape their own violence, removes them from violence, and bestows on them all the institutions and beliefs that define humanity.

The irony that underscores Heaney's poem lies in the fact that vengeance is indeed taken for the murder of Gunnar. Victor Turner, the anthropologist, notes that *Njal's Saga*

> shows pitilessly how Iceland just could not produce the machinery to handle major crises, for inevitably the *Althing* negotiations break down and there is regression to crisis again, sharpened crisis, moreover, that can only be resolved now by the total defeat of one party, even its attempted annihilation.[35]

The cycles of revenge the saga chronicles contain are intended, according to Turner, to describe the final collapse of the Icelandic commonwealth. The poems of *North* suggest a similar fate for Northern Ireland.

Girard has proposed that "Because of their large scale and sophistication, modern Western societies have appeared largely immune to violence's law of retribution." And he continues,

> In consequence, modern thinkers assume that this law is, and has always been, mere illusion and that those modes of thinking that treat it as real are sheer fantasy. To be sure, these modes of thinking must be considered mythic insofar as they attribute the enforcement of the law to an authority extrinsic to man. But the law of retribution itself is very real: it has its origins in the reality of human relationships.[36]

With the poems of *North*, Seamus Heaney reminds his readers of the "law of retribution." The poems themselves deliver a recognition that Girard would second but which the poet himself, to judge from his later, more urbane poetry, might disavow: that man's nature is essentially murderous and that culture has been built upon it only the better to conceal it from his view.

In "Strange Fruit" (*N* 39), a sonnet outside of the sequence of quatrains but sharing their content, the poet offers a rebuke to his own complicity in masking violence in terms of the sacred. The sonnet concludes,

> Murdered, forgotten, nameless, terrible
> Beheaded girl, outstaring axe
> And beatification, outstaring
> What had begun to feel like reverence.

(39)

Just as this sonnet interrupts and, in effect, demystifies the self-hypnotized sequence of quatrains that make up Heaney's myth of "North," the work of such interpretative anthropologists and critical thinkers as René Girard, Walter Burkert, and Victor Turner has examined and demystified the violence that first engenders and then is masked behind the "sacred" sense of life.

Notes

1. Edna Longley's essay "*North:* 'Inner Emigré' or 'Artful Voyeur'?" remains the best and most comprehensive essay on the imaginative contradictions in Heaney's volume. David Lloyd's "'Pap for the Dispossessed': Seamus Heaney and the Poetics of Meaning" is an interesting Marxist reading of the poetry, and one antithetical to the reading offered in this essay. See Edna Longley, "*North:* 'Inner Emigré' or 'Artful Voyeur'?" in *The Art of Seamus Heaney,* ed. Tony Curtis (Chester Springs, Pa.: Dufour, 1975), 65–95. See David Lloyd, "'Pap for the Dispossessed': Seamus Heaney and the Poetics of Meaning," *Boundary 2* 12, nos. 2–3 (Winter–Spring 1985): 319–42.

2. *Violence and the Sacred,* trans. Patrick Gregory (Baltimore: Johns Hopkins University Press, 1977), 31. The identity of violence and the sacred is developed also in René Girard, *"To double business bound": Essays on Literature, Mimesis, and Anthropology* (Baltimore: Johns Hopkins University Press, 1978); *Things Hidden Since the Foundation of the World,* trans. Stephen Bann and Michael Metteer (Stanford, Calif.: Stanford University Press, 1987); *The Scapegoat,* trans. Yvonne Freccero (Baltimore: Johns Hopkins University Press, 1986); *Job: The Victim of His People,* trans. Yvonne Freccero (Stanford, Calif.: Stanford University Press, 1987).

3. Dillon Johnston, *Irish Poetry After Joyce* (Dublin: Dolmen, 1985), 148.

4. Walter Burkert, René Girard, and Jonathan Z. Smith, *Violent Origins: Ritual Killing and Cultural Formation,* ed. Robert G. Hamerton-Kelly (Stanford, Calif.: Stanford University Press, 1987), 6–7. Konrad Lorenz's major work on the "killer instinct" in animals and man is *On Aggression,* trans. Marjorie Kerr Wilson (New York: Harcourt, 1966); Walter Burkert's important works include *Structure and History in Greek Mythology and Ritual* (Berkeley: University of California Press, 1979) and *Homo Necans: The Anthropology of Ancient Greek Sacrificial Ritual and Myth,* trans. Peter Bing (Berkeley: University of California Press, 1983); Burkert and René Girard debate their ideas in *Violent Origins: Ritual Killing and Cultural Formation.*

5. Michael MacDonald, *Children of Wrath: Political Violence in Northern Ireland* (Cambridge: Polity Press, 1986), 3.

6. P. V. Glob, *The Bog People,* trans. Rupert Bruce-Mitford (New York: Ballantine Books, 1971), 132.

7. Seamus Heaney, interview by James Randall, *Ploughshares* 5 (1979): 18.

8. Girard, *Things Hidden*, 32.

9. Ibid., 103.

10. Ibid.

11. Seamus Heaney, interview by James Randall, 16.

12. Girard, *Violence and the Sacred*, 99.

13. Ibid., 99; Girard's emphasis.

14. Ibid., 152.

15. James Joyce, *A Portrait of the Artist as a Young Man* (New York: Penguin, 1968), 253.

16. Girard, *"To double business bound,"* 223.

17. Girard, *Violence and the Sacred*, 14.

18. Glob, *Bog People*, 18-20.

19. Girard, *Violence and the Sacred*, 81.

20. MacDonald, *Children of Wrath*, 5.

21. Girard, *Violence and the Sacred*, 36.

22. Ibid., 37.

23. Both Heaney's and Girard's scapegoats answer to Northrop Frye's definition in *Anatomy of Criticism:* "We may call this typical victim the *pharmakos* or scapegoat. . . . The *pharmakos* is neither innocent or guilty. He is innocent in the sense that what happens to him is far greater than anything he has done provokes. . . . He is guilty in the sense that he is a member of a guilty society, or living in a world where such injustices are an inescapable part of existence." See Northrop Frye, *Anatomy of Criticism* (Princeton: Princeton University Press, 1957), 41.

24. Girard, *Job*, 111.

25. Ibid., 112.

26. Burkert et al., *Violent Origins*, 91.

27. Girard, *Violence and the Sacred*, 69.

28. MacDonald, *Children of Wrath*, 5.

29. Girard, *Violence and the Sacred*, 258–59.

30. Quoted in Glob, *Bog People*, 114.

31. Girard, *Violence and the Sacred*, 255.

32. Ibid., 259.

33. Girard, *Things Hidden*, 198.

34. Girard, *Violence and the Sacred*, 306.

35. Victor Turner, "An Anthropological Approach to the Icelandic Saga," in *On The Edge of the Bush: Anthropology as Experience*, ed. Edith L. B. Turner (Tucson: University of Arizona Press, 1985), 90.

36. Girard, *Violence and the Sacred*, 260.

Works Cited

Burkert, Walter. *Homo Necans: The Anthropology of Ancient Greek Sacrificial Ritual and Myth.* Translated by Peter Bing. Berkeley: University of California Press, 1983.

———. *Structure and History in Greek Mythology and Ritual.* Berkeley: University of California Press, 1979.

Burkert, Walter, René Girard, and Jonathan Z. Smith. *Violent Origins: Ritual Killing and Cultural Formation.* Edited by Robert G. Hamerton-Kelly. Stanford, Calif.: Stanford University Press, 1987.

Frye, Northrop. *Anatomy of Criticism.* Princeton: Princeton University Press, 1957.

Girard, René. *Job: The Victim of His People.* Translated by Yvonne Freccero. Stanford, Calif.: Stanford University Press, 1987.

————. *The Scapegoat.* Translated by Yvonne Freccero. Baltimore: The Johns Hopkins University Press, 1986.

————. *Things Hidden Since the Foundation of the World.* Translated by Stephen Bann and Michael Metteer. Stanford, Calif.: Stanford University Press, 1987.

————. *"To double business bound": Essays on Literature, Mimesis, and Anthropology.* Baltimore: The Johns Hopkins University Press, 1978.

————. *Violence and the Sacred.* Translated by Patrick Gregory. Baltimore: The Johns Hopkins University Press, 1977.

Glob, P. V. *The Bog People.* Translated by Rupert Bruce-Mitford. New York: Ballantine Books, 1971.

Heaney, Seamus. Interview by James Randall. *Ploughshares* 5 (1979): 7–22.

Johnston, Dillon. *Irish Poetry After Joyce.* Dublin: Dolmen, 1985.

Joyce, James. *A Portrait of the Artist as a Young Man.* New York: Penguin, 1968.

Lloyd, David. "'Pap for the Dispossessed': Seamus Heaney and the Poetics of Meaning." *Boundary 2* 12, nos. 2–3 (Winter–Spring 1985): 319–42.

Longley, Edna. "*North:* 'Inner Emigré' or 'Artful Voyeur'?" In *The Art of Seamus Heaney,* edited by Tony Curtis, 65–95. Chester Springs, Pa.: Dufour, 1975.

Lorenz, Konrad. *On Aggression.* Translated by Marjorie Kerr Wilson. New York: Harcourt, 1966.

MacDonald, Michael. *Children of Wrath: Political Violence in Northern Ireland.* Cambridge: Polity Press, 1986.

Turner, Victor. "An Anthropological Approach to the Icelandic Saga." In *On The Edge of the Bush: Anthropology as Experience,* edited by Edith L. B. Turner. Tucson: The University of Arizona Press, 1985.

"Station Island" and the Poet's Progress

SAMMYE CRAWFORD GREER

Seamus Heaney's longtime preoccupation with the relation between his vocation as poet and the political and cultural conditions of Ulster finds its fullest expression to date in his twelve-poem sequence, "Station Island." Placing himself in the traditional fiction of a dream journey through the land of the dead and in the historical and topographical framework of a penitential pilgrimage to the Lough Derg island, Heaney takes advantage of the potential of the poetic sequence to encompass a wide range of historical and cultural matter, to associate and modulate conflicting emotions and varying perceptions, and to achieve realizations that transcend, as well as accommodate, the tensions generated by these interactions.[1] As the sequence progresses, the pilgrim-poet remembers experiences from his youth that reveal the quality of life in Ulster and encounters, in the manner of Dante, "shades," as Heaney says, "from my own dream life who had also been inhabitants of the actual Irish world,"[2] whose testimonies, reproaches, and advice define the condition in which he finds himself as he tries to affirm his identity as both Irishman and poet. The revelatory memories and the exchanges with the shades depict a homeland characterized by acedia, political atrocity, and cultural desiccation and expose the conscience of a poet in extremis, suffering the "contradictory commands to be faithful to the collective historical experience and to be true to the recognitions of the emerging self."[3] In the last three poems, however, the poet experiences a series of realizations that provide a locus from which he can respond creatively to the "entropic conditions" of his homeland while remaining true to the "demands and promise" of his vocation (PW 60; GT 101).

In defining the distinctive features of the modern poetic sequence, M. L. Rosenthal and Sally M. Gall have anticipated the nature of Heaney's exploration of the consciousness of this poet:

Seeking to locate the elements of its oppressed yet volatile state, the associative pressure in such works stirs up sunken dimensions of consciousness and memory from the depths, moving through confusions and ambiguities towards a precarious balance. The process of association and of modulation among shifting intensities is both psychological and cultural in its contexts of reference. It involves the feeling of obsolescence, the need to recover an identifying past. Here enters the heroic or epic aspect of the sequence: its effort to pit primal values and personal, historical, and artistic memory or vision against anomie and desolation.[4]

In "Station Island" the emotional trajectory of this process is downward, ever more deeply and darkly into self-inculpation and artistic despair, following the path of the paradigmatic descent into the land of the dead, until the turn, in the middle of the ninth section, toward the transcendence that characterizes the final part of the sequence. This turn is reinforced by its location at the point of division between the octave and the sestet in the third of the five sonnets that compose section IX. At the beginning of the seventh poem, at the structural center of the sequence, the source of the memories informing this trajectory shifts from the poet's childhood to young adulthood and, concomitantly, from early religious and cultural influences on his growth as a poet to the pressures and burdens imposed by Ulster's sectarian strife on the artistic consciousness of the penitential adult. Memories of moments in his childhood, in the fourth part of the ninth poem and in the tenth poem, take the poet to the moment of revelation in poem X; but this last part of the sequence is characterized by the growth of the poet's consciousness in the present and, in the last poem, by an anticipation of its future maturity. This curve of movement from the beginning to the end of the sequence is counterpointed by an interplay of reciprocal elements located in pairs of poems which stand in polar positions within the sequence (I–XII, II–XI, III–X, IV–IX, V–VIII, VI–VII). Thus, the progress of the sequence "through confusions and ambiguities toward a precarious balance" is informed by complementarities of varying and contradictory forces, and together these dynamic patterns culminate in the series of realizations that define the transcendent artistic consciousness.

The relation of the volume, *Station Island,* and its title sequence to Heaney's continuing exploration of "the antithetical and often incompatible claims of religious or political orthodoxy and artistic independence" has been discussed by several reviewers and scholars and is well analyzed by Carolyn Meyer, who emphasizes Heaney's move in *Station Island* toward "a renewed and revitalized commitment to his poetic art."[5] It remains, however, to define the substance of the realizations presented in the last three sections of the sequence and to consider the nature of the transcendence wherein this commitment is expressed. Especially helpful in understanding the significance of these last three sections of the sequence are the principles Heaney posits in *The Place of Writing* and "The Redress of Poetry," both published since *Station Island*. In these essays he takes on, specifically in the former, "the vexed question of poetry and politics in contemporary Ireland, in order to examine how different political and cultural dispositions get expressed in poetry at a level below the professed meanings and espousals of the poems themselves" (*PW* 20); and he elaborates on the principle of "the imagination pressing back against the pressure of reality" (*RP* 1412). Except for one brief reference, he does not discuss his own poetry, but he could have included his pilgrim-poet as an example of one who discovers the power of poetry to reveal "potential that is denied or constantly threatened by circumstance" (*RP* 1412) or as an Irish poet in whose spiritual passage could be observed, as in Thomas Kinsella's work, "the ancient correspondence between the nation's possibilities and the imagination of its poet . . . discover[ing] itself again in a modern drama of self-knowledge and self-testing" (*PW* 63).

The source of the realizations in the last part of the sequence is the epiphany that the poet experiences in poem X as he recalls the mug that sat on the mantelpiece throughout his childhood. Contrasting with the darkness and the images of sectarian violence and death in the previous section, the morning sounds and light that provide the setting in section X endow the poet with a vision that is the opposite of his nightmare in poem IX. The revelatory nature of the memory that informs this poem is underscored by Heaney's allusions to the traditional setting of evocation: the brilliant light, the drifting smoke, and especially the "drumming" that suggests an incantatory ritual like the one in the last lines of the preceding poem: "the tribe whose dances never fail / For they keep dancing till they sight the deer" (*SP* 206). There comes to the poet's mind the one occasion when the mug was removed from its place on the mantle:

> when fit-up actors used it for a prop
> and I sat in the dark hall estranged from it
> as a couple vowed and called it their loving cup
>
> and held it in our gaze until the curtain
> jerked shut with an ordinary noise.
>
> (*SP* 207)

It is this "translation" of the mug, as he now calls it, that provides him with his epiphany, the significance of which he defines by an analogy to an extraordinary event and with the language of visionary experience:

as the otter surfaced once with Ronan's psalter
miraculously unharmed, that had been lost
a day and a night under lough water.

And so the saint praised God on the lough shore
for that dazzle of impossibility
I credited again in this sun-filled door,
so absolutely light it could put out fire.

(*SP* 207)

He compares the "translation" of the mug and its being "restored to its old haircracked doze / on the mantelpiece" to the miracle of the return of Ronan's psalter, "unharmed" by its immersion in the lough: given new meaning by the miracle, the psalter was transformed yet remained unchanged. The reference to the mug's "parchment glaze," the use of the word "dipped" (as though "immersed") to describe its brief transformation, and the association between "estranged" and "lost" reinforce the sense of its being "restored" in the same way that the psalter was returned to Ronan. For a spell, the commonplace mug was transformed ("glamoured") by the utterances of actors "fit-up" not only in costume but also in emotion and imagination. That night it was an emblem of the commitment and expectations of romantic love; and, now, in this moment of revelation, by means of the analogy between its "translation" and the miracle of the psalter, its symbolic dimensions expand to include the spirituality of early Irish Christianity and the rebirth associated with the Holy Grail and with the archetypal journey across or under water.

In this epiphany the poet realizes the power of poetic utterance to hold "in our gaze" the loving cup that is also the earthenware mug: he realizes the power of poetry to endow the commonplace and the mundane with spiritual potential while faithfully representing the actual. The significance of this epiphany is explained by a fundamental principle posited by Heaney in *The Place of Writing* to "show how topographical place [can] become written place":

one of the first principles of art work . . . might be enunciated in terms of the old schoolbook definition of the meaning of work in any context, artistic or otherwise. This used to be expressed as follows: to work is to move a certain mass through a certain distance. In the case of poetry, the distance moved through is that which separates the historically and topographically situated place from the written place, the mass moved is one aspect of the writer's historical/biographical experience, and each becomes a factor of the other in the achieved work. The work of art, in other words, involves raising the historical record to a different power. (36)

On "its high shelf" throughout the poet's childhood—and probably for as long as anyone can remember ("When was it not there?" [*SP* 207]) —the mug is identified with an ancestral history and, compared to a milestone, with a particular locale. As such, it represents one aspect of the poet's historical/biographical experience and, by extension, the historical record of his homeland. The mug is "the plumb, assured, unshakable fact of an Ulster childhood which cannot be shed," as Heaney says of the Irish elements in MacNeice's poetry (*PW* 45), raised that night in "the dark hall" and raised now, in the "dazzle" of the pilgrim-poet's vision, to a different power.

This fact of an Ulster childhood that cannot be shed appears in various manifestations in *The Place of Writing* as one of the fundamental characteristics of the poetry Heaney discusses in these lectures: from the assertion that John Montague's "Mount Eagle" "freely and opulently rehearses old motifs of attachment and affection and equally freely plays a music of detachment and subversion" (*PW* 71), to the question that anyone might ask about Michael Longley's "The Linen Workers," "What are Longley's father's dentures doing here?" (*PW* 51). In "Station Island" the dynamics of the first half of the sequence arise out of the appearances in each of the six poems of a person or an object that together not only present a biographical record of the poet's early years but also symbolize the religious and cultural constraints under which he labors in this quest for artistic identity. Simon Sweeney, William Carleton, the toy grotto, the young priest, Barney Murphy and the other masters, and "her I chose at 'secrets'" "spring up, unbidden and uncanny," like Michael Longley's father's dentures (*PW* 51), embodying elements of a heritage that the pilgrim cannot leave behind but that he nevertheless transcends in the last three sections of the sequence. The realizations that provide this transcendence also come to him by means of visions of matter from his childhood—"The old brass trumpet / . . . I found once in loft thatch" (section IX), the mug, and a "monk's face / that had spoken years ago" (section XI).

The nature of this transcendence is suggested by the antithetical relationship between poem X and its structural opposite, poem III. Each of the poems is informed by the memory of an object; together they represent the genius loci of the poet's childhood home. If the mug is identified with an ancestral history and place, the toy grotto is associated with the religious faith of the household. It comes to his mind as the prayers in the basilica take the kneeling pilgrim "back among bead clicks and the murmurs / from inside confessionals, side altars / where candles died." It was the boy's "shimmering ark, my house of gold," associated with the worship of the Virgin Mary, whose litany he echoes and whose statue or picture is often set within a grottolike frame, of the sort referred to in the fourth poem when the poet speaks to the ghost of the young priest about "their kitchen grottoes / hung with holy pictures and crucifixes." Moreover, this "seaside trinket," depicted only in images of dryness and sterility, "housed the snowdrop weather" of the invalid girl's death. Altar and crypt, it is the symbolic opposite of the mug on the mantelpiece, associated with communion and sexuality as the loving cup and with vitality and growth by means of the images of the flowers of the grain field that seem to shoot up, "sprig after sprig," around it. In contrast to the visual and verbal prominence of the mug, the grotto was "laid past in its tissue paper for good," like the girl's name, which was seldom spoken in the household; and, while the miracle of the psalter and the revelation that comes to the poet are marked by religious exultation ("And so the saint praised God . . ."), only the sorrowful supplications, *"Health of the Sick"* and *"pray for us,"* are uttered in the litany that concludes the dream vision of the grotto.

This vision leads to a meditation on desolation, which reveals the condition of the pilgrim's spirit: "walking round / and round a space utterly empty, / utterly a source, like the idea of sound" suggests the hollowness of the ritual of encircling the penal beds of stones at St. Patrick's Purgatory and takes the poem back to the "active wind-stilled hush" in which the dream vision originates. The anticipation of fulfillment in this idea of a source, with its links to the mug and to St. John's fountain in poem XI, is undercut by the simile that describes the condition of his spirit, the poet once again turning to childhood and home and another image of desiccation, "the bad carcass and scrags of hair / of our dog." The measure of the poet's transcendence in the final part of the sequence can be taken by the contrast between this metaphor and its antithesis in the tenth poem, the analogy that presents the miracle of Ronan's psalter.

In the poet's epiphany, the earthenware mug is "retrieved by memory and hatched into a second life by the intent imagination," as Heaney says of the particulars of childhood that are recounted in Thomas Kinsella's "His Father's Hands" (*PW* 62). Heaney calls this state of mind "the artistic · impulse itself," defining it as "the need to raise historical circumstance to a symbolic power, the need to move personal force through an aesthetic distance" (*PW* 5). In "The Redress of Poetry," Heaney posits a complementary principle to define this impulse. Referring to Simone Weil's thesis in *Gravity and Grace*, he speaks of "the idea of counterweighting, of balancing out the forces, of redress—tilting the scales of reality towards some transcendent equilibrium"; and he goes on to say: "And in the activity of poetry a similar impulse persists, to place a counter-reality in the scales, a reality which is only imagined but which nevertheless has weight because it is imagined within the gravitational pull of the actual" (*RP* 1412). He further asserts that "the best poetry will not only register the assault of the actual and the brunt of necessity; it will also embody the spirit's protest against all that" (*RP* 1413). The poet in "Station Island" has suffered the assault of the actual and on his pilgrimage is confronted by not only the unshakable fact of an Ulster childhood but also the "vehemence and squalor and helplessly self-validating energies which," Heaney says, "have characterized [Ireland's] history of the last twenty years" (*PW* 52). He has been oppressed by historical circumstance and tortured by a sense of his ineffectuality. In this epiphany, however, he gains an understanding of the power of his art in the face of the "banal reliabilities of the usual" (*PW* 55). As imaginative utterance gave the mug new meaning and vitality, so may his art reveal potential by envisioning historical circumstance in its symbolic context.

"The spirit's protest" is the subject of the eleventh section of the sequence, which articulates and amplifies the realization gained in the previous section. The monk speaks about a principle of replenishment, which not only suggests the form this protest should take but also indicates the nature of the "impossibility" that informs the poet's vision in poem X: "What came to nothing could always be replenished." This principle echoes Heaney's summary statement about the oeuvre of Thomas Kinsella: "he has ingested loss . . . and has remembered it in an art that has the effect of restitution. The place of waste, the place of renewal and the place of writing have become co-terminous within the domain of his poetry" (*PW* 62). The monk professes just such an understanding of the opportunity and the responsibility of the poet's vocation when he speaks

> about the need and chance
>
> to salvage everything, to re-envisage
> the zenith and glimpsed jewels of any gift
> mistakenly abased . . .
>
> (*SP* 208)

Such a calling predicates the affirmative nature of the "spirit's protest" embodied in poetry: in poetry's imagined reality value and meaning can arise out of loss and ruin. When the monk counsels, "Read poems as prayers," he is acknowledging poetry's extraordinary restorative power, as expressed by Heaney as he considers Michael Longley's father's dentures in "The Linen Workers":

> The banal marvel of bodily wholeness restored through the fitting of a set of dentures is a sacramental rite to signify the desired world-miracle of wrongs redressed and wholeness restored through the intervention of the act of poetry itself. (*PW* 51).

The full force of this principle of replenishment is realized in the fountain of Juan de la Cruz. Eternally abounding, vital, "all sources' source and origin" (*SP* 209), it symbolizes infinite possibility. Hidden and secret but watering "hell and heaven and all peoples" (*SP* 209), it represents the sustenance of the spirit and the imagination. As an archetypal symbol of transcendent renewal, it is the antithesis of that legendary place of waste, the popular subject of medieval European devotional literature, St. Patrick's Cave, which marked the nadir of the purgatorial journey to Lough Derg. Through this cave pilgrims entered Saint Patrick's Purgatory, where they were said to look upon Hell itself as they witnessed hideous suffering, encountered raging demons, and endured terrifying tests of their faith.[6] In Heaney's sequence, as replenishment is the opposite of entropy, so the fountain is the counterweight of this island of ancestral guilt and penitential constraint; and, symbolizing St. John's experience of grace within the dark night of the soul, it is the opposite of the "glittering flood" in poem IX, which sweeps the poet from his hallucinatory visions of violence and degradation to the nadir of his spiritual passage:

> I dreamt and drifted. All seemed to run to waste
> As down a swirl of mucky, glittering flood
> Strange polyp floated like a huge corrupt
> Magnolia bloom, surreal as a shed breast,
> My softly awash and blanching self-disgust.
> And I cried among night waters, "I repent
> My unweaned life that kept me competent
> To sleepwalk with connivance and mistrust."
>
> (*SP* 205)

In the eighth poem, in his descent toward this dark night, the poet expresses his sense of ineffectuality in the face of the "assault of the actual and the brunt of necessity" (*RP* 1417), which took the form of the untimely and meaningless deaths of two young men who had been his companions. Reflecting the biographical pattern of the sequence as a whole, this poem presents the poet's sense of his failure in personal and historical circumstances to fulfill the responsibility of his vocation. He confesses to the ghost of his friend, the archaeologist, that in the face of his friend's imminent death, he was

> guilty and empty, feeling I had said nothing
> and that, as usual, I had somehow broken
> covenants, and failed an obligation.
>
> (*SP* 201)

Now, when the ghost asks him one of those questions that would test any poet's insight and mastery of language, the poet "could not speak":

> Ah poet, lucky poet, tell me why
> what seemed deserved and promised passed me by?
>
> (*SP* 202)

His failure to offer solace or understanding to the dying man is underscored by the only words he is finally able to utter; for, ironically, he recognizes the blessing that the archaeologist has bestowed on him: "Your gift will be a candle in our house." When the ghost of his cousin indicts him for neglecting his people and betraying his art by failing to respond forcefully to the ignominy of the sectarian act in which his cousin was slain, the poet expresses his sense of artistic impotence: "I was dumb, encountering what was destined," and "I felt like the bottom of a dried-up lake" (*SP* 203). His cousin's accusation personalizes the concept of the writer's vocation embodied in the ghost of William Carleton, who describes his artistic life in terms of his political and cultural outrage (section II).

In the eleventh poem, however, Carleton's dicta are subsumed in the monk's instructions and St. John's poem. Rather than rejecting Carleton's understanding of the substance and the obligation of poetry, the realization that informs the eleventh section redefines the nature of the act of poetry: not only "remember" but also "salvage everything"; not the "trout kept in the spring" so much as the spring itself, "so pellucid it can never be muddied"; "all that / has gone through us" can be "replenished," not simply ingested and deposited. The image of the fountain replaces the poet's "old jampots in a drain clogged up with mud" and "bottom of a dried-up lake" as well as Carleton's "looped slime gleaming from the sacks" and "maggots sown in wounds." As indicated by the absence of quotation marks to set off the monk's words in lines 6–10 (the only passage in the sequence in which the words of a shade are not enclosed in quotation marks) and by the poet's movement from the past to the present as he introduces the translation of Juan's songs ("Now his sandalled passage stirred me on to this" [*SP* 208]), the poet assumes the voices of both the monk and St. Juan de la Cruz, sloughing off the feeling of artistic impotence and confirming his understanding of the restorative power of his art:

> I am repining for this living fountain.
> Within this bread of life I see it plain
> although it is the night.
>
> (*SP* 210)

As the symbol of his calling and his art, the fountain represents the mystery of poetic inspiration, which can "salvage" and "re-envision" reality. We could say that in his recognition of this mystery the poet understands the "redress" that his poetry can provide:

> If our given experience is a labyrinth, then its impassability is countered by the poet's imagining some equivalent of the labyrinth and bringing himself and us through it. Such an operation does not intervene in the actual but it does constitute a beneficent symbolic event, for poet and audience alike. (RP 1412)

The poet's articulation of the monk's message and Juan's psalm endows him, if not with a priestly role, with responsibility for the beneficent symbolic event, which bestows its own kind of blessing. His assumption of Juan's song hearkens back to the epiphany in the previous poem (X) in which he assumes another saint's voice to celebrate his own experience of the miraculous:

> And so the saint praised God on the lough shore
> for that dazzle of impossibility
> I credited again in the sun-filled door,
> so absolutely light it could put out fire.
>
> (SP 207)

The final confirmation of his artistic identity, however, comes in the words of release spoken by the shade of James Joyce in the last section. Joyce's exhortations echo the admonition of Simon Sweeney, his mirror opposite in the first section, "Stay clear of all processions!" (SP 183); but Joyce would release the poet, rather than attempt to hold him to the imaginative experiences of his past, as does Sweeney: "'Damn all you know,' he said. . . . / 'I was your mystery man / and am again this morning'" (SP 181). Joyce's exhortations also counteract the "lesson" offered by Carleton's ghost, who serves as a foil to Joyce as well as to the monk and St. John.[7] Carleton represents the call of historical circumstance and political responsibility; but Joyce's ghost absolves the poet from this torturous burden: "Your obligation / is not discharged by any common rite" (SP 211). He is referring not so much to the "peasant pilgrimage" as to the activity of poetry: "write / for the joy of it" (note the interplay of "rite" and "write" in the rhyme scheme). In his discussion of Mandelstam and Dante, Heaney's statement about this passage refers to the nature of this absolution and release: the shade of Joyce "speaks here . . . with advice that Mandelstam might

have given"—Mandelstam, whose Dante is "an exemplar of the purely creative, intimate and experimental act of writing itself."[8]

Carleton would place the writer and his work somewhere within the
quagmire of "the demeaning actualities of Ulster" (*PW* 46), while Joyce
directs the poet, in his final words, to a locus outside of any form of abase-
ment, constraint, or enclosure:

> Keep at a tangent.
> When they make the circle wide, it's time to swim
>
> out on your own and fill the element
> with signatures on your own frequency,
> echo-soundings, searches, probes, allurements,
>
> elver-gleams in the dark of the whole sea.
>
> (*SP* 212)

As Maureen Waters says, "The 'earthworms' of the Carleton section finally
give way to more dramatic and exhilarating images of expansion and change,
'elver-gleams' swimming outward."[9] These images suggest a principle that
Heaney associates with the work of recent of Ulster poets:

> . . . MacNeice provides an example of how distance, either of the actual,
> exilic, cross-channel variety or the imaginary, self-renewing, trans-historical
> and trans-cultural sort, can be used as an enabling factor in the work of art in
> Ulster. For with MacNeice, Mahon, Longley and—above all—Muldoon, we
> can begin to consider how important the length of the arm of the lever is
> when it comes to the actual business of moving a world. This takes us back to
> another basic school-book principle of science, the principle of moments, the
> principle in operation when the claw hammer draws out the nail or the crow-
> bar dislodges the boulder. In each case what is intractable when wrestled
> with at close quarters becomes tractable when addressed from a distance.
> The longer the lever, in fact, the less force is necessary to move the mass and
> get the work going. (*PW* 46–47)

The image of the tangent and the circle veritably replicates Heaney's metaphor for the relation between distance and poetry's power of redress. For all
the emphasis on distance in the essay, the trope in the poem originates in
the image of the tangent, which relates to a circle by touching it, as the
Latin root of the word indicates, not by the measure of its distance from it.
For all the importance of the length of its arm, the lever cannot move the
mass without contact with it.

The poet grasps this paradox in the moment of epiphany evoked by the
shade's earlier words of release:

> It was as if I had stepped free into space
> alone with nothing that I had not known
> already. . . .
>
> *(SP* 212)

This "space / alone" is analogous to "the dark of the whole sea," the shade's metaphor for the locus of the poet; and "nothing that I had not known / already" echoes the monk's principle of replenishment and, as "nothing" is naught, or zero, suggests the circle to which the tangent relates. In *The Place of Writing* Heaney calls the tower in Yeats's poems "the 'pure transcendence' of an old Norman castle in Ballylee, a place that was nowhere until it was a written place" (32). Similarly, Heaney's poet realizes that the reality created by the writer was "nothing" until articulated by the writer and yet is constituted only of that which he has perceived or experienced. There is "nothing," the monk would say, until the poet begins "to salvage everything, to re-envisage / the zenith . . ." *(SP* 208). The poet has attained a locus, which is the point at which the tangent touches the circle. He has stepped into the place, the realm, of writing and has professed an understanding of the place, the role, of writing.

It would be remiss not to call attention to the relation between this sequence, which is Part II, and the other two parts of *Station Island.*[10] In fact, "Sweeney Redivivus" could be considered a companion sequence to "Station Island," moving the volume toward "a state of equilibrium that balances, resolves, or encompasses" the "initial pressures" of "Station Island."[11] It seems that, as he swims out on his own, the pilgrim becomes the birdman, his earnestness shed like the "sackcloth and ashes" *(SP* 211). Sweeney, redivivus, emerges out of water, his "head like a ball of wet twine / dense with soakage" *(SI* 98), to enter the sequence, off at a tangent in confirmation of his identity as a Joycean poet. He is also the king, turned mad poet by the saint whose psalter he threw into the lough, a voice speaking to the pilgrim-poet in his exultation. The birdman is, however, still the visionary poet at the place of writing. Now he seeks his inspiration through "a high cave mouth / . . . to the deepest chamber" *(SP* 228), the archetypal, pagan opposite of the purgatorial island and cave; but he seems still to be "repining for this living fountain" *(SP* 210), disposed to

> > meditate
> that stone-faced vigil
>
> until the long dumbfounded
> spirit broke cover
> to raise a dust
> in the font of exhaustion.
>
> ("On the Road," in *SP* 228)

"Sweeney Redivivus" continues the "modern drama of self-knowledge and self-testing" wherein "the ancient correspondence between the nation's possibilities and the imagination of the poet discover[s] itself again" (*PW* 63). Its complex, multiple reciprocities with "Station Island," however, confirm the centrality of the pilgrim-poet's realizations in Heaney's continuing exploration of the consciousness of the artist and leave us with a poet who has, as Heaney says of *The Divine Comedy,* "an overall sense of having come through . . . of faring forth into the ordeal, going to the nadir and returning to a world that is renewed by the boon won in that other place."[12]

> And there I was, incredible to myself,
> among people far too eager to believe me
> and my story, even if it happened to be true.
>
> ("Sweeney Redivivus" *SI* 98)

Notes

1. See M. L. Rosenthal and Sally M. Gall, *The Modern Poetic Sequence.* (New York: Oxford University Press, 1983), 3–18.
2. Seamus Heaney, "Envies and Identifications: Dante and the Modern Poet," *Irish University Review* 15, no. 1 (1985): 19.
3. Ibid., 19.
4. Rosenthal and Gall, *Modern Poetic Sequence,* 10.
5. Carolyn Meyer, "Orthodoxy, Independence and Influence in Seamus Heaney's *Station Island" Agenda* 27, no. 1 (1989): 57.
6. See J. E., "St Patrick's Purgatory," *Canadian Journal of Irish Studies* 10, no. 1 (1984): 7–40.
7. See Maureen Waters, "Heaney, Carleton and Joyce on the Road to Lough Derg," *Canadian Journal of Irish Studies* 14, no. 1 (1988): 62–64.
8. Seamus Heaney, "Envies and Identifications," 18, 16.
9. Waters, "Heaney, Carleton and Joyce," 64.
10. See Meyer, "Orthodoxy, Independence and Influence," 64–65.
11. Rosenthal and Gall, *Modern Poetic Sequence,* 11.
12. Seamus Heaney, "Treely and Rurally," *Quarto* 9 (1980): 14.

Works Cited

Heaney, Seamus. "Envies and Identifications: Dante and the Modern Poet." *Irish University Review* 15, no. 1 (1985): 15–19.

———. "Treely and Rurally." *Quarto* 9 (1980): 14.

J. E. "St. Patrick's Purgatory." *Canadian Journal of Irish Studies* 10, no. 1 (1984): 7–40.

Meyer, Carolyn. "Orthodoxy, Independence and Influence in Seamus Heaney's *Station Island* " *Agenda* 27, no. 1 (1989): 48–61.

Rosenthal, M. L., and Sally M. Gall. *The Modern Poetic Sequence*. New York: Oxford University Press, 1983.

Waters, Maureen. "Heaney, Carleton and Joyce on the Road to Lough Derg." *Canadian Journal of Irish Studies* 14, no. 1 (1988): 55–65.

Aesthetic and Cultural Memory in Joyce and Heaney

MICHAEL PATRICK GILLESPIE

> Shem is as short for Shemus as Jem is Joky for Jacob. A few toughnecks
> are still getatable who pretend that aboriginally he was of respectable
> stemming (he was an outlex between the lines of Ragonar Blaubarb
> and Horrild Hairwire and an inlaw to Capt. the Hon. and Rev. Mr.
> Bbyrdwood de Trop Blogg was among his most distant connections)
> but every honest to goodness man in the land of the space of today
> knows that his back life will not stand being written about in black and
> white. Putting truth and untruth together a shot may be made at what
> this hybrid actually was like to look at.
>
> —*Finnegans Wake*

As I hope the epigraph to this essay illustrates, *Finnegans Wake* arguably
stands as the most effective manifestation of postmodern Irish writing yet
available. It demonstrates in detail and with precision the features that have
characterized the most aesthetically satisfying works of artists from Samuel
Beckett through Seamus Heaney: a profound, near obsessive, attention to
the particular, presented in a manner that may confuse but does not es-
trange readers from the discourse. In this essay I propose examining the
emergence of Heaney from this tradition and commenting upon how habits of reading other Irish writers like Joyce enhance our ability to derive
pleasure from Heaney's poems.[1]

Although, strictly speaking, sources of reader disorientation manifest
themselves differently in Joyce and in Heaney, Hugh Kenner's critical commonplace seems equally applicable to either writer: to some degree, at least,
any work by Heaney or by Joyce is about learning how to read that work.
With this axiom in mind, one can see how the social diffusion within a
Heaney poem or a Joyce narrative actively discourages readers from attempting to respond, for example, to extratextual forces by slipping into
modes of reductive cultural relativism or by succumbing to prescriptive psycho-
analytic determinism. Instead, their work invites efforts to accommodate
the diverse communal elements depicted as shaping the artist's aesthetic

consciousness. Interpretations developed along these lines provide the reader with an ample basis for comprehending the motivation—found in both Joyce and Heaney—behind an ambivalent yet emphatic inquiry into the nature of things. That revelation, in turn, serves as a starting point for delineating a range of possible responses, for neither Joyce's fiction nor Heaney's poetry enforces the need to clarify ambiguity or to articulate a narrow perception of any aspect of the Irish ambiance. Rather, the works of both authors outline—sometimes hesitantly and sometimes with great authority—strategies for embracing multiplicity within one's surroundings. In acknowledging old institutions even while foregrounding the attraction of alternative social systems for guiding behavior, they play upon the variety of potential responses that the polyphony of these different views evokes.

At this point, it may be useful to clarify my application of the term *ambiguity*. *The American Heritage Dictionary* defines the word as susceptible to multiple interpretation, and that articulates (as precisely as language ever can) the sense of the term that I wish to convey. The aesthetic power of the fiction of Joyce and the poetry of Heaney comes from an ability to create within their works the possibilities for multiple interpretation without simultaneously generating frustration over the inherent prohibition of closure that these multiple interpretations enforce. Consequently, I propose here to explore how Heaney, benefiting from the example of Joyce and other Irish authors, can draw upon his own cultural experiences to create poetry nonetheless appealing to a range of readers with diverse social backgrounds. Specifically, Heaney's verse manages to invoke ambiguity without instilling alienation, and it posits the pleasure available through the open acknowledgment of unresolvable alternatives rather than through the submission to prescriptive closure.

The association between Joyce and Heaney, however, goes beyond acknowledging parallels in background and in habits of composition; it shows the influence that Joyce's canon continues to exert upon Irish art. Successive generations have found Joyce's canon standing not only as a model but also as an impediment, establishing a precedent of achievement that both encourages and mocks subsequent Irish writers. Joyce's legacy, of course, does not produce a direct, monolithic impact, and Heaney's own work, to cite just one possible example, remains far too complex to support the easy assumption that any single figure enforces an anxiety of influence.[2] Nonetheless, his own writings (both prose and poetry) amply attest to the formative impact of Joyce's artistic and aesthetic attitudes.[3]

In Heaney's case, however, the contrast between Joyce's cultural, intellectual, and creative experiences and his own make the question of influence or even of analogous aesthetic attitudes both more interesting and more problematic. From the age of twenty-two until his death at fifty-nine,

Joyce lived and wrote outside of Ireland, as a self-imposed exile from the cultural sources for all of his writings. Heaney, on the other hand, has spent the last two decades oscillating between Ireland, England, and America, periodically renewing and revising his conception of the inspirations for his work, while balancing this local color with the experiences of transoceanic commuting. In both instances, countrymen have responded ambivalently to this apparent detachment from the routines of Irish life and politics, yet both Joyce and Heaney have nonetheless produced and sustained moving visions of Ireland, albeit in forms at sharp variance from the work of those who have chosen to remain there.[4]

Especially in terms of their articulation of myths and of mythological figures, both writers offer highly sophisticated revisions of standard Irish tales and characters. Recollecting and refining their impressions from the detached perspectives of artists able to operate beyond the geographic and psychological confines of Ireland, they idealize without sentimentalizing their subjects. Heaney, moving back and forth between cultures, feels keenly aware of what he does because he continually returns to Ireland to confront the source of his mythology. Joyce, living on the Continent and thus removed from direct contact with Ireland, maintains a memory of the Dublin of 1904 frozen in time, and faces no one who will challenge his version of Irish folklore. Although the responses that these two men make to their cultural heritage may seem superficially different, in their most overtly mythological work the basic gestures stand as remarkably similar: Through his translation of the Irish poem *Buile Suibhne,* Heaney presents a sensitive and complex picture of the hero Sweeney. Throughout *Finnegans Wake* Joyce transmutes the figure of Finn McCool from the traditional depictions found in Irish folk culture to the range of postmodern manifestations that crop up throughout the work.

The contrasting styles of these two writers, and specifically the manner by which each develops Irish folklore within his own work, offer useful insights into the way that Heaney manages his relationship with Joyce. Heaney, in fact, defines his artistic bonds to Joyce by applying a mythologizing impulse similar to the one that conditioned his depiction of Sweeney. In celebrating Joyce—his weaknesses as well as his strengths—Heaney consciously evokes Joyce's own adaptations of mythic imagery while simultaneously undermining the inhibiting aspects of Joyce's artistic legacy.[5] Furthermore, in depicting Joyce himself in "Station Island," Heaney—with notable modifications—follows the example set by his predecessor in *Ulysses* and *Finnegans Wake.*

Imposing figures of the Irish Literary Revival—George Russell, George Moore, W. B. Yeats, Lady Gregory—lose much of their prescriptive force through their quotidian depictions in *Ulysses.* Likewise, Heaney replaces the image of Joyce as the threatening, authoritarian competitor that emerges from an anxiety of influence with a more benevolent figure, reconstituted according to his needs and desires, whose attitudes now can be manipulated and made to validate Heaney's own poetic efforts. In consequence, on multiple levels—artistic, cultural, and spiritual—Joyce now exists as an extension of Heaney's artistic consciousness and of his poetry.

As I have already indicated, a clear illustration of the process that Heaney employs to deal with artistic antecedents—both in terms of Joyce and of a myriad of other individuals whose influence intrudes upon Heaney's creative consciousness—appears in the long poem "Station Island." There, through a series of twelve related sections, the unnamed narrator undertakes both a religious and an artistic pilgrimage that merges the spiritual and the aesthetic. By engaging memory and belief, he seeks to gain a measure of insight. In successive passages he encounters a range of ghostly figures representing the multiplicity of values and impulses confronting the contemporary artist (Irish or otherwise), and in the final section he meets the shade of Joyce, who does not so much summarize all previous attitudes as articulate a response that the author of the poem—Heaney—has already eschewed.

Throughout the twelve sections of "Station Island," ghosts conjured up from his cultural consciousness and his personal memories interrogate the narrator, questioning his motives and challenging him to refine his beliefs. In a striking fashion, this process replicates experiences in the life of Stephen Dedalus—recounted both in *A Portrait of the Artist as a Young Man* and in *Ulysses*. In both novels characters from Stephen's past and present intrude upon his imagination and call into question the artistic role that he has adopted for himself.

The parallels that one can draw between such similar representations in Joyce and Heaney go beyond the simple binary association of two authors emerging from similar cultural backgrounds. They alert readers to the artistic, aesthetic, and cultural presuppositions that shape the creative processes of both writers. Our cognizance of these creative assumptions does not remove ambiguities within the discourses—nor should one wish it to—but it does illuminate the dynamics of the process by which each writer investigates the characterizing features of his intellectual heritage.

The first section of "Station Island" introduces the pilgrimage theme while it simultaneously sounds the familiar note of ambivalence towards open adherence to religious ritual. As he moves to join the cortege of praying women, the narrator's memory calls up the ghost of Sweeney the Sabbath-breaker, the narrator's childhood nemesis and a character analogous to the hero Sweeney of Celtic folklore. This Sweeney, ever the iconoclast, frankly challenges the narrator's intention to make the pilgrimage and issues a warning to "stay clear of all processions" (*SP* 183).[6] Coming from the narrator's subconsciousness, Sweeney's distrust of religious practices gives voice perhaps to his own dissatisfaction and echoes, though in a far less frenzied fashion, the position held by Simon Dedalus and Mr. Casey, who, in the Christmas Dinner scene of chapter 1 of *Portrait*, conduct a fierce attack upon Dante Riordan's advocacy of the formal manifestations of the Church and its authority.

> —God and religion before everything! Dante cried. God and religion before the world!
> Mr. Casey raised his clenched fist and brought it down on the table with a crash.
> —Very well, then, he shouted hoarsely, if it comes to that, no God for Ireland![7]

Of course, obvious disparities exist between the two incidents: the Stephen Dedalus who witnesses the above exchange is far younger, for example, than the unnamed narrator who hears Sweeney's milder form of blasphemy. Nonetheless, the emotional ambivalence of the one exchange strikingly replicates that of the other: neither character responds to the respective attacks upon the institution of the Catholic Church, and neither author shows any inclination to resolve the ambiguity inherent in those silences. Joyce makes no comment upon Stephen's reaction and so forces the reader to step forward to assess which of a number of responses might have come to the boy. Heaney's narrator silently joins the "crowd of shawled women" (*SP* 182) who pass, leaving the reader to mull over the possible range of unexpressed feelings.

Though putatively a narrative poem, "Station Island" has temporal and contextual disjunctions between sections similar to the gaps between chapters in *A Portrait of the Artist as a Young Man* and *Ulysses*. Thus, section II makes no effort to provide transitional continuity. Rather, the discourse, while maintaining an interest in literary antecedents, abruptly shifts consideration from one prominent Irish social institution (religion) to another (nationalism).[8]

It begins with the narrator confessing to the ghost of William Carleton: "Your Lough Derg Pilgrim [Carleton's sardonic account of his own final visit to Station Island] haunts me every time I cross this mountain" (*SP* 184).[9] This statement in turn provokes Carleton to reaffirm his own rejection of both Catholic and Protestant nationalism—"hard-mouthed Ribbonmen and Orange bigots." He makes this assertion, apparently, as a way of justifying his own act of pragmatic betrayal—becoming "the old fork-tongued turncoat / who mucked the byre of their politics" (*SP* 185)—

at leaving the Catholic Church for the more financially secure position of a Protestant. This frustrated yet cynical view of Irish politics recalls Stephen's more idealistic though no less bitter dismissal of the invitation proffered by his friend Davin to join the nationalist movement:

> —No honourable and sincere man, said Stephen, has given up to you his life and his youth and his affections from the days of Tone to those of Parnell but you sold him to the enemy or failed him in need or reviled him and left him for another. And you invite me to be one of you. I'd see you damned first. (*P* 203)

"Station Island," however, offers no judgment that would resolve the matter quite so simply. While both Stephen and Carleton fiercely defend their positions, Heaney's narrator tries to reconcile the divergent religious and nationalistic experiences of his youth:

> "The angry role was never my vocation,"
> I said. "I come from County Derry,
> where the last marching bands of Ribbonmen
>
> on Patrick's Day still played their "Hymn to Mary."
> Obedient strains like theirs tuned me first
> and not that harp of unforgiving iron
>
> the Fenians strung. A lot of what you wrote
> I heard and did: this Lough Derg station,
> flax-pullings, dances, fair-days, crossroads chat
>
> and the shaky local voice of education.
> All that. And always, Orange drums.
> And neighbours on the roads at night with guns."
>
> (*SP* 185–86)

The speaker acknowledges the sectarian bitterness highlighted by the others, but he refuses to share their fatalistic attitudes. The pluralism inherent in his response—advocating prayer over militancy and shared experiences over divisiveness—counters the self-righteous extremism of either political position with a tolerant ambiguity that undermines the assurance of ideological polemics.

Despite the emphatic appeal of nationalistic inclinations, however, both Heaney and Joyce insistently return to religion as the institution that informs and stimulates the pace of recollection. In section III of "Station

Island," while praying or at least appearing to pray, the narrator briefly succumbs to nostalgia as he recollects a knickknack that had belonged to a long dead invalid: "A seaside trinket . . . / a toy grotto with seedling mussel shells / and cockles glued in patterns over it" (*SP* 187). Thoughts of this invalid, more a name from childhood than an actual figure, evoke for the narrator images of mortality similar to what Stephen Dedalus feels when, in the Telemachus chapter of *Ulysses*, he moves from a recollection of his failure to pray for his dying mother to the more mundane remembrance of relics of her past.

> Her secrets: old featherfans, tasselled dancecards, powdered with musk, a gaud of amber beads in her locked drawer. A birdcage hung in the sunny window of her house when she was a girl.[10]

The same sense of uneasiness over the connection with religion and memories of deceased family members haunts both men. In Stephen's case it comes from the profound feeling of having disappointed his mother at the time of her death. In the case of Heaney's narrator it seems reflected by a vaguer sort of guilt that, paradoxically, prayer cannot assuage:

> It was like touching birds' eggs, robbing the nest
> of the word *wreath*, as kept and dry and secret
>
> as her name, which they hardly ever spoke
> but was a white bird trapped inside me
> beating scared wings when *Health of the Sick*
> fluttered its *pray for us* in the litany.
>
> (*SP* 187)

In each instance, however, prayer and religion serve to define both the specific interaction and the general protocols for construing the experience.

Section IV of Heaney's poem directly confronts the issue of belief, playing upon the inherent and necessary indeterminacy of the experience of faith to explore the range of positions that one might occupy. As the narrator begins the ritual reaffirmation of religious commitment by repeating the baptismal prayer renouncing Satan and all his pomps, he finds himself confronted with an antithetical image. The ghost of a missionary priest whom the narrator had known as a young cleric now appears. The priest's discourse, reflecting fatigue and disillusionment, bursts out in impatient criticism, possibly aimed at the general practice of one's Catholic faith or perhaps simply directed with carping intolerance at the adherence of the Church to rituals like the pilgrimage to Station Island.

>   What possessed you?
>   I at least was young and unaware
>
>   that what I thought was chosen was convention.
>   But all this you were clear of you walked into
>   over again. And the god has, as they say, withdrawn.
>
>   What are you doing, going through these motions?
>   Unless . . . Unless . . .'
>
>   (*SP* 190–91)

The priest's sardonic attitude towards religion recalls the chillingly pragmatic tones of Stephen's friend Cranly from chapter 5 of *Portrait*. There the agnostic Stephen is shocked by the willingness of Cranly to conform to church practice without offering any evidence of genuine commitment to the Catholic faith.

> [Y]ou need not look upon yourself as driven away if you do not wish to go or as a heretic or an outlaw. There are many good believers who think as you do. Would that surprise you? The church is not the stone building nor even the clergy and their dogmas. It is the whole mass of those born into it. (*P* 245)

Heaney's figures, however, prove far less willing to rationalize either belief or disbelief than do Joyce's, as if the three-quarters of a century separating them has raised suspicions of any form of certitude. Thus, beneath the apparent cynicism of Heaney's missionary, a wavering appears articulated in the stammering qualification "Unless . . . Unless," a doubting of doubt that captures the ambivalence of the modern dis/believer.

Section V of "Station Island" foregrounds an issue always present but often overlooked in the writings of both Heaney and Joyce: the conflict between genuine learning and self-important pedantry. The vision of an old schoolmaster puts the narrator in an ambivalent position, different from those delineated earlier in the poem because of its conflation of the roles and the emotions of the schoolchild and the experienced adult. The narrator's recollection of his old teacher also brings to mind the passing of Anahorish School:

>   dairy herds are grazing where the school was
>   and the school garden's loose black mould is grass.
>
>   (*SP* 193)

This reverie offers a telling comment upon the ambivalence of rate payers towards general education in Ireland—those happy to sacrifice resources

used for public instruction to the production needs of EEC-subsidized com-
modities. Additionally, it presents a slightly updated version of the pragmatic view of learning voiced in the Nestor chapter of *Ulysses* by Garret
Deasy, the master of the school in Dalkey where Stephen works (and a man
also keenly interested in the health of cattle). Although Deasy's tone towards Stephen emphasizes the menacing authoritarian aspect of their association, his remarks and Stephen's reply highlight the same blend of ir-
resolution and expedience in viewing the aims of teaching.

> —I foresee, Mr. Deasy said, that you will not remain here very long at this
> work. You were not born to be a teacher, I think. Perhaps I am wrong.
> —A learner rather, Stephen said.
>
> (*U* 2.401–3)

The coarse, earthy views of Heaney's version of Patrick Kavanagh that
dominate the second portion of section V offer a welcome contrast. Culmi-
nating in this sardonic assessment of the value of pilgrimages—"In my
own day / the odd one came here on the hunt for women" (*SP* 194)—they
feature a healthy antidote to the sterile pursuit of knowledge that the recollections of the first half of the section evoke. Just as such sentiments coun-
terpoint the discourse between the narrator and his old teacher, in much
the same fashion in the Scylla and Charybdis chapter of *Ulysses* the rumi-
nations of Buck Mulligan to Stephen offer sardonic commentary on the
pseudointellectual discourse, featuring Stephen's Hamlet theory, that had
just transpired in the National Library.

> —*I hardly hear the purlieu cry*
> *Or a Tommy talk as I pass one by*
> *Before my thoughts begin to run*
> *On F. M'Curdy Atkinson,*
> *The same that had the wooden leg*
> *And that filibustering filibeg*
> *That never dared to slake his drouth,*
> *Magee that had the chinless mouth.*
> *Being afraid to marry on earth*
> *They masturbated for all they were worth.*
>
> (*U* 9.1143–52)

Through the studied vulgarity of Mulligan and the leering observations of
the Kavanagh figure, both Joyce and Heaney effectively call into question
received opinions on aesthetic worth. With an open delight in the wonders
of ambiguity, the views of Buck and the Green Fool celebrate multiplicity.

They capture our interest without either clearly displacing conventional notions or unambiguously discrediting their own attitudes as alternatives.[11]

Much of the aesthetic power that grows out of the "Station Island" verses comes from this ability to integrate earthy attitudes like those of a Mulligan and a Kavanagh with the motivating forces (alternatively pious, fearful, blissful, and neurotic) that influence contemporary pilgrims. This gentle sense of the complex feelings informing the consciousnesses of the Station Island pilgrims extends the recollections of the narrator beyond an unrelieved tone of penance. Section VI mixes memory and desire and gives itself over to the lyrical evocation of the fleeting sense of guilt, pleasure, and nostalgia conflated into the narrator's composite image of a series of women known through childhood, adolescence, and young adulthood: "her I chose at 'secrets' / And whispered to. . . . I saw her honey-skinned / Shoulder-blades and the wheatlands of her back / Through the wide keyhole of her keyhole dress" (*SP* 195–96). This amalgamated figure calls up a series of analogous girls and women in Joyce: from E. C. in chapter 2 of *Portrait,* who puts her hand in young Stephen's pocket during a tram ride, to the adolescent Stephen's Birdgirl of chapter 4 wading in Dublin Bay, to Gerty MacDowell of the Nausicaa chapter and the whores of the Circe chapter of *Ulysses,* to Issy and ALP of *Finnegans Wake.* Each of these characters acts as a gloss for a portion of the writer's amalgamated vision of the archetypal Irish woman.

Expressing attitudes as the summation of diverse feelings stands as a dominant technique in "Station Island." Thus, almost predictably, the poem's tone moves directly, if abruptly, from the interval of romantic lyricism expressed through youthful sexuality to a depiction of the brutality of political conflict and of sudden, senseless death. The ghost of William Strathern, a murdered Catholic shopkeeper, appears to recount his version of the events that transpired on the night that members of the Royal Ulster Constabulary shot him.

Before Strathern can speak, however, the narrator describes him in a fashion that renders inconsequential the significance of a particular political position by underscoring the horrific results of sectarian intolerance. "His brow / was blown open above the eye and blood / had dried on his neck and cheek" (*SP* 197). As Strathern relates what occurred, the pointlessness of the killing and the implacable determination of the killers give one a disheartening feeling of helplessness. This sensation calls to mind analogous feelings evoked by the outburst of the British soldier, Private Carr, immediately preceding his assault on Stephen near the end of the Circe chapter of *Ulysses.* "I'll do him in, so help me fucking Christ! I'll wring the bastard fucker's bleeding blasted fucking windpipe" (*U* 15.4720–21). On the street in Dublin's nighttown, at least, drunkenness and sexual vitality explain, although they do not mitigate, the behavior of the forces of occupation. Their violence relates to the moment, and it does not inculcate any residual bitterness in Stephen. William Strathern's account of his death, on the other hand, turns the narrator towards a reassessment of the long-term consequences of his own behavior:

> Forgive the way I have lived indifferent—
> forgive my timid circumspect involvement.

> (*SP* 200)

As the poem insistently reiterates, Heaney's episodic evocation of aspects of Irish life foregrounds artistic abilities encompassing far more than the single theme of provincialism. Memories of the dead, for example, persist throughout the work, but taken together they serve the paradoxical function of illuminating a range of Irish lives. One sees this in section VIII when a prayer "at the hard mouth of St. Brigid's bed" calls up from the narrator's consciousness an image of "my archaeologist," Tom Delaney, and the narrator begins to recollect the details of his final hospital visit with Delaney. The tender helplessness of the narrator in the face of his friend's wasting in turn reflects a more Irish attitude. In this context, one can see parallels to the poignant pain of Stephen, in the Telemachus chapter of *Ulysses*, recollecting the details surrounding his mother's painful death from cancer. The stoicism of each figure goes beyond the impotence that one naturally feels in the face of a medically insurmountable catastrophe. It touches on depictions of suffering that universalize the works of both authors.

The second portion of this section, however, works to diffuse any impulse towards the easy and reductive sentimentalizing of human pain. It challenges the reader with stark reminders of how human nature tends to avoid direct confrontation with much of the suffering that comes about through the breakdown of social institutions. Both literally and figuratively it calls forth the spirit of Colum McCarthy, the victim of "sectarian assassination" and the subject of an earlier poem by Heaney, "The Strand at Lough Beg," published in *Field Work*. Here the distinction between the narrative persona and the poet himself becomes increasingly difficult to maintain, for in the discourse Heaney has the murdered McCarthy confronting Heaney's lack of political involvement in a far more chilling and to that degree effective fashion than the criticisms of his contemporaries.

> You saw that, and you wrote that—not the fact.
> You confused evasion and artistic tact.
> The Protestant who shot me through the head

> I accuse directly, but indirectly, you
> who now atone perhaps upon this bed
> for the way you whitewashed ugliness and drew
> the lovely blinds of the *Purgatorio*
> and saccharined my death with morning dew.
>
> (*SP* 203)

Joyce struggled with the same political ambivalences throughout his career: a sense of the profound impact that his Irishness had upon his art colliding with a deep distrust of inclinations to express love of country through violent acts. In *Dubliners, Portrait,* and *Ulysses,* he raises without resolving a range of questions surrounding issues of nationalism. In *Finnegans Wake* he alludes—much more obliquely—to feelings, similar to Heaney's, towards the artistic responses made to the deaths in the Easter Rising, the Troubles, and the Civil War.[12]

Section IX moves to purge the poem of these images of political violence with a final sectarian ghost, an IRA Hunger Striker, depicted in a fashion evocative of Heaney's bog poems. As the Hunger Striker describes the physical changes leading to his death, his body metamorphoses before our eyes to become like one of the figures mummified in peat, to be discovered and reified by subsequent generations.

> My brain dried like spread turf, my stomach
> Shrank to a cinder and tightened and cracked.
>
> (*SP* 204)

In its amalgamation of shifting images from the distant and recent past, the desiccated desperation of the act calls to mind the pathos of Stephen's description, in the Proteus chapter of *Ulysses,* of the Fenian Kevin Egan, a latter-day version of the Wild Geese, living alone and unremembered in Paris. "They have forgotten Kevin Egan, not he them" (U 3.263–64). These two figures of pointless wretchedness created by a fanatical devotion to nationalism—personifications of Yeats's line "Too long a suffering / Can make a stone of the heart" from "Easter 1916"—reverse the movement of accusation. In depicting the futility of their lives, these scenes justify disassociation with the physical-force movement. In essence Yeats' sentiments give Joyce and Heaney political absolution for the course of action that they have chosen in a fashion similar to the way that the Station Island pilgrimage will extend spiritual absolution.

Redefining one's relation to social institutions marks a move towards reintegration with a particular society. The effectiveness of this gesture becomes evident in the next section, where the narrator can lightly touch upon elements of Irish Catholic mythology, in this case the legend of St. Ronan, in a tone neither cynically dismissive nor blindly accepting. Instead, the status of this cultural artifact remains self-consciously indeterminate, affording the narrator a less hostile but no less insistent challenge for commitment than more conventional manifestations of Catholic belief. Like the Telemachus chapter of *Ulysses*, where Stephen infers the need to capture in his own work the essence of Irish life personified by the Old Milkwoman (herself an evocation of Shaun Van Vocht)—"She bows her old head to a voice that speaks to her loudly, her bonesetter, her medicineman: me she slights" (*U* 1.418–19)—section X of "Station Island" emphasizes the defining influence of heritage upon the artist's conception of his environment. Stephen openly longs for the old woman's, and by extension for Ireland's, approval. Heaney's narrator adopts a similar attitude by embracing the concept that one does not become an artist by fleeing from all or even most of the cultural accoutrements of his culture.

This process of absolution and reconciliation that has paced the movement of the first ten sections of the poem moves to the forefront of perception in section XI. In a tacit acknowledgment of the transfiguring experience of the pilgrimage, the narrator recalls a previous visit to the confessional—rather than actually submitting to one on the retreat. The experience blends spiritual and aesthetic forces when the monk (perhaps an artistic descendant of the Capuchin who heard the confession of Stephen in chapter 3 of *Portrait*)assigns the translation of a portion of the writings of St. John of the Cross as penance.

Although Stephen Dedalus does not receive the explicit charge to translate a foreign prayer into the vernacular, that becomes his goal as he matures into an artist. Strictly speaking, of course, Stephen does not so much reject religion as translate it: aesthetics replaces ethics as the moral center of his universe. Examples of this behavior occur with the epiphanic moment in viewing the Birdgirl in chapter 4 of *Portrait* and in composing the villanelle in chapter 5. Implicit in such a gesture, amalgamating art and religious practice, one finds an alternative to the theological isolation that Stephen imposes upon himself at the end of *Portrait*. With the ghost of Joyce continually at the margins of this work, Heaney feels perhaps the need to justify this more ecumenical action that does not replicate Joyce's own artistic direction.

In the final section, using the poem's most effective example of displacement/ventriloquism, Heaney articulates the ambivalence towards artistic and cultural attitudes that has mediated the narrator's experiences throughout the entire poem.[13] The persona of a Joyce figure confronts the narrator with a relentlessly iconoclastic view. Nonetheless, one cannot help feeling that it too succumbs to a predictable, dogmatic, and even clichéd approach that does not fully conform to the multiplicity of Heaney's (or of the historical Joyce's) aesthetics. This artificiality highlights precisely the dual problem of Joyce's presence (in the imagination of the artist and in the public as a whole) that Heaney and other contemporary Irish writers must confront: the artist strives to create under the influences of a subtle personal perception of Joyce's achievements, and yet his or her work inevitably faces a judgment informed by the broad and reductive public sense of Joyce's impact. The hectoring ghost of Joyce in the final stanza embodies that public judgment in much the same way that the supportive spirit of Joyce, evoked through creative analogues in the previous eleven stanzas, illustrates the importance of personal accommodation to such a figure.

Lucy McDiarmid's critique of the final stanza of the poem clearly defines the difficulties inherent in perceptions of these different manifestations of Joyce. She very rightly reminds us that both central figures in the poem—she identifies them in quotation marks as "Joyce" and "Heaney"—emerge from Heaney's imagination and conform to the artistic demands of his process of creation.[14] Her statement implicitly invites one to consider the multiplicity and the polyvocality of the entire poem. She seems to be ignoring her own admonition, however, when a few paragraphs later in her study she uses the words of the ghost to categorize and then to dismiss the narrator's gesture in making the pilgrimage:

> It is Joyce who offers a hand "scribe-cold and bony" to the "convalescent" speaker, helping him off the boat. The ghost's guidance is as much chastisement as encouragement. He refers with great disdain to the "pious exercise" and "your peasant pilgrimage." "I was at nobody's service / the way you are at theirs," he announces, echoing Stephen Dedalus's echo of the satanic *non serviam*. . . . To be "at service" to the community is to be its slave, to surrender and deny individual identity for the sake of some putative larger good. "This was a backsliding enterprise" because Heaney-pilgrim let his artistic self be stifled by a group whose beliefs he did not share. Going on the pilgrimage was a gesture of false deference, mechanical and insincere. "You lose more of yourself than you redeem / doing the decent thing," warns the ghost, and what is lost is the independent expressive self, which becomes as "warped" as the pilgrims' singing.[15]

McDiarmid, in essence, forgets that the Joyce in "Station Island" is no more James Joyce than is the Stephen Dedalus of *Portrait*. Likewise, as she herself notes earlier in the essay, the narrator of this poem is not Seamus Heaney. Further, what the historical Heaney or the fictional one believes is by no means as clear as McDiarmid seems to believe. Instead, as I have tried to show throughout this essay, in the works of both Joyce and Heaney individual characters and specific concepts retain our interest through ambiguities that allow a continuing interpretive elaboration.

This play upon ambiguity stands as the central concern of this essay: like Joyce's *Portrait of the Artist as a Young Man* and *Ulysses,* the tone of Heaney's "Station Island" oscillates between modernism and postmodernism just as the narrative voice swings between a range of religious and secular values. It is worth remembering that, while the poem's narrator ends his pilgrimage by leaving the island, he by no means advocates abstinence from direct contact with the Irish culture that supports and maintains rituals like the trek to Station Island. The ghosts that he meets, on the other hand, wish to retain in one form or another idealized views of a reformed Irish culture without sustaining the physical ties to the masses whose beliefs have defined and will constantly refine that culture. Of course, these voices do not really reflect the views of Sweeney the Sabbath-breaker, William Carleton, Patrick Kavanagh, James Joyce, or any other of the historical figures invoked in the verse. Rather, they facilitate Heaney's articulation of the conflict within his own artistic temperament: the pressures that he feels to shake off the parochialism of Irish life and the need to retain the inspiration provided by his cultural experiences.

Notes

1. Not all critics have found amenable the postmodern form of Heaney's poetry in general and of "Station Island" in particular. Mary Kinzie, for example, finds fault with Heaney's unwillingness to speak definitively or to impose closure. See Mary Kinzie, "Deeper than Declared: On Seamus Heaney," *Salmagundi* 80 (Fall, 1988): 22–57. Desmond Fennell, in a monograph less critical than its title (borrowed from a Heaney poem) implies, takes a closer look at the causes and effects of what he perceives as Heaney's rhetorical strategy. See Desmond Fennel, *Whatever You Say, Say Nothing: Why Seamus Heaney is No. 1* (Dublin: ELO Publications, 1991). An even more flexible approach to Heaney's ambivalence appears in Carolyn Meyer's "Orthodoxy, Independence and Influence in Seamus Heaney's *Station Island*," *Agenda* 27 (Spring 1989): 48–66.

2. I use the term in the sense made popular by Harold Bloom's *Anxiety of Influence* (London: Oxford University Press, 1975).

3. For a sample of Heaney's views on Joyce expressed outside his poetry, see Seamus Heaney's *Preoccupations: Selected Prose, 1966–1978.*

4. Criticisms of Heaney's perceived political/ideological positions come from a range of perspectives. Thoughtful questions about Heaney's early poetry appear in Edna Longley, "Stars and Horses, Pigs and Trees," *Crane Bag* 3 (1979): 474–80. Later, more petulant critiques appear in Terry Gifford, "Saccharine or Echo Soundings: Notions of Nature in Seamus Heaney's *Station Island,*" *The New Welsh Review* 3 (Autumn 1990): 12–17, and Michael Hulse, "Sweeney Heaney: Seamus Heaney's 'Station Island,'" *Quadrant* 30 (May, 1986): 72–75.

Good responses to such criticisms appear in the following: Barry Goldensohn, "The Recantation of Beauty," *Salmagundi* 80 (Fall 1988): 76–82; Conor Johnston, "Seamus Heaney, Sweeney, and *Station Island*," *Eire-Ireland* 22 (Summer 1987): 70–95; and Donald Davie, "Responsibilities of *Station Island*," *Salmagundi* 80 (Fall 1988): 58–65.

A thorough examination of the charges laid against Joyce appears in Dominic Manganiello's *Joyce's Politics* (London: Routledge and Kegan Paul, 1980).

5. Cf. the Dedalan allusion—"Let go, let fly, forget"—in the final section of "Station Island."

6. The attitudes expressed in Heaney's poetry towards the Catholic Church—as a religious, political, economic, and cultural identity—are extremely complex and even contradictory. I do not propose to take them up in detail in this essay, but a very sensitive analysis of these views appears in Darcy O'Brien, "Piety and Modernism: Seamus Heaney's 'Station Island,'" *James Joyce Quarterly* 26 (Fall 1988): 51–65.

7. James Joyce, *A Portrait of the Artist as a Young Man: Text, Criticism, and Notes.* ed. Chester G. Anderson (New York: Viking Critical Library, 1968), 39; hereafter cited as *P.*

8. Some of Heaney's own views on politics, poetry, and nationalism can be found in his essay, "'Place and Displacement': Recent Poetry from Northern Ireland," *Wordsworth Circle* 16 (Spring 1985): 48–56. An earlier view of Heaney's attitudes appears in "'Unhappy and at Home': Interview with Seamus Heaney by Seamus Deane," *Crane Bag* 1 (1977): 66–72.

9. Very different yet detailed analyses of the use of Carleton and other archetypal figures in this poem appear in Maureen Waters, "Heaney, Carleton and Joyce on the Road to Lough Derg," *Canadian Journal of Irish Studies* 14 (July 1988): 55–65 and Henry Hart, "Ghostly Colloquies: Seamus Heaney's 'Station Island,'" *Irish University Review* 18 (Autumn 1988): 233–50.

10. James Joyce, *Ulysses*, ed. Hans Walter Gabler (New York: Random House, 1986), 1.255–57; hereafter cited as *U.*

11. For an alternative approach to Kavanagh, see Heaney, "The Placeless Heaven: Another Look at Kavanagh," in *Tradition and Influence in Anglo-Irish Poetry*, ed. Terence Brown and Nicholas Grene (Totowa, N.J.: Barnes and Noble, 1989): 181–93.

12. Cf. "Ivy Day in the Committee Room" in *Dubliners;* Stephen's conversation with Davin in chapter 5 of *A Portrait;* and Bloom's exchange with the Citizen in the Cyclops chapter (chapter 12) of *Ulysses.* The following passage exemplifies the more oblique tone of *Finnegans Wake:* "After the thorough fright he got that bloody, Swithun's day, though every doorpost in muchtried Lucalizod was smeared with generous erstborn gore and every free for all cobbleway slippery with the bloods of heroes, crying to Welkins for others" (178.08–11).

In an extratextual fashion, these events also commemorate the death of George Clancy, the model for Davin, who as mayor of Limerick was murdered by the Black and Tans during the Troubles. See Richard Ellmann, *James Joyce* (Oxford: Oxford University Press, 1982), 61.

13. This section has appeared in several versions, and the textual multiplicity has caused problems for some critics. Cf. Neil Corcoran's vexed essay, "Heaney's Joyce, Eliot's Yeats," *Agenda* 27 (Spring, 1989): 37–47. For a useful correction, appearing in the same issue, see Stephen Wade's "Creating the Nubbed Treasure (Station Island)," 62–71.

14. Lucy McDiarmid, "Joyce, Heaney, and 'that subject people stuff,'" in *James Joyce and His Contemporaries*, ed. Diana A. Ben-Mere and Maureen Murphy (New York: Greenwood Press, 1989), 131.

15. Ibid., 132.

Works Cited

Bloom, Harold. *The Anxiety of Influence*. London: Oxford University Press, 1975.

Corcoran, Neil. "Heaney's Joyce, Eliot's Yeats." *Agenda* 27 (Spring 1989): 37–47.

Davie, Donald. "Responsibilities of *Station Island*." *Salmagundi* 80 (Fall 1988): 58–65.

Ellmann, Richard. *James Joyce*. Oxford: Oxford University Press, 1982.

Fennel, Desmond. *Whatever You Say, Say Nothing: Why Seamus Heaney is No. 1*. Dublin: ELO Publications, 1991.

Gifford, Terry. "Saccharine or Echo Soundings: Notions of Nature in Seamus Heaney's *Station Island*." *The New Welsh Review* 3 (Autumn 1990): 12–17.

Goldensohn, Barry. "The Recantation of Beauty." *Salmagundi* 80 (Fall 1988): 76–82.

Hart, Henry. "Ghostly Colloquies: Seamus Heaney's 'Station Island.'" *Irish University Review* 18 (Autumn 1988): 233–50.

Heaney, Seamus. "'Place and Displacement': Recent Poetry from Northern Ireland." *The Wordsworth Circle* 16 (Spring 1985): 48–56.

———. "The Placeless Heaven: Another Look at Kavanagh." In *Tradition and Influence in Anglo-Irish Poetry*, edited by Terence Brown and Nicholas Grene, 181–93. Totowa, N.J.: Barnes and Noble, 1989.

———. "'Unhappy and at Home': Interview with Seamus Heaney by Seamus Deane." *Crane Bag* 1 (1977): 66–72.

Hulse, Michael. "Sweeney Heaney: Seamus Heaney's 'Station Island.'" *Quadrant* 30 (May, 1986): 72–75.

Johnston, Conor. "Seamus Heaney, Sweeney, and *Station Island*." *Eire-Ireland* 22 (Summer 1987): 70–95.

Joyce, James. *Finnegans Wake*. New York: Viking Press, 1939.

———. *A Portrait of the Artist as a Young Man: Text, Criticism, and Notes*. Edited by Chester G. Anderson. New York: The Viking Critical Library, 1968.

———. *Ulysses*. Edited by Hans Walter Gabler. New York: Random House, 1986.

Kinzie, Mary. "Deeper than Declared: On Seamus Heaney." *Salmagundi* 80 (Fall 1988): 22–57.

Longley, Edna. "Stars and Horses, Pigs and Trees." *Crane Bag* 3 (1979): 474–80.

Manganiello, Dominic. *Joyce's Politics*. London: Routledge and Kegan Paul, 1980.

McDiarmid, Lucy. "Joyce, Heaney, and 'that subject people stuff.'" In *James Joyce and His Contemporaries*. edited by Diana A. Ben-Mere and Maureen Murphy, 131–39. New York: Greenwood Press, 1989.

Meyer, Carolyn. "Orthodoxy, Independence and Influence in Seamus Heaney's *Station Island*." *Agenda* 27 (Spring 1989): 48–66.

O'Brien, Darcy. "Piety and Modernism: Seamus Heaney's 'Station Island.'" *James Joyce Quarterly* 26 (Fall 1988): 51–65.

Wade, Stephen. "Creating the Nubbed Treasure (Station Island)." *Agenda* 27 (Spring 1989): 62–71.

Waters, Maureen. "Heaney, Carleton and Joyce on the Road to Lough Derg." *Canadian Journal of Irish Studies* 14 (July 1988): 55–65.

Heaney and Havel:
Parables of Politics

PHYLLIS CAREY

Discussing in tandem an Irish poet and a Czech dramatist—who is also serving as president of his country—may seem at first a bit incongruous. But links there are between the Irishman and the Czech. Besides being near in age (Seamus Heaney was born in 1939; Václav Havel in 1936), they have in common a profound respect for Samuel Beckett, whom Heaney has characterized as "the most admirable writer we've known in our time,"[1] and Havel has called "the most important dramatist of the twentieth century."[2] Moreover, Heaney's deep interest in poets from the Eastern bloc— e.g., Osip Mandelstam, Zbigniew Herbert, Czeslaw Milosz, and the Czech poet, Miroslav Holub—derived, as he has indicated, from "the challenges they face to survive amphibiously in the realm of 'the times' and the realm of their moral and artistic self-respect, a challenge immediately recognizable to anyone who has lived with the awful and demeaning facts of Northern Ireland's history over the last couple of decades" (*GT* xx); Havel also survived "amphibiously," his plays banned in Czechoslovakia between 1969 and 1989, and he himself imprisoned several times—once for over three years—as a result of exercising his "moral and artistic self-respect." Furthermore, Heaney is familiar with Havel's writings. On 31 August 1994, when the Provisional Irish Republican Army announced its cessation of military activities, it was Havel's definition of hope that Heaney used to conclude his thoughts about the situation in Northern Ireland.[3]

For both Heaney and Havel, the relationship between their respective artistic endeavors and contemporary political realities became an issue early on. Although the political context of Communist Czechoslovakia differed greatly from the "problems" of Northern Ireland, both writers found their respective political milieus intolerable; both experienced in different ways what Heaney terms in one poem "the ministry of fear." In his *Cure at Troy*, Heaney has joined Havel in writing drama that has explicit political overtones. Through his version of Sophocles' *Philoctetes*, Heaney creates a political parable that resonates at points with Havel's *Largo Desolato*. Examining these plays in juxtaposition mutually illuminates aspects of both Heaney's and Havel's "shaping spirits."

Heaney's version of *Philoctetes* follows the general contour of Sophocles' play: Odysseus and Neoptolemus, the son of Achilles, come to the island of Lemnos to get the bow of Philoctetes, whom Odysseus and his Greek crew had abandoned on their way to Troy when a snake bite rendered Philoctetes prone to fits, limping and reeking. Philoctetes had received the bow from Hercules, and legend had it that without the bow and Neoptolemus, Troy would not fall. Neoptolemus initially goes along with Odysseus's scheme— which involves deceiving Philoctetes—and secures Philoctetes' trust and the bow, only to be overcome later with guilt and remorse. He returns the bow to Philoctetes and agrees to take him back to Greece. Hercules inter- venes at the end of the play, however, to convince both Philoctetes and Neoptolemus to cooperate with destiny and to proceed to Troy, where Philoctetes will be cured and where the two heroes will win glory in the Greek victory over the Trojans.

The main characters in Heaney's version follow the general pattern established by Sophocles: Odysseus is the conniving politician who shapes his stories to suit his purposes; Philoctetes is an innocent victim, who, none- theless, is envenomed physically and spiritually; Neoptolemus, though ini- tially under the influence of Odysseus, learns, with the help of Philoctetes, to follow his own nature.[4]

The changes Heaney makes in the play, however, provide insights into his own political and artistic views. At the center of the conflict in Heaney's version lies the relationship between poetry and politics. In fact, Heaney's projected "cure" is not primarily the healing of the snake bite nor Philoctetes' following his destiny to Troy but rather, the "cure"—in its rich resonance of restoring health, purifying, and caring spiritually—afforded by poetry it- self. The "cure" is an invitation to *see* through poetry, which brings with it the possibility of healing, if not political problems directly, at least the self- absorption that breeds intolerance, a condition Heaney depicts as the root of political woes. One can discern Heaney's poetic redressing of political vision through his recasting of the chorus, through his treatment of the relationship between individuals and society, through his redefining of the nature of heroism, and through his emphasis on awakening to the shapes and shaping of poetic vision.

In using the convention of the chorus more extensively than does Sophocles, Heaney also transforms it from its original designation as the sailors of Neoptolemus to an identification at times with poetry itself.[5] Heaney's chorus defines itself as at the borderline

> Between
> The gods' and human beings' sense of things.
>
> And that's the borderline that poetry
> Operates on too, always in between
> What you would like to happen and what will—
> Whether you like it or not.
>
> $(CT 2)^6$

"Poetry" becomes the enabling voice in the play, at the threshold between individuals and at the border between the past and the present, between exile and community, and between space and time, a position that is emphasized at the end of the play as poetry opens a door into the dark between the living and the dead. Heaney makes poetry a liminality, combining Celtic roots, Greek mythology, and the spiritual resources of Christianity with the Irish "problems." In contrast to Sophocles' use of Hercules as the deus ex machina who reveals to Philoctetes the demands of destiny, Heaney asserts from the very start that "Poetry / Allowed the god to speak" (*CT* 2). Rather than a subordination of the human to the divine, Heaney depicts the divine as a dimension of the human that poetry can awaken. Accordingly, when Sophocles has Hercules appear, Heaney's use of the chorus, as the stage directions indicate, *"Ritually clamant, as HERCULES"* (*CT* 78), draws attention not to the god's intervention in human events but to poetry's power to awaken the spiritual in human experience:

> I have opened the closed road
> Between the living and the dead
> To make the right road clear to you.
> I am the voice of Hercules now.
>
> (*CT* 76)

In Heaney's treatment, poetry becomes the rainbow of hope "for a great sea-change / On the far side of revenge" (*CT* 77). Poetry operates as a "bow" on many levels, one of which spans the relationship between the individual and society, a dominant issue in Sophocles' play, but one that Heaney also transforms by redefining heroism. For Sophocles, "to be a hero . . . is to have a destiny, to bear and painfully realize fate, given by the gods . . . that sets him apart from the mass of men and makes him simultaneously both exemplary and fearful":[7] Philoctetes must put away his bitterness if he is to be cured and go on to heroic feats. Neoptolemus must become attuned to the qualities of true nobility rather than serving as a tool for the unscrupulous Odysseus. In Heaney's version, however, greatness is not the prerogative of a few destined heroes; as Heaney's Neoptolemus points out in a diversion from Sophocles' text, "There's a courage / and dignity in ordinary people / That can be breathtaking" (*CT* 72).

But if ordinary people can experience the dignity of heroes, they are also subject to the extremes of agony and bitterness:

> Human beings suffer
> They torture one another,
> They get hurt and get hard.
>
> (*CT* 77)

In contrast to Sophocles, who focuses on the enormous wrongs done to Philoctetes and elicits pity for his terrible sufferings, Heaney underscores the complicity of all involved, and in so doing, draws attention to his own theme of individual responsibility. The opening litany of the chorus contextualizes the characters—"Philoctetes. / Hercules. / Odysseus. / Heroes. Victims. Gods and human beings" (*CT* 1)—as *all* caught in the mire of narcissism: "Licking their wounds / And flashing them around like decorations" (*CT* 2). The blurring of distinctions between hero and victim, between divine and human, underscores the pathetic nature of the social context when preoccupation with past wounds and perpetuation of more injustices render the entire society paralyzed, at an impasse. The chorus, identifying itself as the bow that links the play with the audience/reader, involves itself and, implicitly, the audience in the "problems" the play addresses:

> I hate it, I always hated it, and I am
> A part of it myself.
>   And a part of you,
> For . . . the chorus
> Is more or less a borderline between
> The you and the me and the it of it.
>
> (*CT* 2)

The "it" of it seems to be primarily the disease, which infecting individuals has spread through the body politic—what Odysseus punningly refers to as "the lie of the land" (*CT* 4), a condition that he encourages Neoptolemus to "study" and exploit. The "lie" is not simply the duplicity that Neoptolemus uses to trick Philoctetes; it includes the central deceit—deriving from self-pity and self-aggrandizement—that the play attempts to deconstruct: that justice consists in revenge. The Trojan War itself is based on that lie; the "wound" of the war (*CT* 73) cannot be healed until individuals are healed. Philoctetes' disease—his insatiable thirst for revenge—feeds on the lie. Odysseus knows how to exploit the lie—to use hatred to bind humans into pliable instruments. Hence his instructions to Neoptolemus to tell Philoctetes of his (Neoptolemus's) own betrayal by Odysseus. In doing so, Neoptolemus feeds Philoctetes' wounded ego and fuels his desire for revenge. The alliance of the two men is calculated initially on the bonds of self-pity and mutual hatred:

> you of all men know
> What it's like when you've been humiliated.
> Still, humiliate me was what they did.
>
> . . . .
> You have heartbreak enough, Philoctetes,
> Without starting to take on another man's.
>
> (*CT* 20)

Such an alliance—begotten in betrayal, mutual self-pity, and calls for revenge—is symptomatic of the society from which the young Neoptolemus emerges. Odysseus, its prime representative, had betrayed Philoctetes ten years previously by ostracizing and abandoning him when he was in distress. Odysseus has also betrayed Neoptolemus by using him in the deceitful plot. Valueless himself, Odysseus assigns to "orders," the "cause," and the gods themselves the responsibility for his own manipulations and connivance.[8] His view of society is based on the wielding of political power; the individual is seen as an instrument to be used to serve the powers-that-be or, in the case of Philoctetes, to be sacrificed for some abstract "common good."[9]

Rather than excuse Odysseus, Sophoclean morality, based on a hierarchical order with divine justice at its apex, places greater responsibility for social ills on the leaders and would-be heroes of society, such men as Odysseus. Neoptolemus alludes ironically to this ethic of responsibility, trying to excuse Odysseus (and himself implicitly) when he proclaims in the Sophoclean version:

> a city's welfare, like an army's lies
> with those who rule, and many who do wrong
> are led astray by what their leaders tell them.
>
> (*P* 385–88)

Heaney's version of Neoptolemus's words makes them doubly ironic in their incrimination of both the speaker and the leadership:

> People in high office are bound to rule
> By the force of their example. Bad actions come

From being badly influenced. What you see
Is what you do yourself.

(*CT* 22)

Heaney's passage suggests by its rich ambiguity a relationship between individuals and leaders in society that is reciprocally responsible. Is "the force
of their example"—with its play on *"force"*—the example of the leaders, or
the example the leaders follow from their people, or both? Who is the source
of the bad influence that brings about bad actions, or is the emphasis here
on bad acts resulting from badly influenced *being*? The last sentence in particular suggests a range of possibilities, while underscoring the major role
that *seeing*—in relationship with *doing*—plays in this drama: What one sees
leaders do influences one's own actions; what one sees leaders do is a reflection of what one does oneself; what one *sees* influences what one *does*.

Heaney's political vision is based on the "sea [see] change" that poetry
can help bring about. Neoptolemus begins to undergo a change in vision
when he sees the bow of Hercules as a transcendent sign of trust between
Hercules and Philoctetes. Although Neoptolemus is in the process of deceiving Philoctetes, Heaney shapes Neoptolemus's words into interlocking
bows that suggest how seeing the object evokes in Neoptolemus a sense of
reverence for its virtue, a quality he had begun to *feel* the need for in himself.[10]

<blockquote>

                                    The bow
Is like a god itself.
                     I feel this urge
To touch it.
           For its virtue.
                            Venerate it.
Can I hold it in my hands?

</blockquote>

(*CT* 36)

Seeing Philoctetes suffer and being utterly impotent to help him,
Neoptolemus gives the only aid possible: his hand in friendship and his
promise to stay. His attempts to *do* anything to relieve the suffering are fu-
tile: "What are we going to do?" (*CT* 40); "But what am I going to do? . . .
There must be something / I could do" (*CT* 41); "But I'm useless" (*CT* 43).

Although the only thing Neoptolemus can *do* is witness the suffering,
something is done to him by that witnessing. He is awakened both to a
genuine compassion for Philoctetes and a recognition of his own "afflic-
tion," the poisoning wound he has inflicted on himself by his exploitation
and betrayal of Philoctetes' trust; he is filled with "self-disgust" (*CT* 49). It is

this gradual "change of heart" (*CT* 69) that moves him from the pliant instrument of Odysseus's manipulation to a consciousness of his own responsibility in a larger human community where "candour" and "justice" are the guiding principles. Giving back the bow and promising Philoctetes to take him home—in effect exiling himself from future glory in Greek society—Neoptolemus defines a new kind of heroism. He promises to take Philoctetes home not out of pity but out of fidelity to his promise. Self-respect becomes a counterweight to self-pity and the basis for a different foundation for society.[11]

Philoctetes, in helping Neoptolemus to see the possibilities of human integrity, in turn, learns from Neoptolemus to see beyond his own wounds. Early in the play, the chorus indicates that every time the crater on Lemnos Island begins to erupt, Hercules' mind "lights up" Philoctetes' mind and reminds him of the blaze "he started years and years ago" (*CT* 2), the fire of his loyalty to Hercules that helped transform the human into the divine. It is a blaze that has been replaced by a scorching sense of betrayal, which has left Philoctetes eaten up in self-pity: "Burnt bones! / Sears and blisters! / . . . I'm scorched to nothing" (*CT* 51). In contrast to Odysseus, the master manipulator, Philoctetes initially sees himself as impotent victim: "What I am / Is what I was made into by the traitors" (*CT* 15). Later, when he learns the full extent of the betrayal, Philoctetes calls on the fire of retribution to "Scorch the earth and brand the hills of Lemnos / With the mark of my ordeal at his [Odysseus's] hands" (*CT* 55). He would immolate the island and himself in his all-consuming hatred.

Although Heaney's Philoctetes prays that his betrayers will all "waken up" the way he did—in "absolute loneliness" (*CT* 18) and agony—it is he who awakens to the long-forgotten power of trust. When Neoptolemus asks to hold the bow, Philoctetes alludes to the light-bringing possibilities of trusting another human: "You've brought back sunlight here. / You've lit the world and now I'm fit to see / A way home to my father and my friends" (*CT* 36-37). Later, when Neoptolemus refuses to abandon Philoctetes, who has been rendered unconscious by his physical agony, Philoctetes awakens to Neoptolemus's presence with the sense that the young man has "made light of everything" (*CT* 47). Just as the spark of trust Neoptolemus had kindled in Philoctetes in turn enables Neoptolemus to see his own treachery, Neoptolemus's return of the bow and call for healing becomes a "lightening" for Philoctetes:[12]

> You're making me see things in such brilliant light
> I can't bear it. I've been in the afterlife . . .

>   .   .   .   .

> Never. Never again can I see myself
> Eye to eye with the sons of Atreus.
>
> (*CT* 73)

Philoctetes, who had earlier sensed that "Justice is going to waken up at last" (*CT* 57), has experienced the awakening of a new vision of justice in himself. In never seeing himself again "eye to eye" with the Atreides, he has left behind the eye-for-an-eye form of justice, the savage law of the beasts on Lemnos, which once mirrored his own bestial sense of retribution.

Philoctetes had previously seen the law of talons operating in the beasts of the island. As he had fed off them, he expects that without his bow, they "will pick me clean. / My life for theirs, eye and tooth and claw" (*CT* 52). Now seeing the savage "justice" of animals, Philoctetes can appeal to a human responsibility in Neoptolemus: "Oh, but, son, you don't want to believe / That's how it is. Change things back again / And change your mind." In his acknowledgment of a nobler nature in Neoptolemus, Philoctetes begins to separate himself from the beasts and, at the same time, to recognize again his own humanity.

It is Neoptolemus, the trusted friend, who helps point the way for Philoctetes into the full light of the present, out of the nightmare of the past: "Stop just licking your wounds. Start seeing things" (*CT* 74), the words echoing the primary imagistic preoccupation and title of Heaney's contemporaneous collection of poetry, *Seeing Things*. Like the flints that Philoctetes used to make a fire on the island, the growing trust and friendship between the two men rekindles the sparks of their humanity. Accordingly, when Hercules speaks in Heaney's version, Philoctetes asserts: "It's as if a thing I knew and had forgotten / Came back completely clear" (*CT* 79). Part of what has come back is Philoctetes' own human nature, which had been distorted by bitterness and the desire for revenge; he has reawakened to the trust that Hercules' gift of the bow once celebrated, and this full awakening is, ironically, "like a dream" (*CT* 79).[13]

The rebirth of trust enables Philoctetes to sail into the future. In Heaney's rich shaping, Philoctetes at the end of the play has become the bow of a ship, "a part of / what was always meant to happen, and is happening / now at last." His burden of self-pity lifted, his head is now "light" (*CT* 80), in the many senses of the word.

Neoptolemus's taking responsibility for the "wrong thing" he did together with his efforts "to right it" (*CT* 64) opens up the possibility for "a change of heart" (*CT* 69) for Philoctetes "on the far side of revenge" (*CT* 77). Pledged to truth (66), to "doing the right thing / And not just saying it" (*CT* 67), Neoptolemus and Philoctetes sail on the "longed-for tidal wave / Of justice" (*CT* 77) that will presumably lead to healing both the individual and "the sore / And cruel stalemate of our war" (*CT* 79). As Seamus Deane aptly phrases it: "Staying faithful to oneself is, paradoxically, truly communal."[14]

Explicitly and implicitly, Heaney uses shapes and shaping to suggest the paradoxical relationship between human freedom and historical events. Although initially the main protagonists are all engaged in "throwing shapes" of their own self-righteousness (*CT* 1), Neoptolemus and Philoctetes learn to recognize the shape of justice not as the ripping out of tongues (see *CT* 57) but as the bow that can balance human desires with the flow of history. Neoptolemus, at first following the model of the "adaptable" Odysseus and bending into shapes to suit the occasion—"slithering" as Philoctetes terms it (*CT* 69)—learns from Philoctetes the "straight and true" (*CT* 47) nature that will enable him to return the bow to Philoctetes. Philoctetes, on the other hand, must himself bend from his fixation on revenge before he breaks (*CT* 75). Both men—the one manipulated, the other obsessed—paradoxically find their freedom in *obeying*: Philoctetes: "All that you say / Is like a dream to me and I obey." Neoptolemus: "And so will I" (*CT* 80). But Heaney has redefined obedience earlier in his re-working of the Neoptolemus-Odysseus exchange when Neoptolemus returns the bow to Philoctetes: Neoptolemus says, "The commands that I am hearing overrule / You and all you stand for" (*CT* 67). In obeying the higher commands of his conscience, Neoptolemus "redress[es] the balance" (*CT* 65). Despite the obvious political pressures and advantages of keeping the weapon, Neoptolemus freely chooses "to right the wrong" and in so doing provides a counterweight to the machinations of Odysseus.

Going of their "own free will" (*CT* 72) to Troy at the end of the play is an exercise in inner freedom, where Neoptolemus and Philoctetes act as citizens of what Heaney in one poem calls "the republic of conscience," upholding the "unwritten law" (*HL* 12–13) of human conscience in the service of justice, which "isn't only Greek" (*CT* 67). This inner freedom liberates Philoctetes from his former self-absorption to a sense of self in history—"like the sixth sense of the world" (*CT* 80); the cave of his deadly hatred and self-pity is redefined in his last speech as a vessel for new life and hope.

Sophocles' play ends with the chorus briefly bidding farewell. Heaney expands the chorus's last speech, having them pass on their choral voice to "the sea-nymphs in the spray." The final words—"What's left to say"— seem to belong to the chorus, to Philoctetes and Neoptolemus, to the author leaving his place of writing, to the audience/reader leaving the play, and to poetry, offering a counterbalance of imagined possibilities to the betrayal, despair, and hatred that intolerance brings:

I leave
Half-ready to believe
That a crippled trust might walk

And the half-true rhyme is love.

(*CT* 81)

The voice of Hercules had earlier asserted that "Lives that suffer and come right / Are backlit by immortal light" (*CT* 78). The last lines of the play suggest by allusion that "immortal light" which the human heart is capable of reflecting, if imperfectly as in a dark mirror: "There are three things that last for ever: faith, hope, and love; but the greatest of them all is love" (1 Cor. 13:13).

Although Heaney's political vision of a society based on individual self-respect freely following one's conscience may seem improbable in the context of Northern Ireland and to a world bent by regional hatreds and revenge, there are fascinating affinities between his political vision and that which helped shape the 1989 "Velvet Revolution" in Czechoslovakia. Václav Havel, whose drama and political writings span the previous twenty years, had in 1975 diagnosed a modern disease that resembles the sickness of the Greeks in Heaney's *Cure at Troy*, who, like Neoptolemus originally, have lost a sense of personal responsibility. As Havel puts it, "A person who has . . . no sense of responsibility for anything higher than his or her own personal survival, is a *demoralized* person."[15] But while the Greeks abdicated responsibility to their leaders, Havel sees modern humans surrendering to the "consumer value system" (*PP* 62), which, as Havel points out, is merely a projection of a demoralized society. What Havel has continued to advocate is "a new-found inner relationship to other people and to the human community. . . . the rehabilitation of values like trust, openness, responsibility, solidarity, love" (*PP* 118).

In Havel's political vision, it is the individual living in integrity who has the potential to spread "the virus of truth": "a single, seemingly powerless person who dares to cry out the word of truth and to stand behind it with all his person and all his life, ready to pay a high price, has, surprisingly greater power, though formally disfranchised, than do thousands of anonymous voters."[16] Neoptolemus, returning the bow to Philoctetes in *The Cure at Troy*, is such a person, ready to give up all prospects for his own future in fidelity to his promise. Though seemingly impotent, his reliance on truth makes Odysseus's conniving transparent, leaving him with the only power possible for totally demoralized persons: *brute* force. Like Heaney, shaping and reshaping images of light, moreover, Havel sees in individual moral acts a power of illumination that can help reform society:

> [T]he crust presented by the life of lies is made of strange stuff. As long as it seals off hermetically the entire society, it appears to be made of stone. But the moment someone breaks through in one place . . . —when a single person breaks the rules of the game, thus exposing it as a game—everything suddenly appears in another light and the whole crust seems then to be made of a tissue on the point of tearing and disintegrating uncontrollably. (*PP* 59)

But if Havel's political and philosophical writings state his political vision explicitly, his drama serves as a negative version of that political vision. Havel says his plays are designed "to warn, to predict horrors, to see clearly what is evil. Face to face with a distillation of evil, man might well recognize what is good."[17] *Largo Desolato*, which resonates in interesting ways with Heaney's *Cure at Troy*, works through distortion and absence as a negative political parable.[18]

The plot centers on Leopold Nettles, a philosopher, who has exiled himself in his own apartment, in fear of the "authorities"—realistic representatives of Communist Czechoslovakia and embodiments of the Thought Police in Orwell's *1984*—who have taken offense at a paragraph in one of Leopold's philosophical works. Though not suffering the physical deprivations that Philoctetes experiences, Leopold, like Philoctetes, writhes in self-pity in addition to his paranoia; although the totalitarian political context may have initially caused his dilemma, he has increasingly imprisoned himself in his own rationalizing and self-doubts. Leopold is visited by several representatives of one cause or another, who become a modern "chorus" of sorts, reflecting the pressures on him to champion one cause or another or to conform to the status quo: e.g., two paper-mill workers who want Leopold to turn his philosophy into practical political action; Leopold's friend Bertram, who speaks for the intellectuals and fears that Leopold will not be a martyr for the intelligentsia; two representatives of the authorities who want Leopold to deny his identity; and two women, Lucy and Marguerite, who want to "save" Leopold through sex. Psychologically disintegrating because of all the roles he has tried to play, Leopold finally tries to take responsibility for his writing at the end of the play, but as the official representatives inform him, such a claim is superfluous; he has already surrendered his identity. His "case" has been "adjourned indefinitely. . . . for the time being."[19]

In his use of the characters as "chorus,"[20] Havel underscores their lack of individuality. None of the characters except Leopold have surnames: the

ideological representatives are known only as First Sidney and Second Sidney
(First Sidney drinks, and Second Sidney smokes), First Chap and Second
Chap. Although Leopold lives with Suzana, she is an "insignificant other,"
a functionary of her schedule, bringing in the groceries, going out to the
cinema, and more concerned about her silver and her frying pans than the
seemingly desperate state of Leopold. His girlfriend, Lucy, and Suzana's
companion, Edward, are apparent adjuncts of the living arrangements. Lucy
tries unsuccessfully to revivify Leopold's passion; she is paralleled in the
final scene of the play by Marguerite, a young admiring student of Leopold's
writings, who speaks some of the same lines Lucy used.

That all the characters are variations on the theme of inner emptiness
is apparent in Havel's clever and humorous use of repetition and cliché.
Lines are repeated by different characters, and Leopold himself ends up
parroting lines others have spoken to him.[21] The society that emerges in
this microcosm is bereft of friendship, loyalty, mutual respect, and the ability to recognize truth. Leopold, though preyed on by the other characters
initially, ends up using their lines to try to seduce Marguerite.

Like Heaney, Havel underscores the complicity of all the individuals
who contribute to this societal disease; the mutual exploitation and dys-
functional relationships have evolved from the pervasive lack of individual
inner integrity. For Havel, as for Heaney, the individual and society are
reciprocal realities. Leopold's refusals to take responsibility for his words
and actions lead inevitably to his loss of identity both personally and so-
cially at the end of the play. He becomes as anonymous as the "chorus" of
other characters.

Like Heaney in *The Cure*, Havel also addresses explicitly the relationship between leaders and their people as well as the question of heroism in
modern societies. As the Greeks in *The Cure* blame those higher up in the
system for what they do themselves, the First Chap points out to Leopold
that "we don't make the decisions. . . . And we can't be expected to know, of
course, what the relevant authorities will make of this whole business—"
(*LD* 31). The other characters in the play expect Leopold to be the hero
who will relieve them of the need to act responsibly. The Sidneys repeat
with variations the refrain: "There's lots of people looking to you—" (*LD* 6,
8, 40); "we're ordinary people" (*LD* 7, 8, 42, 45, 46). Bertram expresses the
apprehensions of Leopold's friends "that you'll be able to fulfill the expectations which . . . are rightly expected of you . . . to do justice to those great
obligations, to the truth, to the world, to everyone for whom you set an
example" (*LD* 17). Scene 5 ends with several of the characters chorusing
their individual complaints of how Leopold has let them down and culmi-
nating in a common refrain:

Edward. Some hero.
Suzana. Some hero.
Bertram. Some hero.
Lucy. Some hero.

. . . . . .

Second Sidney. Some hero.

(*LD* 46)

Havel dramatizes the absurdity of Leopold's "heroism" in part to reveal the convoluted demoralization that has fostered it. Bertram speaks of the "expectations which . . . are expected" (*LD* 17); Second Sidney points out, "The respect in which you're held puts you under an obligation—" (*LD* 8). The other characters hold Leopold responsible for the moral responsibility they have abdicated to him. He is their excuse not "to be."[22] As the play progresses, it becomes increasingly clear that Leopold can neither play all the variations of the hero role in which he is constantly being cast nor act on his own integrity.[23] In scene 6 of the play, after trying to seduce Marguerite, he swears dramatically that he will not give up his "own human identity" (*LD* 55); his "heroics," however, are to no avail. Like Heaney's Odysseus, who finds virtue in being adaptable, Leopold by the end of the play has adapted himself into nonidentity; the representatives of the "authorities" become a mere stamp of approval for the self-disintegration that has already taken place.

Havel devotes the final scene (scene 7) to collapsing any illusions about Leopold's heroism. The silent scene replicates the beginning of the play with Leopold sitting on the sofa. He goes through the same actions as scene 1 and then *"goes to the footlights and bows"* (*LD* 56), where he is joined by the other *characters.* The last scene implies that the characters and their role-playing are just that, characters playing roles. *Largo Desolato* is a drama about humans who play interchangeable roles but who refuse to *act* as responsible persons. Although the political system contributes to the dehumanizing process, Havel's focus is on how the characters themselves have surrendered to the system.[24]

The efforts the other characters make to "awaken" Leopold to their various demands provide an ironic link with Heaney's use of this theme in *The Cure at Troy.* Leopold trembles when the representatives of the "authorities" promise him that by disclaiming his essay, "here's a chance—with one stroke of the pen—to rid yourself of everything that's piled on your head, all the shit—a chance for a completely fresh start, it's once in a lifetime!" (*LD* 31). Their offer of a new life, however, depends on Leopold's forsaking his identity by denying responsibility (his *author-ship*) for his own past.[25] Similarly, both Lucy and Marguerite hope to make Leopold "come alive again" by awakening his passion (*LD* 23, 54). Marguerite vows, "I'll save you. . . . I'll bring you back to life" (*LD* 53–54). But just as Philoctetes' wish that the Greeks would "waken up" (*CT* 18) is doomed, Havel implies through Leopold's deterioration that awakening must come from an inner response. As Heaney's Odysseus never "awakens" to personal responsibility and the capacity to trust, Havel's play likewise suggests that neither further false deeds nor other people can save one from the burden of being a human being. Heaney's Neoptolemus attests to "a courage / And dignity in ordinary people" (*CT* 72); Havel's play implies by its negative distortions that courage and dignity are part of the very definition of being human.

While Heaney's poetic art foregrounds the possibility for humans to change their isolation and bitterness into trust and hope, Havel's drama works through negativity—the banal, the trite, the mechanical, the self-absorbed—to jar the audience to recognition. In both artistic visions, the foundation for human relationships in society comes to the fore. In elucidating their visions of society, both writers in their respective plays and elsewhere have redefined the notion of "home."

In *The Cure at Troy* when Philoctetes begs Neoptolemus to take him home (*CT* 26), he speaks of the island of Lemnos as "a home where I never was at home" (*CT* 29). His "homesick[ness]" (*CT* 26) includes an alienation from the island itself. Later, when Neoptolemus reveals his treachery, Philoctetes begins to identify with the island: "What's left here now but me / And the place itself? The island's all there is / That'll stand to me" (*CT* 51). He sees in the "nature" of the place a steadfastness and integrity lacking in human interaction. When he meets the conniving Odysseus face to face and cannot quell his desire for revenge, Philoctetes calls on that steadfastness: "Ground of my island, be with me now" (*CT* 55). He begs the fires of Vulcan to inscribe the treachery of Odysseus on the island itself.

It is not, however, the island that will bear the marks of Philoctetes' revenge; rather, it is Philoctetes who will forever bear the imprint of the island. As he becomes reconciled with his past sufferings and prepares to leave, instead of bidding farewell to Lemnos as Sophocles' Philoctetes does, Heaney's Philoctetes metaphorically takes the island with him: "this island's going to be the keel under me and the ballast inside me" (*CT* 80); the place has become part of the man, just as Philoctetes himself feels "a part of what was always meant to happen, and is happening now at last" (*CT* 80).[26] At the end of the play, one has the sense that Philoctetes' going to Troy is paradoxically a going "home" in the broader sense of being a part of a future he was not capable of envisioning in his bitterness. In Heaney's complex interweaving of the themes of the play, one can see a reshaping of the notion of "home" from the place of one's origins, to a recognition of the influences that have helped shape one's identity, to a sharing in trust with another, to an openness of the human heart to imagined possibilities as it journeys through time.

While Heaney redefines "home" with an eye toward the temporal and the imaginative, Havel, who resigned from the presidency of Czechoslovakia on 20 July 1992, in response to the Slovakian desire for their own "homeland," implicitly in his drama and explicitly in his essays calls for a rethinking of "home" that would take humans beyond the nationalistic and sectarian boundaries that currently divide them.

In *Largo Desolato*, there are no specific references to Czechoslovakia. The given names of the characters are international in flavor, e.g., Leopold—reminiscent of the "exile," Leopold Bloom—Lucy, Suzana, Edward, Sidney. Although all of the action takes place in Leopold's living room, the stage set with its two "glass-panelled doors" in the back wall and the "peep-hole," which affords Leopold his only view of the outside world, have metaphysical overtones. Leopold deals with the many characters who come through his doors, but as the play itself suggests—by its self-irony as play and the emptiness of the characters—the place is more like a railway station than a home: there is no one, humanly speaking, at home.

Leopold's use of territorial terms when he is rejecting Lucy suggests a distortion of "home," which Havel has discussed elsewhere. Leopold speaks of Lucy's defending her territory "while quietly but relentlessly trying to enlarge it" (*LD* 22). He himself says he fears being "colonized" (*LD* 23), but that is exactly what happens throughout the course of the play. Leopold uses the "non-verbal, existential space" (*LD* 50) he has written about in one of his philosophical works as a ploy to seduce Marguerite, a way of enlarging his own territory. Havel suggests in many subtle ways that defending and enlarging "territory" has usurped the place of genuine human relationships.

Though conspicuously absent in *Largo Desolato*, the idea of "home" for Havel is inseparable from human identity and has little to do with territory:

> I . . . reject the kind of political notions that attempt, in the name of nationality, to suppress other aspects of the human home. . . . A civic society, based on the universality of human rights, best enables us to realize ourselves as everything we are—not only members of our nation, but members of our family, our community, our region, our church, our professional association, our political party, our country, our supra-national communities—and to be all of this because society treats us chiefly as members of the human race, . . . as particular human beings whose individuality finds its primary, most natural and, at the same time, most universal expression in our status as citizens, in citizenship in the broadest and deepest sense of that word.[27]

In contrast to the territorial conception operating in *Largo Desolato*, Havel's description above emphasizes the individual human being "at home" in the concentric circles of human interaction, with individuals living responsibly in ever-widening communities. Heaney's poetic definition of "home," on the other hand, emphasizes the flow of time, from an individual's origins to the possibility of standing fast in self-respect, to holding trust with another, to the hope "that a further shore / Is reachable from here" (*CT* 77).

Heaney and Havel are political writers primarily because their imaginative visions of human possibilities implicitly pose a threat to social orders based on manipulation, deceit, and intolerance. In the face of such political power, Heaney demonstrates the "revelation of potential" that poetry can offer (RP 1412). Such "potential" includes "miracles / And cures and healing wells" (*CT* 77), which are nothing more—and nothing less—than the "self-healing; / The utter, self-revealing / Double-take of feeling" (*CT* 77), which allows a person like Philoctetes to see the reality that is "denied or constantly threatened by circumstances" (RP 1412) and to regain hope that self-respect and human trust can link individuals in a humane community. Havel offers what he calls "the power of the powerless," the belief—as he thinks the Velvet Revolution exemplified—"that the world might actually be changed by the force of truth, the power of a truthful word, the strength of a free spirit, conscience and responsibility—with no guns, no lust for power, no political wheeling and dealing."[28]

The political parables of the Irish poet and the Czech playwright-president bear the marks of the differing "times" and "troubles" of Northern Ireland and Czechoslovakia. Nonetheless, the "shaping spirits" of Heaney and Havel are kindred in the hope that both compels their art and nourishes the human spirit of their readers. Both writers appeal to seemingly powerless modern humans to reassume their humanity. Both writers beckon a "crippled trust" (*CT* 81)—twisted and fragmented by political manipulation, cynicism, and violence—to arise and walk. As Heaney paraphrased Havel in the Dublin *Sunday Times* to express his hope for Northern Ireland,

> Hope, according to Havel, is different from optimism. It is a state of the soul rather than a response to the evidence. It is not the expectation that things will turn out successfully but the conviction that something is worth working for, however it turns out. Its deepest roots are in the transcendental, beyond the horizon. The self-evident truth of all this is surely something about which a peace process might reasonably be grounded.[29]

Notes

1. Seamus Heaney, "Bard of Hope and Harp," interview by John Walsh, *Sunday Times*, 7 October 1990, sec. 7, p. 4.

2. Václav Havel, "Václav Havel on Beckett," *Beckett Circle* 12 (Fall 1990): 4. Beckett

dedicated his play *Catastrophe* (1982) to Havel when Havel was in prison; Havel wrote *Mistake* (1983) as a response to Beckett's play (see *Index on Censorship* 13, no. 1 (February 1984): 11–14.

3. See Seamus Heaney, "Light Finally Enters the Black Hole," *Sunday Tribune,* 4 September 1994.

4. Sophocles' *Philoctetes* has generated many fascinating versions in this century. For versions by André Gide, Oscar Mandel, and Heiner Müller, see Oscar Mandel, *Philoctetes and the Fall of Troy: Plays, Documents, Iconography, Interpretations* (Lincoln: University of Nebraska Press, 1981). The translation of Sophocles' *Philoctetes* used in this essay is by Robert Torrance in the Mandel volume. It is abbreviated as *P* and is cited by line number.

5. Sophocles had changed the role of the chorus from Aeschylus's and Euripides' versions of Philoctetes' story. In the two previous dramas the chorus is composed of the natives of Lemnos. Sophocles' change draws attention to Philoctetes' isolation on the island. See R. W. B. Burton, *The Chorus in Sophocles' Tragedies* (New York: Oxford University Press, 1980), 226. Heaney's chorus in identifying itself as a threshold, an "in-between," seems to underscore from the start both complicity and poetic openings.

6. In "The Government of the Tongue," Heaney designates the borderline of poetry as what gives poetry its governing power: "In the rift between what is going to happen and whatever we would wish to happen, poetry holds attention for a space, functions not as distraction but as pure concentration, a focus where our power to concentrate is concentrated back on ourselves" (*GT* 108).

7. Charles Segal, *Tragedy and Civilization: An Interpretation of Sophocles* (Cambridge: Harvard University Press, 1981), 294.

8. Late in the play when the scheme to lure Philoctetes to Troy is known, Neoptolemus himself blames "the cause, a plan, big moves, / And I'm a part of them. I'm under orders" (*CT* 51). It is Philoctetes who, knowing he has been betrayed yet again, deflates the notion of a society constituted by obeying orders and finding a common bond in revenge: "He [Neoptolemus] knows all this / Solidarity with the Greeks is sham. / The only real thing is the thing he lives for: / His own self-respect" (*CT* 53). Although Philoctetes' words are ironic at this point in the action (he has yet to rediscover his own self-respect), like other lines in the play, they contain the seeds of truth that later come to fruition.

9. Philoctetes' bow, one of the central symbols of the play, which is viewed differently by each of the characters, is seen by Odysseus as the ultimate tool to be possessed and exploited in order to achieve the predetermined goal.

10. Cf. Heaney's comment on Zbigniew Herbert's poem "A Knocker," where Heaney alludes to poetry's capacity to make "us *feel*, and by means of feeling carries truth alive into the heart" (*GT,* 100, emphasis Heaney). Note also that the rich resonance Heaney achieves in his shaping of the bow imagery in *The Cure at Troy* includes echoes of "The Harvest Bow," where the poet, like Neoptolemus holding the bow of Hercules, "finger[s] it like braille, / Gleaning the unsaid from the palpable." In the "still warm" knots of the harvest bow, the spirits of humans and nature live on, drawn together into art, whose purpose—as Heaney has quoted from Coventry Patmore via Yeats—is peace: *"The end of art is peace."*

11. Cf. Heaney's comments on the activity of poetry: "to place a counter-reality in the scales, a reality which is only imagined but which nevertheless has weight because it is imagined within the gravitational pull of the actual" (*RP* 1412).

12. "Lightenings" was the original title Heaney had in mind for *Seeing Things*. The term refers to the deathbed experience of "a lift of the spirit," as well as to physically making lighter and brighter. See Seamus Heaney, "Seeing Things: John Breslin Interviews Seamus Heaney," *Critic* 46 (Winter 1991): 28. The term seems appropriate in this context in all of its connotations.

13. The "awakening" theme is underscored by the images of death and rebirth. Philoctetes' life on Lemnos has been a death of his existence in society: "ten years of being gone / And being forgotten" (*CT* 73); his difficult rebirth into the human community implies his coming out of the darkness of his cave. The "fire on the mountain" (*CT* 77) and Philoctetes' vision of Hercules "shining in the air" (*CT* 78) affirm the rebirth of Philoctetes into society and into a more human consciousness: "The outcry and the birth-cry / Of new life at its term" (*CT* 78). Heaney universalizes this theme in his use of contemporary death imagery—"The innocent in gaols," "A hunger-striker's father" in a graveyard, a police widow "at the funeral home"—juxtaposed with images suggesting a rebirth of hope—"miracles / And cures and healing wells" (*CT* 77).

14. Seamus Deane, "Oranges and Lemons," *New Statesman & Society* 4 (5 April 1991): 18.

15. Václav Havel, "The Power of the Powerless," trans. Paul Wilson, in *Living in Truth*, ed. Jan Vladislav (London: Faber and Faber, 1986), 62; hereafter cited in text as *PP*.

16. Václav Havel, "Politics and Conscience," trans. E. Kohák and H. Scruton, in *Living in Truth*, 156.

17. Václav Havel, *Disturbing the Peace: A Conversation with Karel Hvížďala*, trans. Paul Wilson (New York: Knopf, 1990), 199; hereafter cited in the text as *DP*.

18. While acknowledging that *Largo Desolato* "was inspired by my own experiences, certainly more directly than any other play I've written," Havel has asserted "it is not an autobiographical play; it is not about me, or only about me as such. The play has ambitions to be a human parable, and in that sense it's about man in general." See Havel, *DP* 65.

19. Václav Havel, *Largo Desolato*, trans. Tom Stoppard (New York: Grove, 1985), 55; hereafter cited in the text as *LD*.

20. *Largo Desolato*, as its title implies, uses the motif of music on many levels. The stage directions call for "impressive orchestral music . . . at the beginning and the end of the play and also during the intervals between the scenes." The unusual title suggests fascinating possibilities. Perhaps the most famous *Largo* of this century is the familiar "Going Home" of the Czech composer Anton Dvořák in his *Symphony from the New World*. A different level of the musical theme occurs in the language itself, where repeated lines become refrains, and sound replaces linguistic meaning. *Desolato* suggests not only the sterility of the humans and their language but also, etymologically, the solitariness of Nettles in his isolation.

21. Repetition and cliché are stock devices Havel uses in many of his plays to underscore, among other things, the devaluation of meaning in language and in modern society and the standardization to which humans willingly succumb. Some Western critics, missing the satire on language and the lack of human identity, have seen Havel, the dramatist, as prosaic and uncreative as a result. Ironically, such criticism addresses a major concern of Havel's negative aesthetic: that one cannot vicariously feed on artistic creativity. Expounding on his own definition of "absurd theatre" and how he sees his own plays, Havel notes that such plays "throw us into the question of meaning by manifesting its absence. Absurd theatre does not offer us consolation or hope. It merely reminds us of how we are living: without hope" (*DP* 54).

22. The question of Being lies at the root of Havel's philosophy and his drama. For an overview of the philosophical and political essays that have been translated into English, see my "Contemporary Drama 101: Václav Havel," *Thought* 66 (September 1991, 317–28. For an overview—which also traces the Hamlet theme—of Havel's translated drama, see my "Living in Lies: Václav Havel's Drama," *Cross Currents* 42 (Summer 1992): 200–211.

23. Cf. Havel's comments in *Disturbing the Peace*: "The role of theatre, as I understand it and as I have tried to practice it, is not to make people's lives easier by presenting positive heroes into which they can project all their hopes, and then sending them home with the

feeling that these heroes will take care of things for them. To my mind, that would be doing the lion's share of the work. I've already talked about how each of us must find real, fundamental hope within himself. You can't delegate that to anyone else" (*DP* 199).

24. Havel as president has expounded on the reciprocal relationship between individuals in society and their leaders, pointing out more explicitly the roles of leaders: "Politicians are indeed a mirror of their society, and a kind of embodiment of its potential. At the same time—paradoxically—the opposite is also true: society is a mirror of its politicians. It is largely up to the politicians which social forces they choose to liberate and which they choose to suppress, whether they rely on the good in each citizen or on the bad." See Václav Havel, *Summer Meditations*, trans. Paul Wilson (New York: Alfred A. Knopf, 1992), 4.

25. Cf. Havel's words in *Letters to Olga*, where individual responsibility and identity are recurring themes: "Responsibility establishes identity; it is only in the responsibility of human existence for what it has been, is and will be that its identity dwells." *Letters to Olga*, trans. Paul Wilson (New York: Henry Holt, 1989), 268.

26. Cf. Havel's description of becoming president of his country: "That special time caught me up in its wild vortex and . . . compelled me to do what had to be done. . . . History—if I may put it this way—forged ahead and through me, guiding my activities." See Havel, *Summer Meditations*, xvii.

27. Václav Havel, "On Home," *New York Review of Books*, December 1991, 49.

28. Havel, *Summer Meditations*, 5.

29. Seamus Heaney, "Light Finally Enters the Black Hole." Havel has defined hope frequently in his writings. See, e.g., *Disturbing the Peace*, 181, and "Never hope against hope," *Esquire*, October 1993, 68.

Works Cited

Beckett, Samuel. *Catastrophe. Index on Censorship* 13 (1 February 1984): 11–12.

Burton, R. W. B. *The Chorus in Sophocles' Tragedies*. New York: Oxford University Press, 1980.

Carey, Phyllis. "Contemporary Drama 101: Václav Havel." *Thought* 66 (September 1991): 317–28.

————. "Living in Lies: Václav Havel's Drama." *Cross Currents* 42 (Summer 1992): 200–211.

Deane, Seamus. "Oranges and Lemons." *New Statesman & Society* 4 (5 April 1991): 18–19.

Havel, Václav. *Disturbing the Peace: A Conversation with Karel Hvížďala*. Translated by Paul Wilson. New York: Knopf, 1990.

————. *Largo Desolato*. Translated by Tom Stoppard. New York: Grove, 1985.

————. *Letters to Olga*. Trans. Paul Wilson. New York: Henry Holt, 1989.

————. *Mistake. Index on Censorship* 13 (1 February 1984): 13–14.

————. "Never hope against hope." *Esquire*, October 1993, 68.

————. "On Home." *The New York Review of Books*, December 1991, 49.

————. "Politics and Conscience." Translated by E. Kohák and H. Scruton. In *Living in Truth*, edited by Jan Vladislav, 136–57. London: Faber and Faber, 1986.

————. "The Power of the Powerless." Translated by Paul Wilson. In *Living in Truth*, edited by Jan Vladislav, 36–122. London: Faber and Faber, 1986.

————. *Summer Meditations*. Translated by Paul Wilson. New York: Alfred A. Knopf, 1992.

———. "Václav Havel on Beckett." *Beckett Circle* 12 (Fall 1990): 4.

Heaney, Seamus. "Bard of Hope and Harp." Interview by John Walsh. *The Sunday Times,* 7 October 1990, 7.2–7.4.

———. "Light Finally Enters the Black Hole." *The Sunday Tribune,* 4 September 1994.

———. "Seeing Things: John Breslin Interviews Seamus Heaney." Interview by John Breslin. *The Critic* 46 (Winter 1991): 26–35.

Mandel, Oscar. *Philoctetes and the Fall of Troy: Plays, Documents, Iconography, Interpretations.* Lincoln: University of Nebraska Press, 1981.

Segal, Charles. *Tragedy and Civilization: An Interpretation of Sophocles.* Cambridge: Harvard University Press, 1981.

Seamus Heaney's *Seeing Things:* "Retracing the path back . . . "

CATHARINE MALLOY

In *Seeing Things*, Heaney continues his celebration of "the marvels of exist-ence" that Elmer Andrews noted about Heaney's early collections *Death of a Naturalist* and *Door into the Dark*.[1] There is a sense Heaney has come full circle: from *North*, where he needed to escape "the tight gag of place / And times" (*N* 59) through *Field Work*, where the "points at which the public event, the statistics, intersect with the personal life of the poet,"[2] to *Sweeney Astray*, Heaney's revelatory translation from the Irish of *Buile Suibhne*, to *Station Island*, the collection indebted to Sweeney's significance and Dante's influence in the poet's life. In *Seeing Things*, however, Heaney's explorations of the past yield unexpected pleasures. Although the continuation of a Dantesque pilgrimage is suggested by the speaker's approach, in this col-lection, he comes "to credit marvels," (50), rejoicing in the epiphanies ris-ing from his orchestration of, and engagement with, language as a shaper of experience. By re-viewing people, things, places both exuberantly and benignly at the same time, the speaker is able to express a momentary wis-dom: he "sees." Heaney, in speaking of Dante and Eliot, sums up Virgil's purpose as guide, but his summary of the Latin poet could just as well define the role of language as it functions for the speaker in *Seeing Things*:

> Virgil comes to Dante, in fact, as Dante comes to Eliot, a master, a guide and authority, offering release from the toils and snares of the self, from the *diserta*, the waste land.[3]

But while language's authority does serve Heaney as a guide, his or-chestration of the various discourses in *Seeing Things* actually frees him from dependence on any one particular strain. Although allied to language by language, he is not enslaved by it; his utterance guides, illuminates, acts as a torch offering a vision of the past as well as release from it.

The speaker in these poems attempts to retrieve and see "things" and events and people through dialogical utterances[4] just as he has in much of his work since and including *Field Work*, but the events are transformed from the past even as they capture a moment in time or a remembered thing.[5] By expanding the consciousness of the speaker through discursive emanations and encouraging retrieving and reseeing "things," memory assists the speaker as he uses language to re-view and see "things" from the past as if he is seeing them for the first time. The attendant wonder and innocence is present, but the dialogic transformation effected by language's ability to direct him back to the past as well as to release him from it works to inform both speaker and reader.

The ability to see things anew may derive from the speaker's penchant for recalling the quotidian and then paying attention to how the everyday reassimilates itself through language in a way that informs and directs. Memory functions to augment discourses that attempt not so much to perfect a recollection as to see it for its evocation of something true and lasting. The remembered event may be seen with multiple facets: as it originally happened and as time has changed and broadened the speaker's perception of it. Memory, therefore, does not serve so much to embellish a recollected event as to unleash its possibilities for meaning.

The discursive emanations from these memories help to reshape the speaker's past as he reflects upon their relevance for the present. Distance from past events allows the speaker to initiate new dialogues that influence the old, dormant, suspended ones, freeing them from immutability by inviting a gathering of new discourses to assist him in redressing a past event. Advancing multiple possibilities for meaning, the speaker's remembrances of things and events are perceived through language's many facets rather than distorted by the lens of time. Therefore, whatever the speaker is trying to reclaim in order to enlighten, enrich, inform or accommodate the present is not limited by his former perception of it. Rethinking past experiences allows, as Heaney has said, "a certain distance from your first self,"[6] but it allows, as well, a reclaiming of remembered visions by reseeing them.

The deliberateness of the speaker's language recalls events with familiar, often colloquial speech, but the discourse evolving from and interacting with his utterance often redresses what transpired in the original event. The past is not framed and secured by the speaker so much as it is incorporated into the present and used to illuminate any number of things. Seeing the past is not limited by the speaker's reflection upon it, because the discursive revelations issuing here act "as a dialogue of different times, epochs and days, a dialogue that is forever dying, living, being born: co-existence and becoming are here fused into an indissoluble concrete unity that is contradictory, multi-speeched and heterogeneous."[7] The speaker's need to retrieve some "thing" from his past attests to his lingering innocence as well as to his need for "things" to function in connection with passages or cross-ings in the present as he ratifies the daily. The physical, the visible, aids his exploration of the invisible, and naming things invites discursive resonances from his past to coalesce with languages that speak to the present.

Many of the poems in this collection, therefore, arise from remember-ing a visible object. There is "The Ash Plant," "The Pitchfork," "A Basket of Chestnuts"; "The Settle Bed," "The Schoolbag," "The Cot," "The Sky-light"; there is a poem about "wheels" and a poem about the game of "Scrabble." All are concerned with "seeing things" as in the triptych that names the collection and in which the speaker begins to not only "see" things but to "see" through them as well. He explores things and discovers that those things once seen or used in one way may now be seen or used for another purpose. The many voices entering the discourse and guiding the speaker to reshape and re-view his recollections of these things inform his way of seeing and knowing, enhancing his vision as he moves onward, an enlightened wayfarer.

The aforementioned things serve to call up discourses as aids to self-understanding while en route and although they shift in the "Squarings" portion of the volume from concern with the concrete object to a concern with measuring, settling, and traversing, language continues its role as illu-minator and guide: "Lightenings," "Settings," and "Crossings" invite ex-ploration, encourage discovery, and continually offer assistance in the speaker's journey.

Diverse discourses in "The Ash Plant" reveal characteristics of the poet's father as well as underscore traditional Catholic beliefs relating to the last judgment. The familiar thing, the ash plant, becomes the most assiduous connection between father and son, but it is through language that the variousness of the connection between father and son is revealed.

The Ash Plant

> He'll never rise again but he is ready.
> Entered like a mirror by the morning,
> He stares out the big window, wondering,
> Not caring if the day is bright or cloudy.

(19)

The image[8] of the sentry lingers: father is watchful, attentive, vigilant; the language of the Church, ironically contorted, reinforces its hold as the old man continuously, if benignly, remains aware of death's approach. Al-though the "lofty station" accorded the old man through his baptism may be "forgotten," it is so deeply etched in his consciousness that he is not fearful of death; he is "ready" to rise *to* life's end, because he knows he will rise *from* it: belief in resurrection sustains him, prevails. While judgmental, his old saying "I could have cut a better man out of the hedge!" parallels father to Father: "God might have said the same, remembering Adam." The religious, paternal, and filial voices entering the discourse are ambivalent: the father will not "rise," but he is ready to rise again. In addition, the familiar, domestic language helps to recreate the image of a father comfortable in his surroundings: no plans for moving are immanent. Accordingly, the language is in the present tense: the "tree / In damp opulence above damp hedges," his "head goes light . . . he can stand his ground." The old gentleman wields the stick before him, flattening any discursive undulations he encounters along the way. He may be "disencumbered as a breaking comber," but because of his impending "lightening" he may also have glimpses of departing gently. Ironically, while "he'll never rise again," he is "ready"; he "finds the phantom limb of an ash plant which steadies him" so he can "stand his ground / or wield the stick like a silver bough," should it become necessary.

Recalling more than a father's last moments on earth, the speaker is enlightened by the discursive revelations, and his understanding of death and resurrection is sharpened. The father, although feeble, is seen as resilient, unvanquished; he is "like a sentry . . . wakening . . . yet in position": father as judge, father as flawed before another Father. But with that "phantom limb" he wields, the old man demonstrates his reluctance to give up, suggesting a resolute and relentless spiritual dimension that argues against the purely physical, whether it is "ash plant" or dying body. In his space, "an upstairs outlook on the whole country," he advances premonition of change, of crossing to some different place; his propensity for seeing despite the day's cloudiness or brightness is affirmative, final, confirming that not all that is realized and understood is visible, not all that is known is known rationally.

Those intimate assertions that affirm the speaker's links to the past and his place in it often are disclosed in a way that makes them seem to be heard from a great distance, but with perfect clarity. In the title poem, three events are reconstructed: a remembered outing in a boat; the recollected vision of a cathedral's facade; the scene of a young boy who, in retrospect, sees his father, perhaps, for the first time. All three, when imagined from a critical distance, stir up many voices[9] to articulate the experiences and to open possibilities for meaning that could not be known when the events first happened.

Beginning with "Sunlight, turfsmoke, seagulls, boatslip, diesel," the speaker is transported by his verbal recitation of these objects' names to

"Inishbofin on a Sunday morning." But the entire boating expedition is colored as much by a child's language registering awe and wonder as it is with an adult's language associating the outing with a life's journey:

Seeing Things

I

Inishbofin on a Sunday morning.
Sunlight, turfsmoke, seagulls, boatslip, diesel.
One by one we were being handed down
Into a boat that dipped and shilly-shallied
Scaresomely every time. We sat tight
On short cross-benches, in nervous twos and threes,
Obedient, newly close, nobody speaking
Except the boatmen, as the gunwales sank
And seemed they might ship water any minute.

(16)

The boater, frightened at the "shiftiness and heft" of the craft, is kept in "agony" at the thought that the boat may tilt and tip and that he may drown. The language of risk and shift suggests a precarious balance and the speaker is filled with fear and doubt about a safe crossing. But the memory of that crossing shifts eventually, eliciting languages reaching toward a fuller, more complete understanding of the journey. No longer wary as he was when he first experienced the event, he begins to float on the "deep, still, seeable-down-into water," knowing how riskily they all traveled; but his fear dissipates when he remembers that one's fate may be predetermined by Someone looking on "from another boat."

The allusive language connecting the "ferryman" to the mythical Charon underscores the puzzling omniscience of the speaker in the last four lines of the poem and the images suggested by these tandem ferrymen lake-going in a "boat that dipped and shilly-shallied" connects the physical act of sailing to the discourse suggesting that life may be something other than an even sail. This internally persuasive discourse is "fundamentally and organically fused with the image of [the] speaking person,"[10] but the speaker nonetheless orchestrates the other discourses invading the dialogue even as he may resist them. There is a sense he is keenly aware of the implications of his now redirected boating excursion. The polarities in the text, its reference to the boat's "quick response and buoyancy and swim," struggle with the speaker's "agony" and fear of drowning in a physical sense but reaffirm, as well, the speaker's spiritual connectedness to Dante's journey and to the Church: the "shiftiness and heft / Of the craft itself" actually "panicked" the child. Will he be lost? Or will he survive the precarious wayfaring he is destined to continue, whether in the "dark wood" or on the "deep" water?

Complicating the memory of this event, religious and philosophical languages continue to assist the speaker to see the boating experience as one defined and enriched by the time that has passed since the event took place. His perception gathers not only a remembered image, but the multiple implications that are drawn from the remembered scene.[11] Now he looks "from another boat / Sailing through air, far up," yet he knows "How riskily [they] fared into the morning." That they all may have tipped into "The deep, still, seeable-down-into water" no longer alarms him, for now another journey is implied. There is a sixth sense at work here suggesting that the speaker is still en route, connecting his crossing over the water with a crossing of another kind, and it may be this sixth sense that draws out the other languages in the recollected scene where it collides with the reimagined "Obedient" and "newly close" language of childhood: trusting anyone, boatmen, ferryman, or even God, is an act risking disappointment.

Discursive variety continues to intrigue in the second poem of the triptych as well where the question of trust once again is broached. What becomes emblematic and encourages exploration even as it "grounds" the speaker's beliefs is the "facade of a cathedral," which the speaker not only objectifies but assimilates through the resonances sounding from the "dialogue of languages"[12] operating in the reassimilated event. The "carved stone of the water / Where Jesus stands up to his unwet knees / And John the Baptist pours out more water / Over his head" bespeaks events biblical and ritualistic, ordered and linear, clear as in "bright sunlight." This "story," perhaps remembered from childhood, is reenforced and reconstituted by time as well as by the art in the "carved stone" depicting the biblical scene.

On the stone tablet the catechetical becomes enriched with the botanical. The botanical is seen; the catechetical is unseen: "in that utter visibility / [the stone becomes] alive with what's invisible: / Waterweed, stirred sandgrains hurrying off, / The shadowy, unshadowed stream itself . . ."

Seeing Things

II

Claritas. The dry-eyed Latin word
Is perfect for the carved stone of the water
Where Jesus stands up to his unwet knees
And John the Baptist pours out more water

Over his head: all this in bright sunlight
On the façade of a cathedral.

(17)

All is not linear; all is not memory; all is not visible; and yet, poetry can reify
possibility, waver like heated air, ineluctably, like "the zig-zag hieroglyph
for life itself." Perhaps the speaker "sees" that all life is "alive with what's
invisible," but recognition of this theological principle occurs through his
hearing of coexisting dialogues: catechetical, "*Claritas.* The dry-eyed Latin
word / Is perfect"; biblical, "Jesus stands . . . [and] John the Baptist pours";
botanical, "waterweed . . . [and the] stream itself"; artistic, "the carved
stone," "the facade," the "Lines / Hard and thin," the "hieroglyph." While
the speaker's trusting, innocent language may yet infiltrate the drama of
voices, his revisioning of the cathedral's facade draws in the dissident discourses that influence and expand his current perceptions. It is the reciprocity of discourses that encourages this expansion and allows, as Bakhtin
suggests, that "the transmission and interpretation of the divinely inspired
(as opposed to the profane) word are acts of religious thought and discourse
having the greatest importance."[13] The speaker's divining and sifting through
the different languages shapes his continuous exploration: of faith, of art, of
the journey.

Enabling the speaker in the third poem of the triptych are the dialogues echoing from a remembered encounter with his father. The child is
not invited to accompany his father "to spray / Potatoes in a field on the
riverbank," because he is too young: "The horse- / sprayer / Was too big
and new-fangled, bluestone might / Burn me in the eyes, the horse was
fresh, I / Might scare the horse, and so on" (18). Fatherly language, au-
thoritative language, and even condescending language resound and are
historically real and heteroglot. But the son, by his deciphering of the remembered event through language, hears from its resonances both the vul-
nerability and the authority of his father. Clearly, both father and boy know
their place, but when the father returns the young lad sees him "out the
window, scatter-eyed / And daunted, strange without his hat, / His step
unguided, his ghosthood immanent," and voices the tumult that subverts
his father's position of authority. The accident of the horse, cart, and sprayer
being "pitched" easily into the river exposes the frailty rather than the authority of the man, distinguishing the father's position (vulnerable) as well
as the son's (enlightened). The boy's mythical separation from his father
when everything went "tumbling off the world" is changed by this illumination as is the direction he takes after the event where, again, language serves
as a guide for shaping perceptions.

Using language laden with theological overtones, the speaker stresses that "That afternoon / [he] saw him face to face," as he really was: "daunted," "unguided," "strange." Perhaps in "That afternoon" the lad passed from innocence to experience, from son to man: "there was nothing between us there / That might not still be happily ever after." Was there "nothing" between them? Or is what was between them then still vital and alive? Or was there "nothing," for the first time, between them to separate them? "Nothing" becomes a "word with a loophole" and a "word with a sideways-glance"[14] inviting multiple interpretations and encouraging play even as it functions to lead the speaker along.

Seeing events from a distance enables the speaker to become intimate with his own discourse and to realize that it is "wrought out of others' words."[15] The speaker, like a ventriloquist, mouths the words of his father, the words he remembers, but by hearing intrusive discourses as well, he discerns that the voices infiltrating his dialogues may influence but not necessarily control him, may guide but not necessarily manipulate him. The memory of his "undrowned father" challenges the speaker to acknowledge the event differently now from the way it happened, but the fullness given to the event recollected and transferred to the present is achieved through the mingling of voices passing from then to now.

Discourses are continuously roused by the speaker as he remembers and relates to past events. Even the ordinary helps him to "see" the invisible: centrifugal force in "A Basket of Chestnuts" (24); transcending time in "Markings" (8); impulse and willfulness in "Crossings xxix" (86) and, with its conglomerate of languages, perpetual motion in "Wheels within Wheels" (46). The verbal lift issuing from the language of physics equates with the floating sensibility experienced by the speaker as he spins the bicycle wheels, but even more compelling than the play with wheels is the speaker's exhilaration at his play with words. The remembered circularity of the wheel spins into the free energy of language, igniting glimmers for possibility not realized or known when the wheel spun in the original event.

And the tipped-over bicycle thwarted by its inability to move a body from one place to another suits the grown man with his helpless illusions about going back.

> Something about the way those pedal treads
> Worked very palpably at first against you
> And then began to sweep your hand ahead
> Into a new momentum—that all entered me
> Like an access of free power, as if belief
> Caught up and spun the objects of belief
> In an orbit coterminous with longing.

(46)

The young lad knows that by turning the pedals the wheels will spin, but this perception is challenged by the man's feeling a "new momentum" that conflicts with his former "innocent" understanding of the phenomenon of power. Unlike the lad in "Death of a Naturalist," he is not up close to the phenomenon, so his distance from the event lends credibility to a whole new way of seeing: he remembers "the way those pedal treads . . . entered" him. There is that epiphanic sense of recognition concerning his "objects of belief" heightening, ironically, his inexplicable sense of yearning. The languages of philosophy and desire collide in that reimagined thing: the upside-down bicycle with its spinning hoops, the speaker's "regenerate clays" entering an "orbit coterminous with longing." And yet, after the event, "Nothing rose to the occasion" again until "Cowgirls" stood "in a circus ring . . . At the still centre of a lariat" reminding him of *"Perpetuum mobile,"* kinetic energy, and language's power to rouse. Guided by language's effusion, the speaker comes to know that perpetuum mobile, too, has the power to influence perceptions.

Although the remembrance of the physical sensation of upside-down pedaling encourages the speaker to advance his understanding of the sensation, it is the dialogue comprised of intruding languages that encourages advancement of a different order. He knows now of restlessness and longing, of the futility as well as of the exuberance associated with daily life and the quotidian. The sensations he felt as a young boy spinning the pedals of an upside-down bicycle are sensations he converts discursively to mean more than the physical relevance of perpetual motion. Now the recollections serve to illuminate both the innocence of his boyhood and the experiences of his manhood with their attendant responsibilities. By crossing languages of childhood and innocence with languages of adulthood and experience, the speaker is challenged rather than appeased. The outward display of colliding languages, like the "whooshing mud," invites the speaker's recognition of his own "regenerate clays" by subverting the importance of the "mud" and recalling, perhaps, the words from the Ash Wednesday ritual: "you are dust and unto dust you shall return."

Articulation of the most profound mysteries issues forth from the playfulness with language where "objectness" is juxtaposed to the language of hope that is "coterminous with longing." Incantatory, but filled with a sense of loss and longing, the discursive revelations yield more than the quantifiable, the scientific, the physical, and suggest that languages in dialogue with one another often serve to illuminate what is invisible. In "Wheels within Wheels," much that becomes known *is* invisible: desire, innocence, death, disappointment.

Events remembered discursively consistently illuminate by the variousness of the languages that comprise them. Often the events, effected and shaped by time and distance, serve to light the speaker's way by illuminating his former way of knowing, as in "Scrabble" (31), for example, where the memory of a friend assumes a renewed vitality through the speaker's recollection of a board game used by players to play with words. The languages of game and reality invite the speaker to approach the board anew and to listen to what the words may be saying to him. Here, "love [is] / Taken for granted like any other word / That was chanced on and allowed within the rules," but taking love for granted is much more serious than the frivolous act of taking words for granted in a game of words. And yet, the paradoxes of language and love and friendship become increasingly more insistent as the poem relates their importance by way of the game. Considering that his friend, an archaeologist, "hears" the "scraping, clinking tools" that are words, their importance cannot be overestimated:

Scrabble

in memoriam Tom Delaney, archaeologist

Bare flags. Pump water. Winter-evening cold.
Our backs might never warm up but our faces
Burned from the hearth-blaze and the hot whiskeys.

. . . .
Year after year, our game of Scrabble: love
Taken for granted like any other word
That was chanced on and allowed within the rules.
So 'scrabble' let it be. Intransitive.
Meaning to scratch or rake at something hard.
Which is what he hears. Our scraping, clinking tools.

(31)

Both the futility of discourse to adequately and precisely convey meaning and its attendant kinetic energy is replicated here, echoing itself, needing "all of language, all of its aspects, and all of its elements" to reveal its potential[16] although its full potential is never actualized. The possibility of language, of a word like love, is directly related here; and while its possibility for meaning is intimated, it is late in occurring. When the game was played, one senses, "love" was "taken for granted," but not anymore. Love is placed in the poem just as the small wooden squares are placed on the game board: carefully, knowingly. That the word is confined to the board (or to the poem) does not limit its resonances, for it, like all discourse, is hardly more than "scraping, clinking tools." While the gravediggers' language scrapes noisily, what the archaeologist "hears" is his friend's voice suggesting language is no more profound than the words arranged and placed on a Scrabble board. And yet, words on top of words, or words in a row on a board game, or words in rows of poetry attest to the attempts language makes toward meaning. Energetic and active, the conversations expose levels of meaning without having one necessarily surface at the top as *the* meaning. Recalling the dialogues in "Scrabble," the speaker sees the event as both a familiar one and one he is seeing for the first time, hearing words he has heard before, too, as if he is hearing them for the first time.

Often dialogism may erupt by remembering things: "The Pitchfork" of "Riveted steel" (23), the "Basket of Chestnuts . . . golden bowelled as a moneybag" (24), "The Biretta," which "like Gaul . . . was divided / Into three parts" (26). Inspired by things and their shapes but moving beyond them, the speaker advances from sight to insight. For example, a "schoolbag" becomes a "word-hoard" (30) and the "headboard" of an inherited settle bed echoes "the long bedtime / Anthems of Ulster" (28). The language of vision, of "seeing," assists the evolutionary language of "becoming" as the speaker consistently reviews objects and events from his past, inevitably "seeing" in another way. Dialogism invites conversations that reveal what could not have been foreknown; for example, there is "the pitchfork . . . That came near to an imagined perfection" when "he tightened his raised hand and aimed with it" (23), but it is "imagined" and only "near" to whatever kind of perfection the speaker is trying to define. And yet, the process of this flight, "like a javelin," parallels his far-reaching, dreamy, romantic language when he thinks of "probes that reached the / farthest . . . starlit and absolutely soundless" (23). Ironically, the "perfection—or nearness to it—" still becomes "imagined," but it ceases to exist "out there." The language of the imagination parallels the flight of the pitchfork through space but moves beyond it "to an imagined perfection" relying "Not in the aiming but the opening hand." In short, the hand opening, like the process of discourse itself, replaces the romantic "aiming" with implementation and recognition; the convergence of various languages assists the speaker's process of both "seeing" and "becoming." He understands that to visualize a remembered object is one thing, but to extrapolate from that vision something that is invisible is another.

Through "seeing" the process of "becoming" is enabled, but what lingers after the re-visioning of a specific thing is the glimmer of possibility. These dialogues of recognition, rather than separating the speaker from the event, serve to imprint his consciousness with their timeless relevance. In "Fosterling" (50), for example, a remembered picture from childhood evokes more than the painted "canals" and "windmills" on the canvas. The speaker says he can't "remember never having known / The immanent hydraulics of a land / Of *glar* and *glit* and floods at *dailigone*. / My silting hope. My lowlands of the mind." Those "lowlands of the mind" prefiguring

"Heaviness of being" parallel, perhaps, the speaker's perceptions concerning poetry "Sluggish in the doldrums of what happens," but the discursive shift, from the speaker's "seeing" the picture to his "seeing" and "credit[ing] marvels," redresses his entire perspective, not only on life, but on poetic inspiration as well; he waited "so long for air to brighten, / [and his] heart to lighten." The remembered picture augments his "vision," but the stabilizing language of "inplaceness" and "immanent hydraulics" is invaded and overcome by the language of poetry. His "silting hope" becomes encompassed by language, by his "lowlands of the mind," and poetry, too, becomes "Sluggish in the doldrums of what happens," doesn't easily sing, as it did in "Song," with "the music of what happens." And yet he understands that the time has come for him to "credit marvels," to have "Time to be dazzled."

Language, with its ability to inform, is permeated like the speakers who use it with possibility and potential. Dialogism advances languages' possibilities by offering, as Dennis Donoghue suggests, "not the mind's imposition of order upon sentiments and images . . . but recognition of all the constituents of the scene, including most particularly those which are in danger of being suppressed."[17] So, the poems here may capture either a moment in time or a remembered thing, but they also expand the consciousness of the speaker as it shapes, and is shaped by, discursive emanations.

In Part II of *Seeing Things*, measurement and possibility, as well as traversing and journeying, encourage the speaker to draw, measure, settle, or cross something in "Lightenings" (53), "Settings" (67), "Crossings" (81), and "Squarings" (95). There are the "anglings, aimings . . . re-envisagings" of poem iii in "Lightenings" (57); the "time marked by assent and by hiatus" in poem xiv in "Settings" (70); the "journey of the soul with its soul guide" in poem xxvii in "Crossings" (85); the light breaking "on the road beyond Coleraine" in xlviii in "Squarings" (108). In the first poem of "Lightenings" the idea of a journey is connected to the remembered image of a beggar "shivering" on a doorstep, and his presence affects and influences the kind of journey the speaker is pondering:

> And after the commanded journey, what?
> Nothing magnificent, nothing unknown.
> A gazing out from far away, alone.
>
> And it is not particular at all,
> Just old truth dawning: there is no next-time-round.
> Unroofed scope. Knowledge-freshening wind.

(55)

Standing at a window observing—seeing—a "beggar shivering," the speaker is moved. But the "knowledge freshening wind," suggesting enlightenment and illumination, works to alter the observer's empathy, replacing it with a kind of fatalism. That the "particular judgement" and the "commanded journey" are mentioned serves only to emphasize the sad futility of the beggar as well as the inevitability of death and its inability to soothe. Incongruous as the Beatitudes' "blessed be the poor in spirit for they shall inherit the earth," the theological language becomes, if not subsumed by the ordinary utterances, at least diminished by them; it is the beggar's deathlike silence that invites its de-emphasis. Because the silhouetted beggar is mute, his silence separates him dramatically from any association with the Word in a religious sense. But at the same time he provokes other discourses by his wordlessness. The silence issuing from the recollection of the beggar on that "stone doorstep" tells of old "truth dawning" and eventually informs the speaker that, indeed, "there is no next-time round"; but the beggar's wordlessness remains insistently invasive as the image of him in the doorway continuously reappears before the speaker, forcing him to view the event in a new way.

The theological is not always de-emphasized by a remembered image, however; it may be underscored. In poem xxiv (80), for example, images provide the shape from which some sense of "omnipresence" may be approached and, possibly, understood. The shape of the "harbour wall" in this poem becomes a "masonry of silence," but from that image a "fullness" is apprehended. The interweaving of the laconic and the silent together with the grammatical language of "antecedent" and "apposition" adds another dimension to a possibility for meaning.

Settings

xxiv

Deserted harbour stillness. Every stone
Clarified and dormant under water,
The harbour wall a masonry of silence

. . . .

Air and ocean known as antecedents
Of each other. In apposition with
Omnipresence, equilibrium, brim.

(80)

The speaker's "Perfected vision" becomes more than "cockle minarets"; the "Fullness," rising from the antecedent air and ocean is juxtaposed to

"Omnipresence" and suggests a divine ubiquitousness impossible to en-
close; "things" are approached and "seen" as they are discursively constructed. Although the speaker recalls the "kesh and turf stacks" (xlii) and
the hare's "form" in the snow (xliii), he uses these images to shape other less
visible, but not less lucent, concerns. These remembered images act as
magnets to draw out the more elusive—the philosophical, the theological,
for example—but it is language's pull that implements, assists, and shapes
the discursive constructs and the revelations continuously emerging from
these constructs.

In poem xlviii, for example, attempts by the speaker to root himself to
something tangible are displaced by language referring and endorsing concerns that are distinctly not empirical. Speaking about what is "manifest"
and "Seventh heaven" and the "whole truth," the speaker broaches the
abstract, the invisible. The salty air he encounters "on the road to Coleraine,"
while concretizing his experience, invites introspection as well.

xlviii

Strange how things in the offing, once they're sensed,
Convert to things foreknown;
And how what's come upon is manifest

Only in light of what has been gone through.
Seventh heaven may be
The whole truth of a sixth sense come to pass.

(108)

Trying to shape his recollection with language as he reframes the Bann
"between the painted poles," the speaker offers syntactical variations that
only serve to underscore his search for meaning: when the light "breaks"
over him "The way it did" then, "That day [he'll] be in step with what
escaped [him.]" It is only by joining past tense and future tense that the still
point of a "whole truth of a sixth sense [may come] to pass." What is "foreknown" through things sensed emerges because of the discursive constructs
illuminating a particular thing or event from the past. "Seeing," for the
poet, involves moving ahead and turning back through the back-and-
forthness, the resonances of language. There are the discourses of desire
and memory and philosophy and others challenging his imaginative process, and this seesawing forces him to retrieve scenes and things from his
memory, attesting not only to his function as an orchestrator of many voices,
but also to his availability as a listener.

In poem xxxvi in the "Crossings" section of the volume, the biblical language of the dark valley acts like a Dantesque imprint upon the poem. Here, destiny and vocation merge in the language of "policemen's torches" that "Clustered and flicked and tempted us to trust / Their unpredictable, attractive light."

xxxvi

And yes, my friend, we too walked
Once. In darkness. With all the streetlamps off.
As danger gathered and the march dispersed.

Scene from Dante, made more memorable
By one of his head-clearing similes—
Fireflies, say, since the policemen's torches

Clustered and flicked and tempted us to trust
Their unpredictable, attractive light.

(94)

Reimagining the event causes the speaker to shape its most lasting resonances into poetry. Although the two friends are aware of the political implications connected to the "policemen's torches," they were not then imagining themselves as "herded shades" boarding "Charon's boat." In retrospect, the event is magnified, clarified by the language of the historical moment, the language of poetry, the language of the spirit. The speaker remembers that "march" when "danger gathered" and he knows how far he has come since then.

Seeing Things invokes memory as an aid to exploration, as an aid to "seeing," but memory here is reconditioned and does not function in the conventional sense. Dialogism and the discursive constructs sounding within the poetry work to illuminate the facets of a recollection even as the speaker's intimacy with his past sustains the dialogues and invites their continuous examination. Languages flow forth in the speaker's act of remembering and serve to influence his way of "seeing."

There is a feeling of lift and at the same time of illumination as the wayfaring speaker progresses, but there is also a sense of marking time, staying it at various intervals, defying its linearity for one glimpse of a thing or event that serves, ineluctably, to light his way; for as poet and wayfarer Seamus Heaney knows, to use the words of John Fowles, that he must have "whole sight; or all the rest is desolation."[18] And Heaney also knows that his poetry has been shaped by the remembered experiences of his past. Approaching the spirit level, Heaney rejoices in the evanescent miracles of every day.

Notes

1. Elmer Andrews, *The Poetry of Seamus Heaney: All The Realms of Whisper* (New York: St. Martin's Press, 1988), 42.

2. Tony Curtis, *The Art of Seamus Heaney* (Bridgend, Mid Glamorgan: Poetry Wales Press, 1982), 9.

3. Seamus Heaney, "Envies and Identifications: Dante and the Modern Poet," *Irish University Review* 15, no. 1 (Spring 1985): 11.

4. See Mikhail Bakhtin, *The Dialogic Imagination: Four Essays*, ed. Michael Holquist, trans. Caryl Emerson and Michael Holquist (Austin: University of Texas Press, 1981). In *The Dialogic Imagination*, dialogism is defined as "the characteristic epistemological mode of a world dominated by heteroglossia. Everything means, is understood, as a part of a greater whole—there is a constant interaction between meanings, all of which have the potential of conditioning others. Which will affect the other, how it will do so and in what degree is what is actually settled at the moment of utterance. This dialogic imperative, mandated by the pre-existence of the language world relative to any of its current inhabitants, insures that there can be no actual monologue" (425).

5. Jurij Lotman, in *The Structure of the Artistic Text*, divides dialogues into internal and external exchanges. The internal (between an earlier and later self) he considers to be in the temporal rather than the spatial realm (9). The persona in *Seeing Things*, although often crossing from one space to another, consistently maintains his equipoise. Through dialogism, past events are transformed and present in the "now" with an integrity made possible only through this dialogic transformation. See Jurij Lotman, *The Structure of the Artistic Text*, trans. Gail Lenhoff and Ronald Vroon (Ann Arbor: University of Michigan Press, 1977).

6. Thomas C. Foster, *Seamus Heaney* (Boston: Twayne, 1989), 133.

7. Bakhtin, *Dialogic Imagination*, 365.

8. Bakhtin discusses the importance of the image to provoke dialogism. See ibid., 277.

9. Ibid., 291. He explains this intersection of languages as a "unique, specific common plane where specific points of view on the world" may be discerned.

10. Ibid., 347.

11. Stratification in texts is discussed in ibid., 288-294, where Bakhtin advances his theory concerning the diversity of language and its lack of neutrality in any given text.

12. Ibid., 365.

13. Ibid., 351.

14. Ibid., xxi.

15. Ibid., 345.

16. Tzvetan Todorov, *Mikhail Bakhtin: The Dialogical Principle*, trans. Wlad Gozich (Minneapolis: University of Minnesota Press, 1984), 67.

17. Dennis Donoghue, *We Irish* (Berkeley: University of California Press, 1986), 129.

18. John Fowles, *Daniel Martin* (Boston: Little, Brown, 1977), 3.

Works Cited

Andrews, Elmer, *The Poetry of Seamus Heaney: All The Realms of Whisper*, New York: St. Martin's Press, 1988.

Bakhtin, Mikhail. *The Dialogic Imagination: Four Essays*. Edited by Michael Holquist. Translated by Caryl Emerson and Michael Holquist. Austin: University of Texas Press, 1981.

Curtis, Tony. *The Art of Seamus Heaney*. Bridgend, Mid Glamorgan: Poetry Wales Press, 1982.

Donoghue, Dennis. *We Irish*. Berkeley: University of California Press, 1986.

Foster, Thomas C. *Seamus Heaney*. Boston: Twayne, 1989.

Fowles, John. *Daniel Martin*. Boston: Little, Brown, 1977.

Heaney, Seamus. "Envies and Identifications: Dante and the Modern Poet." *Irish University Review* 15, no. 1 (Spring 1985): 5–19.

Lotman, Jurij. *The Structure of the Artistic Text*. Translated by Gail Lenhoff and Ronald Vroon. Ann Arbor: University of Michigan Press, 1977.

Todorov, Tzvetan. *Mikhail Bakhtin: The Dialogical Principle*. Translated by Wlad Gozich. Minneapolis: University of Minnesota Press, 1984.

Ways of
Seeing Things

DARCY O'BRIEN

In 1972 Seamus Heaney left Northern Ireland to live in the Republic of Ireland, or the South, as it is often called on the island. Other than his forsaking the family farm for boarding school in Derry, it proved to be the most important move of his life. He had abandoned his teaching job at Queen's University, Belfast, for what he conceived of at the time as "the freelance life" in a nineteenth-century forester's lodge on the old Synge estate in County Wicklow. The modest rent on what he, his wife, and their children came to call Glanmore Cottage was paid in advance for a year. The family had no savings; what Seamus could earn from writing and from public readings and lectures would merely supplement Marie Heaney's schoolteacher's salary, but she was fully supportive of the risk her husband took. "I don't know how I arrived at the decision," he told a friend at the time. "It would be more accurate to say that the decision arrived at me."

Three years later, still at the cottage, he published *North*. Holed up in his Wicklow fastness, his thoughts had been all of Northern slaughters. Another three years after that, in the middle of what may be described as a funk, he began translating Dante. Heaney was then thirty-seven years old. For starters, the work was an exercise, a sort of poet's calisthenics, part of a broader attempt to learn to lengthen his lines, experiment more with rhyme, and loosen his syntax, toward some unspecified goal or seeking. Initially, he was inspired by Robert Lowell's translations from Brunetto Latini. Dante then grew on him, became for him a constant aesthetic and spiritual companion and remains so to this day. It is fair to say that Dante is as much the wellspring of *Seeing Things* (1991) as he was of *The Waste Land* or the *Cantos*, but in a far different way.

How was it that Dante came to mean so much to Heaney? What internal and external circumstances contributed to the hold that medieval mind has had on the modern one? How did *Seeing Things*, in all its various beauties, come into being as a reaffirmation of something so old, so nearly ancient, so seemingly distant from the contemporary sensibility?

For anyone who is not Irish, it is difficult to understand how momentous the move from North to South was for Seamus Heaney. It is the same island—even the same country, according to the Constitution of the Republic, though not in political fact. For Heaney, however, the transplanting meant a voluntary exile in many ways as traumatic as Dante's involuntary one from Florence to Verona and elsewhere on the Italian peninsula. Although the comparison may at first seem disproportionate—Dante faced execution if he returned and remained separated from his wife and children—Heaney's self-banishment also involved the political, as well as rejection of many he left behind, as some of them understood and did not like. The chief effect on him was a psychological one; he did not, at the time, fully comprehend, and would not for twenty years, the degree to which his choice meant a cutting loose, though never a cutting off. Wishing to move his children away from a war zone was a factor but not the determinant. His articulated sense of the decision, as fated more than made, indicated the degree to which he acted impulsively rather than from reason or certainty.

The publication of *North* in 1975—both the content of that book and the mixed reaction to it—showed how defining an event his decision had been. To put the matter bluntly, he could never have written *North* in the North, and its existence sealed off permanently any ideas he may have had of returning to live there. He would not, like Dante, have faced burning at the stake, but his soul would have curled up black at the edges and his talent gone to ashes.

The trying and confusing period he had entered became the motive force of his art; to have tried to resolve the conflicts into which he had plunged himself would have been to stop writing, or at least writing well. *North* brought him far greater fame than he had known before, as well as hostility from the "anvil brains of some who hate me," as he had called them in "Exposure," meaning the politically correct persons, in Irish-Catholic Nationalist terms. These included Irish Republican Army members or sympathizers of various stripes, from actual Provos to those—including certain politicians, members of the clergy, and academics—who publicly condemned sectarian and political murder but were quietly in favor of it. Subtly in print, more viciously in whispers, Heaney was accused of *betrayal*— for having abandoned the North for the indolent, hedonistic, hypocritical South and for having written of his native grounds as if the conflict there might have an irrational motive that had less to do with political ideals than with blood lust.

For the weight of *North* came down on the side of what one might call

the Hannah Arendt heresy: that evil, specifically the impulse to violence, is
an ordinary and perennial thing that knows no political boundaries and
that it springs, in all its savagery and weakness, from that unfashionable
concept, human nature, and from tribal allegiances based on blood, not
beliefs. Indeed the reaction to the book among some Irish Catholic Nation-
alists was comparable to that among some Jews offended by *Eichmann in
Jerusalem* who could not bear the idea that an architect of mass murder was
just a run-of-the-mill sort of guy and even that some of his victims bore
responsibility for their fate. To paraphrase Tatyana Tolstaya, with reference to Stalin's victims, why blame only the shepherd? What about the
sheep? Heaney's variation on this heresy asked, why blame only the British? What about ourselves?

Worse, his poetry was now embraced by the British. Turning up the
heat, Conor Cruise O'Brien praised *North* lavishly; to receive an endorsement from him was almost as good as getting your name on an I.R.A. hit
list, as Cruise O'Brien's was, when as a member of the Irish government he
banned members of paramilitary organizations from appearing on televi-
sion and radio. (I do not mention hit lists lightly. I recall hearing John
Pope Hennessey's name on a tape-recorded IRA hit list introduced into
evidence at a trial in Dublin in 1977; his offense was to have an Irish name
and be director of the British Museum.) In a conversation with me, Cruise
O'Brien did voice one misgiving. He questioned whether, by acquiescing to
murder as a historical commonplace and admitting (as in "Punishment")
his own instinctive tribal loyalties, Heaney might not be unconsciously sanc-
tioning violence or even glorying in it, like a man rushing to the spectacle of
a house on fire or a car crash or the sacrifice of the Mass.[1]

Indeed the sensibility revealed in *North* was a deeply Catholic one, however uneasy it was with Irish-Catholic politics. It was the same sensibility
that Cruise O'Brien had detected in French, British, and Irish Catholic
writers years before in his *Maria Cross* (1954). This aspect of *North* left many
readers puzzled, cold, or both, and led one critic to dismiss Heaney's por-
traits of "famine, plague and slaughters" as "nothing but jumping on graves."
The comment, made by a British Protestant academic living in Ireland at
the time, was rendered only in conversation (to me), not in print; but it was
representative of qualms about the book that persist within the circle-graves
of academe, where neither religion nor arguments against the perfectibility
of mankind play well.

The popularity of the book also rendered it academically suspect. For a
volume of mostly unrhymed verses addressed to the etymologically inquisi-
tive, the book sold astonishingly well: some thirty thousand copies in the
first two years after British publication. People were spotted buying it whim-
sically in railway stations; it marked the onset of Heaney's rise as a pop star,

obscure compared to Mick Jagger, less well-known than that other Northern Irish artist, Van Morrison—but for a serious poet in the age of rock, famous. Sales in the United States lagged only because Heaney's American publisher at the time refused to buy more than nine hundred copies. His American audience would remain small until Farrar, Straus brought out *Field Work* (1979). (In the interim W. W. Norton had declined to add Heaney to their list because, the editor-in-chief apologized, "Americans don't buy British [*sic*] poets." I had made the suggestion to him myself, because he was my own editor then and seemed in all other ways a perceptive gentleman.) But the growth of Heaney's audience was well underway all over the English-speaking world and in Europe. Translations of his works proliferated; invitations to read poured in from everywhere.

To some within the ranks of the professoriat, those who in Patrick Kavanagh's words "didn't believe in the poet 'ating"[2] and revere inanition as the precondition to inspiration, Heaney's fame, charismatic personality, and even his tranquil domestic situation in Dublin were causes for misgivings. Father of three, living en famille with a new mortgage taken out on a large house by a famous strand on which Stephen Dedalus, properly keyless and homeless and soon to be passed-out drunk, had mulled protean matters; sociable; apparently unsuicidal; outwardly unenraged; inclined, it was rumored, to episodes of joie de vivre—he seemed all wrong for the part. He did not fit the accepted poet's mold, as satirized by Kavanagh in *his* "Portrait of the Artist": he had "deserted no wife to take another,"[3] was not known to be suffering from any venereal disease, had not denounced either his critics or the public; nor, unlike Kavanagh, was he rotting in a room or out cadging whiskies or pissing on gas fires in approved artistic fashion. Having accepted, not without some resistance, the responsibilities of a householder, he was by 1977 chairman of the English department at Carysfort College in Blackrock (County Dublin), an unglamorous position that required more of his time reading the compositions of prospective secondary-school teachers than he could give to writing poetry. If he went on like this, his life would defeat biographers. Now, Dylan Thomas, Delmore Schwartz, John Berryman, Sylvia Plath—those were *real* poets!

Within himself, however, anxieties multiplied; battles raged (in Joyce's infelicitous phrase applied to Ibsen) behind his forehead. It was not merely that he was sure his fame would not last: that may have been the only thing about which he felt certain, and it gave him as much comfort as distress. Anticipating that one day, perhaps tomorrow, he would sink back into obscurity gave him pleasure, the way the idea of falling into psychosexual degradation pleased T. E. Lawrence, who was reassured that there was an animal level beneath which a human being could not descend. Ascent was the more disquieting phenomenon, because one had no idea how high one might reach, or should reach. No, failure had its attractions: it won friends; it would mean being able to relax, play with the dog, admire Marie's herb garden, attend better to his students. His true fear was that he had perhaps succeeded too well in cutting ties, in breaking free from the clichés and lockstep assumptions of Irish history and life. He had begun to map out poetic and intellectual territory for himself, but there were no discernible boundaries. Had he become his own man, as it were, only to become no one's?

"Neither internee nor informer . . ." ("Exposure"), neither pro-British nor a member of an illegal organization committed to the conquering by force of "that part of the national territory as yet not reintegrated"—he feared that he was in danger of becoming a nowhere man, or had become one. He knew also that he did not know what to do next.

The controlling, overriding metaphor of his four published books, that of digging into things, had culminated in the bog people and was used up. The question of Irishness itself ("'What ish an Irishman?'") had become redundant, for him as, increasingly, for the nation, excluding those Orange and Green who would never surrender that conflict. He had spent the three previous years, the ones after *North*, honing his craft in a beautiful series of sonnets and other poems, including a celebration of the lush pleasures of eating oysters that had earned him scorn as a privileged glutton. *He was not even a Marxist!* What was he? Unsure what to do next, he thought of his old pseudonym from apprentice days, *Incertus*, or the Uncertain One, which lay there "like a mouldering tegument."

Edward McGuire caught Heaney's mood and aspect perfectly—miraculously one might say—in the painting of the poet that appeared on the back cover of *North* and hangs in the Ulster Museum in Belfast. Heaney, "grown long-haired / And thoughtful," sits at a table before a large, open book. His hands rest listlessly against the edges of the pages, gripping nothing, not even a pen; his feet turn inward; the table is dressed with what looks like an altar cloth, but there is no sacrifice and no Communion. Is he looking out at the painter, or at us, or at something in the middle distance? One cannot tell; he may be staring at nothing. Nor can one quite decide how to characterize the expression on the poet's face. Is he unhappy? Angry perhaps? Only bored? It may be the look of someone irritated at having to endure a party or maybe life. Light gleams from the top of his shoes, but he cannot see them; they are under the table.

One cannot help wondering whether the painter had in mind the famous portrait of Dante in exile in Verona; one could ask him, but Edward McGuire is dead. It was in this frame of mind, in this poverty of spirit, in this uncertainty, that Seamus Heaney began translating Dante. What, as I have said, commenced as exercise, at length became much more than that. "A man dabbles in something, and it becomes a life," Kavanagh said—did he say everything?[4] Eventually, working and reworking the passages over several years, Heaney evolved this:*

> In the middle of the journey of our life
> I found myself astray in a dark wood
> Where the straight road had been lost sight of.
>
> How hard it is to say what it was like
> In the thick of thickets, in a wood so dense and gnarled
> The very thought of it renews my panic.
>
> It is bitter almost as death is bitter.
> But to rehearse the good it also brought me
> I will speak about the other things I saw there.
>
> How I got into it I cannot clearly say
> For I was moving like a sleepwalker
> The moment I stepped out of the right way . . .

As I write out these lines, Seamus Heaney's translation of the familiar, yet renewed, opening of the *Inferno*, I am astonished and moved by their lucidity, their *claritas*, the deceptive ease of their movement, and their power. It is the power of a certainty of vision. No wonder, given his state of mind when he began work on them, that Heaney was enraptured by them and ultimately by his own sure handling of their intimate, affecting narrative pull. I can hear his voice, not only Dante's, different as the use of language is from Heaney's usual style: there are no knots for the reader to loosen, and there are only hints of Irish-Gaelic or Hiberno-English syntax and metaphor.

As I write, Heaney has yet to publish these or most of the other lines he has translated from the *Inferno;* only two of his books (*Field Work* and *Seeing Things*) contain any of that work. Nor is an essay by another's hand the place to print any extended portion of a poet's work for the first time. But, with omissions marked, I wish to carry on a little further through Canto I, so as to give more of the texture and quality of Heaney's version and make subsequent remarks on it:

---

*Excerpts from Heaney's translation of the *Inferno* are taken from Heaney's manuscript with permission of the author. Portions of his translation have subsequently been published in *Dante's Inferno: Translations by Twenty Contemporary Poets,* ed. Daniel Halpern (Hopewell, N.J.: The Ecco Press, 1993), 3–15.

But when I came to the bottom of a hill
Standing off at the far end of that valley
Where a great terror had disheartened me

I looked up, and saw how its shoulders glowed
Already in the rays of that planet
Which leads and keeps men straight on every road.

Then I sensed a quiet influence settling
Into those depths in me that had been rocked
And pitifully troubled all night long—

And as a survivor gasping on the sand
Turns his head back to study in a daze
The dangerous combers, so my mind

Turned back, although it was reeling forward,
Back to inspect a pass that had proved fatal
Heretofore to everyone who entered.

I rested a little even then since I was weary
And began to climb up the waste slopes once more
With my firm foot always the lower one beneath me

When suddenly the spotted fluent shape
Of a leopard crossed my path
Not far up from the bottom of the slope,

Harrying me, confronting my advance,
Loping round me, leaping in my face
So that I turned back downhill more than once.

The morning was beginning all above,
The sun was rising up among the stars
That rose with him when the Divine Love

First set those lovely things in motion,
So I was encouraged to face with better hope
The beast skipping in its merry skin

By the time of day, the sweetness of the season . . .

After confronting the lion and the she-wolf, afraid that he will "sink
back into the depths," Dante meets Virgil who, explaining the savagery of
the she-wolf, advises the traveler:

"Therefore, for your own good, I think the best course
Is to follow me and I will be your guide
And lead you from here through an eternal place

Where you will hear desperate screaming and will see
The long-lost spirits suffering their pain,
Lamenting the second death they have to die.

And then you will see those who are not distressed
In the fire because they hope to come,
Whenever their time comes, among the blessed.

If you want to ascend among these, then you
Will be guided by a soul worthier than I
And I will leave you with her when I go;

For that Emperor above does not allow
Me or my like to come into His city
Because I was a rebel to His law,

His empire is everywhere but His high seat
And city are there, in His proper kingdom.
O happy is the man he calls to it."

And I said to him, "I ask you, poet,
In the name of that God you were ignorant of,
And to help me to escape my own worst fate,

Lead me to that place described by you
So that I may see St. Peter's Gate
And those other ones you spoke of in their sorrow."

Then he set off and I began to follow.

Needless to say, these passages must be read aloud to be appreciated for what they are: not merely a new translation into English but distinctly a Seamus Heaney poem. Heaney has also translated the whole of Cantos II and III, using part of the latter as the end-piece to *Seeing Things;* and he made Ugolino materials from Cantos **XXXII** and **XXXIII** the end-piece to *Field Work.* Canto I, however, provides the key to why he devoted himself to Dante, with an obsessiveness comparable to Dante's devotion to Virgil.

What Heaney has done, somehow—and this is where analysis stumbles before the she-wolf of great poetry—is to transform Dante's vision into a dream, or a nightmare, with which the late-twentieth-century reader can identify. If there exists in the world a creature, and I dare say there are one or two, who has read a lot of Heaney but has never encountered Dante in any form, such an odd one would be able to identify this Canto I as a poem that manifests the familiar Heaney cadence and diction, especially the tone of awe and wonderment characteristic of Heaney's latest work. The book of his that comes first to mind, however—or to the mind's ear and the deep heart's core—is *Sweeney Astray* (1983), which is itself a version from another language, the Irish. I shall never again be able to think of Sweeney astray and aflight in his woods without recalling Dante astray and frightened in his "thick of thickets"—a phrase so Sweeneyesque, so early-Irish, and so distinctly Heaney. Heaney also happens to be unique among the several English translators in using the word "astray" in line two, "I found myself astray in a dark wood . . . ." Dorothy Sayers, to pick an example at random, renders it, "I woke to find myself in a dark wood," which is accurate enough but lacks the sense of frantic, swerving lostness. What makes the Heaney version his own is not only the individual choices of words but the entire, cumulative effect.

This effect is profoundly psychological. That is what makes it our own, for as everyone knows we are still living in a period which, since the romantics, since Coleridge certainly, through Poe and the symbolists and Freud and all the rest, embraces the psychological as the predominant metaphor, whether of Beauty and Terror or of Ego and Id, whether Boris Karloff or Stephen King. Heaney has transformed into contemporary terms what in the hands of other translators is more an object for study than a source of feeling, something intricate but remote—in a word, medieval. I do not mean to suggest that Heaney slights the medieval elements or saps them of their iconographic power, nor that he has produced a *Dante Alighieri Superstar*. He has not cheapened the original but reshaped it and infused it with his own genius, which is something both of our time and slightly ahead of our time because it anticipates, like all great poetry, wishes and dreams we do not even know we are having yet.

If I may be forgiven the use of a psychobabble term, Heaney has turned Dante's imagined experience into a "midlife crisis" that is unnervingly familiar to us all and that, surely, reflects the poet's own. More elegantly put, Heaney conveys what Scott Fitzgerald meant by his most-quoted line, that "in the dark night of the soul, it is always three o'clock in the morning."[5] Heaney's cantos are *The Crack-Up* revisited. They are also *Dorian Gray* and *Big Two-Hearted River* and Quentin Compson and *Howl* and *Play It As It Lays* and Sylvia Plath and Philip Larkin and, yes, even Gilbert Pinfold; they are the "Circe" episode, *The Trial*, *Nausea*, *Murphy*, and dozens of other literary and cinematic masterpieces, with *Sunrise* and *The Night of the Hunter* coming to mind among the latter. They could be subtitled *In Our Time*, "the journey

of *our life*" (italics added) as Heaney so matter-of-factly phrases Dante's opening line.

The language of Canto I is so simple, beautiful, and direct, the syntax
so close to contemporary speech, that to read it aloud is easy; the words
flow as if improvised; it is like becoming the ghost of Lester Young playing
"Satin Doll." When "thick of thickets" fills the mouth, one remembers that
the composer is also Sweeney (yes, rhymes with Heaney) derived from the
wordplay, the belief in onomatopoeia, and the paring-knife precision of
early-Irish nature description. Later, as with Dante's own language, the
diction assumes greater density and "has all the force of dirt hitting a
windscreen."[6]

That last image is another of Heaney's, taken from the 1985 essay "Envies and Identifications: Dante and the Modern Poet," which he published
in the spring of that year in the *Irish University Review*. Heaney surveys the
pervasive influence of Dante on modern poetry, beginning with W. B. Yeats's
"Ego Dominus Tuus," which itself is a quotation from *La Vita Nuova*. He
goes on to cite Geoffrey Hill, Wilfred Owen, Thomas Kinsella, Ezra Pound,
and T. S. Eliot to remind us of poets for whom the presence of Dante mat-
tered greatly. He adds a brief, lyrical account of the importance of Dante to
Osip Mandelstam, who included the *Commedia* as one of the few books he
was able to take with him from St. Petersburg when he was banished into
imprisoned exile for having written a poem against Stalin. And he closes
with an overview of the most obviously Dante-inspired poem he had published up to that time, "Station Island" (1984), in which the shades of friends,
neighbors, a murdered cousin, and other Irish writers appear to him and
give advice or admonishment. At the last, James Joyce, sneering, crackling
with scorn on the Tarmac of the Lough Derg parking lot, urges Heaney to
challenge orthodox ways and obedient attitudes, to "let go, let fly, forget,"
and strike a personal note.

Heaney tells us that what he first loved about the *Commedia* was "the
local intensity . . . the strong strain of what has been called personal realism
in the celebration of bonds of friendship and bonds of enmity" and the
ways in which Dante could combine "the political and the transcendent."[7]
Heaney emulated these qualities in "Station Island," where he explored
exactly those strains endemic to Ireland that had induced his personal funk
and caused him to turn to Dante and to translate him: "The main tension"—the one that had forced the decision to leave Northern Ireland—"is
between two often contradictory commands: to be faithful to the collective
historical experience and to be true to the recognitions of the emerging self.
I hoped that I could dramatize these strains by meeting shades from my
own dream-life who had also been inhabitants of the actual Irish world."[8]

The most extensive and complex discussion in Heaney's essay is of T. S.

Eliot's views and uses of Dante's language. Surprisingly, at any rate to those of us who had always thought, or were taught, that Dante's great innovation was the use of the vernacular, Eliot emphasized the universal qualities of the Florentine idiom, rather than its localness. His argument was that the Italian language in Dante's day, unlike the languages of Shakespeare or Racine in theirs, gained by being so close to medieval Latin and therefore could convey what all of the various peoples of Christendom thought together, cutting across political, ethnic, and linguistic boundaries.

Heaney, however, argues that Eliot was recreating Dante in his own image, whatever truth there may be in Eliot's analysis of the presence of universal Latin in the Italian. Heaney points out that Eliot made his remarks on Dante in 1929, five years after publication of *The Waste Land,* and that they reflect Eliot's preoccupations with the more abstract concerns of his later poetry. *The Waste Land* itself is more localized in language and image than the *Four Quartets,* as in for instance the London Bridge passage with its allusion to the *Inferno,* "I had not thought death had undone so many." "Here," Heaney says, "Dante was actually giving Eliot the freedom to surrender to the promptings of his own unconscious, and the language is more allied to Shakespearian-local-associative than to the latinate-classical-canonical. For the moment, the imagination is in thrall to romantic expressionism, bewildered on the flood of its own inventiveness."[9] But even in *The Waste Land,* the language is demotic only sporadically; by *The Four Quartets,* Eliot has made the language so universal, so unlocalized, that the poetry becomes subservient to values and judgments, "an austere embodiment of universal myth."

For Heaney—obviously referring to his own standards for poetic language—Dante's diction, syntax, vocabulary, and imagery are both local *and* universal: that is the greatness of them. Heaney contends that Eliot and Pound, coming on Dante first as students, learning to read him in an academic context, found in him an avenue toward isolating themselves from parochial, demotic, American, and, later, English culture. They canonized him "as the aquiline patron of international modernism" but in the process alienated themselves from the very power of his specificity, his localness, his embracing of language as not something to be "written on official paper," but the very breath of ordinary life.[10]

Heaney tells us that his own view and use of Dante is much closer to that of Mandelstam than to that of Eliot or Pound: "This Dante is essentially lyric; he is stripped of the robes of commentary in which he began to vest himself with his epistle to Can Grande [della Scala], reclaimed from the realm of epic and allegory and made to live as the epitome of a poet's creative excitement."[11] Unlike Eliot and Pound, Mandelstam came to Dante not as a student but as a prisoner and an involuntary exile from his native place; and he found in him that love of the local, the celebratory exultation in the physical force and highly personalized associations that idiom—the vernacular, the sound-signature of rude, common life—can convey. This Dante showed Mandelstam a road not toward orthodoxy—whether Catholic or Anglo-Catholic and royalist (Eliot) or fascist / anti-Semitic (Pound) or Stalinist—but back toward the truly universal, that of the particular.

The political implications of this argument are obvious enough. They are against any sort of group-think; they are Jeffersonian, weary and wary of the general and the abstract and of the politically correct in any form, Left or Right. They embrace individualism in all the ways herd-minded people, poets or politicians or professors, despise. Subtly, they amount to Seamus Heaney's political and poetical manifesto. And they evolved from his leaving Northern Ireland and discovering Dante.

Why did Heaney choose to publish his translations of the Ugolino passages as the first example of his work on Dante? The act of rendering those lines into English was for him, I believe, a kind of exorcism of the anxiety-ridden interlude that followed the publication of *North*. If Ugolino's sin was betrayal, so was Heaney's, according to his detractors. He had become an "inner-émigré," a "wood-kerne / Escaped from the massacre" ("Exposure"), gnawing, as it were, on his own head. The Ugolino lines are intensely, violently local; they acted on Heaney as caustic soap for the soul, as a purgative. The power of this translation stems, talent apart, from its being so personally felt:

> I walked the ice
> And saw two soldered in a frozen hole
> On top of other, one's skull capping the other's,
> Gnawing at him where the neck and head
> Are grafted to the sweet fruit of the brain,
> Like a famine victim at a loaf of bread.
> So the berserk Tydeus gnashed and fed
> Upon the severed head of Menalippus
> As if it were some spattered carnal melon. . . .

Sweeney Astray followed in 1983; *Station Island* (the poem and those surrounding it in the volume, including verses "voiced" for Sweeney) came the next year. There ensued another contemplative period not dissimilar to that of his second book, *Door Into the Dark* (1969). Many of the poems of *The Haw Lantern* (1987) have an unearthly quality. They make me think of a space probe: winking, distant lights here and there, mere glimmerings, the voice faint, static-plagued. Rereading this volume as I trace the way toward *Seeing Things*, I imagine an astronaut who sees unseen things but is having difficulty transmitting and is in danger of drifting out of orbit and beyond. Heaney Aloft.

Dante was most powerful among the voices guiding him back to earth. If Dante leads us from the earth down to hell, through purgatory and upward to heaven, Seamus Heaney's inner voyage took him at last to an Earthly Paradise. *Seeing Things* may be the most joyful book of serious poetry produced in this century, unless one counts the posthumous publication of Gerard Manley Hopkins's verse in 1918. There are many affinities with Hopkins, not merely the usual similarities in diction found between him and many modern Irish poets but complicities of vision, by no means always Christian in Heaney's case but here and there undoubtedly so. Both are poets of incarnation who rejoice in the discovery of lineaments of the ineffable. One had almost lost hope that poetry could ever again celebrate as well as weep.

If *North* was Heaney's politics and *Field Work* his poetics, *Seeing Things* is his cosmology. In returning to the parochial, the local, the remembered, and the specific once again, this time he has unearthed the transcendent. Once more he uses a passage from the *Inferno* as his end-piece, the lock on the door and also the key. "The Crossing" is his version of Canto III (lines 82–129); it tells of Charon and the Styx. Long before reaching this final crossing, one has noticed that the entire volume is marked and held together by crosses, squarings, and other geometric designs. Religious, geophysical, astronomical, botanical, and other patterns taken from religion and nature pervade. Some are mundane—the crisscrosses of a game of marbles or a soccer field—others obviously allusive to the Crucifixion, the universe. Like Yeats before him, Heaney has hammered his thoughts into unity with the aid of Euclid.

And inevitably like Dante, Heaney manages to be intensively local in language and subject, yet so hallucinatory and otherworldly also that one has to look back to St. Augustine to try to express the technique and its effect. "All doctrine," Augustine wrote in *On Christian Doctrine*, his handbook to the reading of the Scriptures,

> concerns either things or signs, but things are learned by signs. Strictly speaking, I have here called a "thing" that which is not used to signify something else, like wood, stone, cattle, and so on; but not that wood concerning which we read that Moses cast it into bitter waters that their bitterness might be dispelled, nor that stone which Jacob placed at his head, nor that beast which Abraham sacrificed in place of his son. For these are things in ways that they are also signs of other things. There are other signs whose whole use is in signifying, like words. For no one uses words except for the purpose of signifying something. From this may be understood what we call "signs"; they are

things used to signify something. Thus every sign is also a thing, for that which is not a thing is nothing at all; but not every thing is also a sign.[12]

Heaney's method in *Seeing Things* is to begin with a thing, usually a memory of a person, place, or event, and to transubstantiate it into a sign—not of any orthodoxy, but of some pattern, shape, or trajectory of action, that implies order and imparts mysterious joy. It is this last quality, effect, or result that distinguishes *Seeing Things* from Heaney's earlier work and allies it still more closely to Dante, as well as to St. Augustine, doctrine aside. The order is perceived or hinted and at that moment in reading one of the poems, we partake in the joy of the discovery. To read these poems is to understand what Einstein meant by the joy of scientific discovery, what he meant when he said that to hear the prodigy Yehudi Menuhin play the violin was to have proof of the existence of God.

What Heaney has done in this book is to reinvigorate poetry with a religious element that has diminished in Western art since the Enlightenment. He has rekindled the *numinous*. If Eliot attempted the same in the *Four Quartets*, he fell short, producing verse as cold, as calculated, as remote from ordinary emotions and experience and as paradoxically secular as an Anglican service. One now understands why the *Quartets* do not convince, why they come across more as a simulation of religious experience than as the thing itself: Eliot had the wrong idea about Dante's language. He fell into the error of asking signs alone to carry the burden of spiritual significance, rather than remembering that signs must be things before they can signify.

In his method and effect, Heaney's great exemplar in this century, different as they are in so many other ways, was Yeats, who after the airiness of his early poems learned to feed the heart not on fantasies but on "mythologies rooted in the earth." One could cite "no ideas but in things," except that in practice William Carlos Williams's verse was all things and no ideas, except ones about poetry. Like Yeats's, Heaney's delineations of the actual impart another, unseen actuality. Let me illustrate this achievement of the numinous with reference to one poem from *Seeing Things*. It is untitled, identified as "xviii" under the subheading "Settings" in Part II, "Squarings." The setting here is a local fair. If the poem had a title, it would be called "The Rope-Man":

> Like a foul-mouthed god of hemp come down to rut,
> The rope-man stumped about and praised new rope
> With talk of how thick it was, or how long and strong.
>
> And how you could take it into your own hand
> And feel it. His perfect, tight-bound wares
> Made a circle round him: the makings of reins

And belly-bands and halters. And of slippage—
For even then, knee-high among the farmers,
I knew the rope-man menaced them with freedoms

They were going to turn their backs on; and knew too
His powerlessness once the fair-hill emptied
And he had to break the circle and start loading.

                                                        (*ST* 74)

I cannot resist saying, What can one say? If you don't get it, you don't get it. Permit me an aside, but what passes for literary criticism these days, apart from gagging theory, is so much affected by the need to explain the obvious to undergraduates, that one has difficulty knowing where not to begin. It seems enough to have written out, printed, this poem, to convey its beauty and the wonder of it. Surely that it conveys the thrill of performance and of rude vigor, sexual power and the timidity of the folk encircling that hairy man, the temptations of freedom and its rejection—all this must be apparent. But it may be useful to emphasize the geometry of the thing, the circle—of life that is broken by death?—formed by the rope.

Heaney, modestly and maybe somewhat disingenuously, has called this and other "twelve-liners" in the volume "snapshots, quickies, passes en passant." I, requiring profundity, craving *magnificence* and finding it here, think of the nobility Fellini was able to evoke from Anthony Quinn as the circus performer in *La Strada*. I am also assailed by memories from youth and know I must have missed their grandeur, evoked now through Heaney's conjuring: Clyde Beatty cracking his whip at a tiger; my father trying and failing to teach me how to box; Gorgeous George and Baron Leone in the early days of televised professional wrestling; the man hawking a useless implement called "the glass knife" on a local TV channel; the way my father told stories and slumped into melancholy when, like the rope-man, he lost his audience.

That is the effect of *Seeing Things*, of which the twelve-liners are only a part. Each poem in the book—I think chiefly because of the geometry, the circles and squares and crosses that demarcate nearly every verse—sets the mind spinning inward and outward toward distinct patterns, certainties of the belief in them. This is not only a matter of free association, as with the romantic-symbolist-surrealist-expressionist verse of the old days, but of pattern. Among the thoughts sparked by these poems are those of what we know, or think we know, of science. Has it occurred to Heaney, I wonder, that Yeats's gyres, his hypothesis of the pattern of universal energy, adumbrated the basic structure of DNA, a spiral? Heaney's own patterns include spirals but also many other sorts of markings, orderings, and boundaries. The result is soothing as well as stimulating. I cannot help but think of Bart Giamatti's reminder to us that the proportions of a baseball diamond are perfect and that the word *paradise* comes from the Persian and means *enclosure, park,* or *green.* More to the point, the verb and adverb from which the noun *paradise* derives are the Persian words for *form* and *around.*[13] Forming a pattern, an enclosure around experience is the aesthetic of *Seeing Things.* *Measuring* is I think the dominant metaphorical verb of the book. Measuring discovers *Paradiso.*

Dante's leveling and parceling (strips of canvas wrapped around a rope, sailors used to mean by this word); Yeats's plummet-measuring; Heaney's father's weighing and joining and his mother's spooning, slicing, trimming, and clipping—this is a poet whose anxieties of influence derive from actual at least as much as from literary parents. And he advances the idea of poetic form to encompass the scientific discoveries and theories with which every modern mind is imbued, especially ideas about light, the phenomenon that makes all seeing possible. In "A Basket of Chestnuts," the twelfth poem of Part I of *Seeing Things,* he recalls sitting for the Edward McGuire portrait, back in those crepuscular days, and remembers that a basketful of gleaming chestnuts rested between him and the painter but was not included in the finished portrait. He had thought McGuire would use the chestnuts as "a decoy or a coffer for the light / He captured in the toecaps of my shoes." Now the light-capturing chestnuts glow warmly in the poet's mind to illuminate the communion that took place between himself and the dead painter: light as intimation of immortality.

Astrophysical light and hints of something beyond "the vestibule of stars" are everywhere in *Seeing Things.* While evoking a lost world of ungeared bicycles, fairs, solitary fishing, millstones, quarries, tripartite birettas and other curiosities, Heaney stimulates associations with matters that transcend discarded technologies and fashions. "If I could come on meteorite!" he burst out in the dreary time of "Exposure," his premature elegy for lost poetic vision. Nearly twenty autumns later, "the comet's pulsing rose" at last is visible everywhere, in a game of Scrabble or in the hieroglyph of heat waves. It is a *Commedia.*

A writer shapes experience by imposing the order of syntax; a painter frames, or does not, what gets stroked and scraped and dripped; a musician embraces harmony and rhythm or breaks them. A poet pauses at the end of a line or a stanza, or does not; a novelist, any narrative writer, uses chapters or scenes to control the linear energy of action, or cuts everything up. We have been educated—*to an effing standstill!* as the paranoid schizophrenic with a cape pulled over his face who was barred from the Bailey in Dublin used to shout—to believe that in the form, or in the lack of it, lies the meaning of a work of art, or the absence of it. Samuel Beckett told us something, nothing, by creating perfect forms that were only that, forms, with zero content.

Seeing Things escapes the self-referential aesthetics of modernism and the nonaesthetics of postmodernism to suggest, as the at-present-unfashionable Robert Frost often did, "For Once, Then, Something." To read the book is to encounter what great art used to do, what religious art has always done: to imply something beyond itself, something other than the personal or the political. This aesthetic is today so much scorned that to reaffirm it must have taken a certain daring. That the book begins with a passage from the *Aeneid* evoking the difficulties of ascending from the underworld and ends with crossing the Styx must mean something, too.

Several years ago, I think it was in the summer of 1979, I sat in the passenger seat of Seamus Heaney's Volkswagen as we crossed the border into Northern Ireland at Newry. Like all the crossing points, this one is notorious for ambushes, remote-control explosions, random sniper fire; on that day as on most, however, nothing happened. When, as we wended through a one-way street in the heart of the town, British soldiers in an open truck ahead of us leaped out to point black machine guns at the windows of houses, one of Seamus's two sons, who were in the back seat, asked, "What are those men doing, Dad?"

"They're trying to provoke violence," Seamus said, and we got out of there rapidly.

We visited settings and crossings, ending up at the Heaney family farm in Belaghy, County Derry. Seamus's parents and various relatives were there. I met an aunt who had loved a German prisoner of war thirty-five years ago; I thought I'd write a book about her. Seamus had already (in "Stations") described the internee from the Luftwaffe who had painted Tyrolean landscapes on light bulbs when visiting the farm on a weekend pass.

In the morning we sniffed the turf-sweet air, standing in the yard near the disused pump, the one he writes about as the omphalos of his youth. Not a sound. You would have to go to Nebraska to find such silence in the States. All around us were the things he had made into his signs—the river, the small fields with soft names, crossroads, the flax-dam he had remembered for the horrors of its frogspawn. To my surprise, it was nothing but a short narrow ditch. As usual, I thought of Kavanagh:

> Ashamed of what I loved
> I flung her from me and called her a ditch
> Although she was smiling at me with violets.[14]

For me the moment was what Heaney describes in *Seeing Things* as a "lightening." I noticed how bare and beautiful this farmyard was and considered how mean-spirited I had been with the riches of my own youth—a baroque movie theater on the corner, a park with such a wonderful diamond, a neo-Gothic waterworks made of concrete, my mother dipping French bread into cocoa, my father coming diffidently to call, my grandmother's coffin carried by six policemen, the barbershop that was a bookie joint—so much that I had ignored, my personal mythology denied in search of something that was fake. I became electric with envy that morning—not of Seamus's childhood, it was like any other; mine had been the neon one. I was envious because Heaney had made something miraculous of what anyone else would have counted for nothing, while I was dissipating California wonders.

This was a man, it came to me, who would have made violets of anything and who never, even if he had to leave them to express them, denied the glories of his hills and yards.

He was idle that morning, wandering without direction around the yard, some Derry cowboy escaped from *At Swim-Two-Birds*. He ambled—sashayed?—over to the pump. He lifted its lid. At his excitement I came over to peek in and saw that a bird, frightened by us but faithful to her task, sat trembling inside that metal incubator.

> finch-green, speckly white,
> nesting on dry leaves, flattened, still,
>
> suffering the light. . . .
>
> There was a single egg, pebbly white,
>
> and in the rusted bend of the spout
> tail-feathers splayed and sat tight. . . .

The poem, which he called "Changes," arrived a year later as a Christmas greeting. Eventually he made it part of *Station Island*.

So that is how it's done, I thought when I received the gift and saw how he had transformed the happening into something other. He had made it into an imagined experience shared with, I think, his father. I felt a bit let down at being left out, but my pleasure in the art of it modified my pique.

I was embarrassed, and still am. It was like having been present at a conception, so much more a private matter than a birth. So that is how he makes a poem. So matter-of-fact, and yet not.

Notes

1. Conor Cruise O'Brien, conversation with the author, July 1976.
2. Patrick Kavanagh, *Self-Portrait* (Dublin: Dolmen Press, 1963), 11.
3. Patrick Kavanagh, "Portrait of the Artist," in *Collected Poems* (London: Martin Brian & O'Keeffe, 1964), 121.
4. *Collected Poems*, xiii. The full text is "A man (I am thinking of myself) innocently dabbles in words and rhymes and finds that it is his life."
5. The full text is "In the real dark night of the soul it is always three o'clock in the morning." F. Scott Fitzgerald, *The Crack-Up* (London: New Directions, 1956), 344.
6. Seamus Heaney, "Envies and Identifications: Dante and the Modern Poet," *Irish University Review* 15, no.1 (Spring 1985): 12.
7. Ibid., 18.
8. Ibid., 19.
9. Ibid., 13.
10. Ibid., 16.
11. Ibid.
12. Augustine, *On Christian Doctrine*, trans. D. W. Robertson Jr (New York: Liberal Arts Press, 1958), 8–9.
13. A. Bartlett Giamatti was a Renaissance scholar, president of Yale University, and in his last, best incarnation, commissioner of baseball. He often cited this etymology. See George Will, *Men At Work* (New York: Macmillan, 1990), 5.
14. Patrick Kavanagh, *Collected Poems*, 127.

Works Cited

Augustine. *On Christian Doctrine*. Translated by D. W. Robertson Jr. New York: Liberal Arts Press, 1958.

Dante. *The Divine Comedy*. Translated by Dorothy Sayers. London: Penguin Books, 1967.

Heaney, Seamus. "Cantos, I, II, III, *L'Inferno*." Photocopy of typescript, in the present writer's possession.

———. "Envies and Identifications: Dante and the Modern Poet." *Irish University Review* 15, no. 1 (Spring 1985): 5–19.

Kavanagh, Patrick. *Collected Poems*. London: Martin Brian & O'Keeffe, 1964.

———. *Self-Portrait*. Dublin: The Dolmen Press, 1963.

Will, George. *Men at Work*. New York: Macmillan, 1990.

List of Contributors

JONATHAN ALLISON (University of Kentucky) is editor of *Yeats's Political Identities* (1995) and of *Patrick Kavanagh: A Reference Guide* (forthcoming). He has published essays on such writers as Yeats, Heaney, Kennelly, and Muldoon.

JOHN R. BOLY (Marquette University) has published a volume on W. H. Auden, *Reading Auden: The Return of Caliban*. In addition, he has published essays in *Diacritics* and *Twentieth-Century Literature*. He is currently working on a book entitled "Legible Texts, Literate Readers: Hopkins, Lawrence, Thomas, and Heaney."

RAND BRANDES (Lenoir-Rhyne College), in addition to coediting with Michael Durkan a Heaney bibliography (forthcoming), has published in the following journals: *Salmagundi* (1988), *The Irish Review* (1990), and *Studies in Contemporary Irish Literature* 1991).

PHYLLIS CAREY (Mount Mary College) is coeditor of *Re: Joyce 'n Beckett* (1992). In addition, she has published essays on James Joyce, Samuel Beckett, and Václav Havel, as well as interviews with Czeslaw Milosz and (with Catharine Malloy) Seamus Deane.

SEAMUS DEANE is general editor of the *Field Day Anthology of Irish Writing* (1992) and also the author of book-length studies: *A Short History of Irish Literature* (1986); *Celtic Revivals: Essays in Modern Irish Literature, 1880-1980* (1987); and *The French Revolution and Enlightenment in England, 1789–1832* (1988). In addition, he has published several volumes of poetry: *Gradual Wars* (1972), *Rumours* (1977), *History Lessons* (1983), and *Selected Poems* (1988). Deane has authored some seventy essays, including two pamphlets in the Field Day series.

MICHAEL PATRICK GILLESPIE (Marquette University) has published widely in Irish studies: *Inverted Volumes Improperly Arranged: James Joyce and His Trieste Library* (1983), *James Joyce's Trieste Library: A Catalogue of Materials* (1986), *Reading the Book of Himself: Narrative Strategies in the Works of James Joyce* (1989), *Oscar Wilde: Life, Work, and Criticism* (1990). Gillespie has published essays in scholarly journals and newspapers such as *The Explicator, Renascence, James Joyce Quarterly, Contemporary Authors,* and the *Irish Literary Supplement.*

SAMMYE CRAWFORD GREER (Wittenberg University) has given many papers on Irish Studies and has published in the following journals: *The South Carolina Review, Clio,* and *Eire-Ireland.*

DAVID LLOYD (Le Moyne College) has published numerous critical articles on contemporary poetry, some of which have appeared in the following journals: *Ariel* (1979, 1981, 1987), *Twentieth Century Literature* (1988), *The Biographical Dictionary of Contemporary Catholic American Writers* (1989), *Poetry Wales* (1990), and *World Literature Today* (1992). His anthology, *The Urgency of Identity: Contemporary English-language Poetry from Wales* was published in 1994.

CATHARINE MALLOY (Mount Mary College) wrote her doctoral dissertation on Seamus Heaney and has read papers on Heaney at the International Association for the Study of Anglo/Irish Literature (University of Leiden, the Netherlands, 1991), the American Conference for Irish Studies (University of Wisconsin, 1991), and the Modern Language Association (San Francisco, 1991); she has published essays on Heaney, most recently in a special Heaney issue of *The Colby Quarterly* and collaborated with Phyllis Carey in an interview with Seamus Deane.

DARCY O'BRIEN (University of Tulsa) is the author of eleven books of criticism, fiction, and nonfiction narrative. These include *The Conscience of James Joyce (1968), W. R. Rodgers (1970),* and *Patrick Kavanagh (1975),* criticism; *A Way of Life, Like Any Other* (1978) and *Margaret in Hollywood* (1991), fiction; and *A Dark and Bloody Ground* (1993) and *Power to Hurt* (1995), nonfiction.

CHARLES L. O'NEILL (St. Thomas Aquinas College) received National Endowment for the Humanities Awards for summer seminars on "Yeats and His Circles" at the University of Rochester and on "Narrative Theory and Narrative Practice: Reading, Interpreting and Teaching James Joyce's *Ulysses*" at Columbia University. He has published essays in *Spirit* (1989), *Irish Literary Supplement* (1986), and *The Essay: Redefining a Genre for the Humanities* (1989). In addition, he writes a regular column for the *Irish Times.*

Index

195